D1021601

THE PIANO TEACHER

The True Story
of a Psychotic Killer

Robert K. Tanenbaum and Peter S. Greenberg

A SIGNET BOOK

NEW AMERICAN LIBRARY

PUBLISHED BY
THE NEW AMERICAN LIBRARY
OF CANADA LIMITED

Copyright © 1987 by Robert Tanenbaum

This book previously appeared in a hardcover edition published by New American Library and published simultaneously in Canada by The New American Library of Canada Limited.

First Signet Printing, August, 1988

2 3 4 5 6 7 8 9

SIGNET TRADEMARK REG. U.S. PAT. OFF. AND FOREIGN COUNTRIES
REGISTERED TRADEMARK — MARCA REGISTRADA
HECHO EN WINNIPEG, CANADA

SIGNET, SIGNET CLASSIC, MENTOR, ONYX, PLUME, MERIDIAN AND NAL BOOKS are published in Canada by The New American Library of Canada, Limited, 81 Mack Avenue, Scarborough, Ontario, Canada M1L 1M8
PRINTED IN CANADA
COVER PRINTED IN U.S.A.

For Patti Tanenbaum, who by example makes us all strive to be the best we can. And for Uncle Don B., the best detective in the business.

—R.K.T.

For Karen Greenberg, my sister, who gave me the strength and moral support to finish this book, and, most important, a woman who has always encouraged me to be myself.

—P.S.G.

Acknowledgments

The authors acknowledge the zealous and meticulous research efforts of Linda Kent, without whom this book would not have been possible.

CHAPTER ONE

It was an unseasonably warm fall Monday night in New York City. Suzanne Reynolds, an attractive twenty-five-year-old secretary, decided to walk to her regular 5:30 P.M. appointment. There was no need to change. She wouldn't need a sweater or a jacket this evening. Her thin red coat would suffice. At 5:10, she left her cluttered office on Twenty-sixth Street and headed uptown.

Suzanne was a newcomer to the East Side. She had left Florida eighteen months earlier because she craved the action New York City promised. The opportunities were bigger and they seemed better. Also, Suzanne was fascinated with show business. She was a pretty, bubbly, and some would say, a sexy redhead. Reynolds had been told more than once back in Florida—and was now convinced—that she had the looks, the personality, and the stamina to make it. She was going to be an actress.

Soon after she arrived in Manhattan, Suzanne began taking acting and voice lessons. They seemed mandatory, unwritten requirements, and she eagerly signed on. Reynolds possessed at least the first prerequisite for moving north: she had ambition.

Ambition like Suzanne's was not easily rewarded at

D. L. Blair, the sales promotion company where she worked to pay for her acting lessons. Reliability was. And Suzanne was a very reliable $125-a-week secretary. She helped supervise the other girls and distinguished herself within the company by never talking about her personal life, never having friends visit her at work, and by always keeping her ambitions to herself.

Next to acting and singing, Suzanne wanted more than anything to travel. All of her friends had vacationed in Europe and she wanted to be next. Her salary barely paid the rent and the phone bill, but Suzanne was determined. She thought the classwork would end soon. Then, she hoped, with the money she would earn from some theater and night club work, she could afford to cross the Atlantic.

Twice each week Suzanne took acting classes. And once each week, she took voice lessons. Monday night was voice night.

Three months earlier, she had found the right voice teacher, a thirty-one-year-old piano player named Charles Yukl. A good pianist, classically trained and extremely well mannered, he played professionally in the Catskills on weekends. During the week he worked a host of happy hours at West Side piano bars. He was a slender, quiet man who lived in a small, unpretentious apartment on East Twenty-eighth Street with his wife and pet dog. He also managed the apartment building.

Charles Yukl wasn't an arrogant or pretentious cocktail lounge pianist, he just liked to play the piano. At least that's what he said. He was also inexpensive. He charged Suzanne Reynolds and his other students five dollars an hour for their lessons.

Suzanne had worked on a new routine with him the week before. It was standard nightclub fare—songs like "Alexander's Ragtime Band" and "Hello Dolly" interrupted by some transitional dialogue Yukl wrote to bridge the music. But the routine wasn't quite ready yet, and she was anxious to work a few more tunes into the repertoire before going out on her first auditions. Yukl said she was close to getting it all together. Tonight, he said, they would make a tape.

It was already dark outside when she arrived at his building. She was five minutes late, and quickly walked up the stairs to Yukl's third floor apartment. On the door to the apartment was taped a note on a white piece of paper with scrawled handwriting: "Hi. Just went out to walk the dog. The door is open. I'll be right back. Charlie."

Suzanne let herself in. As soon as she opened the door she saw the big dog sitting quietly in the small living room. There was not much to the room—a small, brown couch, two small end tables, a few plants, a wood-laminated coffee table, and, of course, the piano.

It always struck Suzanne as strange that a man would keep a Great Dane in such a tiny apartment. She sat down on the couch to wait. For a moment, the room was quiet. Then, Suzanne heard a noise coming from the bathroom. It sounded like someone running the bathwater.

Charlie must be in there, she thought. He must have forgotten to take the note off the door. Perhaps she should announce her arrival.

"Okay, you lucky boy," Suzanne bellowed in her usual effervescent way, "I'm here."

The door to the bathroom opened quickly and out came a naked, dripping man. "Oh," Yukl apologized. Suzanne looked quickly away. "I didn't realize you were here," he offered. He stood there for a few more seconds, then abruptly retreated to the bathroom. Yukl

grabbed a towel. "I'm sorry," he called out. "I'll be
with you in a minute." Suzanne thought nothing of it.
She shrugged and headed over to the small upright
piano. New York, she had always been told, was full
of colorful characters. Charles Yukl was just one of
them.

Two minutes later, Yukl came out of the bathroom
dressed in an unironed short sleeve button down shirt
and slacks. He didn't go to the piano. He walked
silently, nervously over to a small chair, sat and stared
at the floor.

"Charlie, are you okay?" Suzanne asked. He didn't
respond. "You want to forget about tonight? I could
come back." Yukl shook his head. "N-n-no," he stuttered. "Y-y-y-you can stay."

His behavior this evening was strangely different.
The drapes were closed. The room was dimly lit. She
could see that he had been drinking. A half empty
bottle of vodka sat on the table. And his wife wasn't
home.

"I'm sorry about the bathroom," he murmured,
barely audible. He was still sitting in the chair. Without waiting for Suzanne's response, he began to ramble, making little sense. He started to mumble things
about sex. "Did you get excited at seeing me?" he
asked. She didn't notice that his eyes had begun to
widen.

Suzanne tried to change the subject. Men had come
on to her before. She could handle this guy. "Let's get
to work, Charlie," she said. "We can talk about that
later." But he was still sitting across from her on the
chair, mumbling. He seemed lost in a host of confused
thoughts. Suzanne waited for him to snap out of it, but
he didn't. "Charlie?" she asked. "Charlie, are you all
right?" He looked up at her.

Suddenly, he blurted out, "Did you bring the songs?"

Good, she thought. We're back on track. Maybe this silly episode is over. "Sure," she said, reaching for her purse. "Thought you'd never ask. Got 'em right in here."

As Suzanne opened her brown leather handbag, the clasp snapped and everything fell on the floor: compact, lipstick, apartment keys, handkerchief, address book and wallet.

Charlie jumped quickly out of his chair. Both he and Suzanne got down on the floor to retrieve the items. "Where's the sheet music?" he asked. They both looked. "Where is it?" he repeated himself quickly.

Suzanne realized it wasn't in the bag. She had forgotten it. "It's not in the purse. I'm sorry, Charlie, I guess I left it at home this morning." She managed a silly, embarrassed laugh. "But we could work on another tune."

He stood up suddenly, almost jerking himself from the floor. "You're a slob. You're a goddamn slob," he yelled. Yukl had always been quiet around Suzanne. But now he was loud. He began pacing nervously around the small living room, staring directly at her. He made a fist and began pressing it hard into the palm of his left hand, mortar and pestle style. This time she could not avoid looking at his eyes.

"C'mon," she said soothingly, trying to hide her growing nervousness as she moved over to sit on the couch. "I said I was sorry. So, I'll sing something else. Or maybe I should leave. What do you think?" Indeed, it was a rhetorical question for Suzanne. She could no longer give this guy the benefit of the doubt. She had to exit. *Now.*

Suzanne got up from the couch. Charlie now turned toward her as she rose with the handbag. He was no longer looking at her. His eyes were focused on his hands as he grabbed her by the shoulders and violently pushed her up against the piano. Her buttocks pressed down hard against the white and black keys, producing an atrocious diminished chord.

"Hey," she shrieked, "what are you—" Before she could finish, he yanked at her blouse and ripped it, trying to pull it off. Incredulous at first, she didn't struggle, hoping he might stop. But Yukl didn't stop. He kept grabbing for the blouse. She tried to fight back—she swung at him with the now-full handbag, but he saw it coming and put up his left arm to block it. She tried again to use the bag.

This time he grabbed her arm, and held on. He was a little man, but he was strong. She grabbed for his arm and squeezed it, hoping to stop any further advances. For the briefest moment there was silence as they stood in the living room, faced each other, and arm-wrestled. The nails on his right hand began to dig into her skin.

"Charlie," she cried, trying to push away from him, "you're hurting me." He just stared back at her, his face contorted in rage. In the corner of the room, she caught a glimpse of the Great Dane. The dog was sitting, quietly watching the struggle.

He forcefully pushed her away and onto the couch. "You're a slob," he repeated and started toward her again.

Yukl was crazy. She had to get away. She was no longer just nervous. Suzanne was now very frightened.

The situation was not manageable. "We can work on the songs next week, okay?" she asked, hoping he would give her an opening to say good-bye and leave quickly. He didn't answer. His eyes were still glued on her scarf. "Okay?" No answer. "Look, Charlie," she said, raising her voice for the first time, "this isn't very funny."

Charlie didn't hear a word she said. He turned and

ran toward the closet. He swung open the door, reached inside, and grabbed a large black necktie. She had run out of time. Suzanne bolted from the piano and headed for the front door, twelve feet away. She made it. But then she suddenly stopped. Pausing for no more than a second or two, she turned and went back to get her red coat. It was a fatal mistake.

Charlie had twisted the tie around his hands. Before Suzanne could even reach the front door bolt, he came up behind her. He jumped up, threw the tie over her head and around her neck, quickly crisscrossed his hands around each end of the tie and pulled hard in opposite directions. She reached up to grab it but she was too late. His grip was firm.

She was only inches away from the door. She could feel her arteries futilely trying to pump blood to her head. She reached out for the door and managed to grab hold of the lock. But Yukl pulled her back.

As she moved backward, Suzanne took her elbow and jabbed Yukl in the rib cage, then tried to use the fingers on her left hand to gouge his eyes. But somehow, Yukl kept his right knee planted firmly in the small of her back while he pulled on the tie. She couldn't reach him. He drew her head closer to his. "Don't scream," he said soothingly, "P-p-please don't scream," he stuttered, his voice growing more quiet.

Suzanne had only one choice. She wrenched around, moving her full body weight in an attempt to face Yukl. But he held on, and swung around with her. She tried to push him away. But his grip was too firm. She gasped and fought for breath.

She spun around once more. This time she managed to face him. With what little strength was left, she used her right hand and tried to hit him. He blocked it and landed a right punch in the middle of her face, drawing blood and breaking her nose. The Great Dane retreated to the kitchen.

Instinctively Suzanne put her hands up to her face and looked at her fingers, now dripping with blood. Yukl used the moment to spin her around and again thrust his knee in her back. Charlie tightened the silk noose. She gasped again. When she tried to scream, she couldn't. Suzanne grabbed one last time for the tie, but Charlie's grip was still too tight. Now Charlie was pulling her into the bedroom, fifteen feet away.

She tried to pull away. She was taller than he by a full three inches, but height was no longer a factor. She started to backpedal as he now pushed her closer to the bathroom. Blood was running down her face. Suzanne could sense the air leaving her lungs all too fast. She reached out one last time for him and tried to grab his cheeks, or his hair, or anything.

Charlie maneuvered around her flailing arms. Her eyes widened as she looked into his face for the last time. His expression was rigid, his eyes fixed in position. His forehead was sweating. And his mouth was wide open. But he wasn't looking at her. He was still staring at the tie. He pulled the tie again and again and spun her around. She tried to kick him, but couldn't. He twisted her head violently. Her hands stabbed the air uselessly as the last of her oxygen was consumed.

Her knees buckled as she began to collapse. Yukl twisted the tie once more. But it was no longer necessary. Suzanne was already falling backwards. He released his grip and watched with a slow motion fascination as her arms dropped limply, her mouth opened, her lifeless legs gave way, and the corner of her head hit the rim of the bathtub with a final, hollow-sounding crack.

The voice lesson was over. Suzanne Reynolds was dead.

The struggle had taken less than two minutes. There were no screams. There were no witnesses. And there was no apparent motive other than what seemed to be the obvious: Charles Yukl had experienced an unstoppable psychotic episode. He had had an irresistible impulse to kill, and he had succeeded.

Yukl sat in the bathroom for a few moments with the body. He was sweating, breathing heavily as he inspected the corpse. Reynolds' eyes were fixed open, staring up at the ceiling. Some blood had trickled into the bathwater. He leaned over and lifted her head up by its hair, removed the tie. He rose and, clutching the silk weapon, walked a few feet back to the small kitchen and opened the old white refrigerator. Inside was a carton of milk, some eggs, and what was left of a six pack of Rheingold, his favorite beer. He took out one of the red and white cans. He drank it quickly. Then he had another.

The beer felt good. It relaxed him. There was silence now, broken only by a few car horns on Twenty-eighth Street. Even the dog knew its place at a time like this and stayed in the kitchen.

On top of the earlier vodka, the second beer hit Yukl hard. He put his left hand down on the sink to steady himself.

His heart was pounding faster now than when he had killed her. He was excited. His whole body shook with a strange exhilaration, and he smiled as he felt himself having an erection.

Susanne Reynolds' blood had already dried on his brown shoes, but Yukl didn't notice. He went over to the body and unbuttoned her blouse, already badly torn. He unfastened her wine-colored wool skirt, and tried to slip it off. It was stuck under the deadweight of the body. He yanked it harder, and it finally moved freely. Next he tore at her white lacefringed half-slip, then her stockings. He grabbed her head and pulled it up. The blood had dried and caked on her face, running from her nose to her chin. "You're a goddamn slob," he repeated. He dropped the head back down.

He was moving faster now. He rolled her over, unfastening the snaps of her black lace brassiere. Then he removed her black bikini panties. He rolled the body over again. One hundred and fifteen dead, very heavy pounds. It wasn't easy.

He dragged her back into the living room. He sat down on the couch. "Goddamn slob," he mumbled. Then he remembered he had left the water in the bathtub. He walked quickly back in and pulled the plug and the now-rose-colored water slowly drained from the tub.

Charlie looked at his watch. It was six o'clock. His wife would be home soon. He started to leave the bathroom when he remembered something. He opened the medicine cabinet near the bathroom door. Sitting on the glass shelf was a Duridium single-edge razor blade. He put it in his pocket and walked back into the living room.

He opened the apartment door. It was quiet out in the hall. It was also dark. Yukl had yet to put a new bulb in the vestibule. Returning to Suzanne's lifeless body, he attempted to lift her, but struggled unsuccessfully under the weight. So he grabbed Suzanne's arms and started to pull, moving slowly across the old shag carpet and out into the hallway. Charlie looked quickly around the deserted stairwell. It was still very quiet.

He had to move fast now. He pulled the body along the dirty floor. When he reached the stairs, he turned around and started backing down as the body took each stair with a thud. First the head hit, then the shoulders, the back, the legs and the ankles. Once there had been a cheap linoleum tacked onto the stairs. It had long since been removed. But the tacks and staples remained, and ripped the skin off as the body passed over each step. Skin stuck to the staples, and blood formed a narrow streak that ran down the stairs.

In less than a minute Yukl had reached the second floor. As the manager of the building, Yukl knew there was a vacant apartment on the floor. Charlie found the door open and pulled the body inside.

He closed the door. It was dark. It was cold. The room was empty except for a ceiling light fixture left in a corner.

He sat for a moment on the low bare white-wall bookshelves and stared again at the body, lying faceup on a decaying fiber carpet mat. Though the room was dimly lit by the street lamp outside the window, Charlie went back upstairs and returned with a flashlight.

He felt safe now. He took off his shirt. Then his pants and shoes. He got down on his knees and straddled the body. He rubbed his hands over her cold and flaccid breasts. Then he squeezed them mercilessly.

He removed his underpants and rolled the body over. As with the bloodstains on his shoes, he didn't notice all the blood and broken skin left by the stairway carpet tacks.

Charlie got on top of the body now and began rocking back and forth, riding the dead girl. He then slid his body down Suzanne's back. He placed his lips and mouth all over her, oblivious to the blood, and worked himself into a sexual frenzy. It was as if an internal stopwatch was ticking. With a mad precision he beat at the body, slapping her face, her neck and shoulders. He was breathing heavily now as he continued his gruesome ritual for another few minutes. He had an orgasm, and punched the corpse hard in the face when he was done.

"Goddamn slob." He kept saying it. But Charlie wasn't finished. His level of excitement had only increased. He got up from the body and went over to the top of the bookcase, where he had placed his trousers. He removed the razor from the right pocket, turned the body over, and started to slash violently with the sharp blade. He cut deep into the breasts, the forehead, the chin. He couldn't stop. He cut deeper into the stomach and abdomen, the thighs, the legs, and the crotch. Then he slashed at her stomach again.

It was 7:30. Charlie dressed, and calmly walked out into the hall and returned to his apartment. His wife had not yet come home. He found an old paper grocery bag in the kitchen and retrieved all of the clothes. He returned the crumpled black tie to a hanger in the closet. He had another Rheingold and combed the apartment for any remaining evidence. He then grabbed a leather leash and without further hesitation took the dog for a long walk down Twenty-eighth Street.

A few doors down he took the clothes out of the grocery bag and dumped them in an outside trash container. He threw away the leather handbag on Twenty-ninth Street—right on the street itself. He returned to the building as his wife, Enken, arrived. Charlie calmly and quickly took her to the vacant apartment and showed her the body.

At 9:45, the cops at the Thirteenth Precinct received a call that a body had been found at 29 East Twenty-eighth Street. The caller was a man named Charles Yukl.

Patrolman Charles McMillen took the radio call and arrived at the apartment shortly after ten. Yukl told McMillen that Reynolds had been in his apartment for a voice lesson earlier that day. He explained that at 9:40 he returned from walking his dog, noticed the apartment door open, entered, found the body, and promptly notified the police.

McMillen put out an immediate call for assistance. Detectives were summoned. So was the medical examiner. While photos of the badly beaten, bruised and mutilated body were being taken a floor below, the questioning began.

The detectives talked to Yukl for more than three hours. His story remained straightforward, consistent. They talked some more. Intuitively, the cops suspected that Yukl knew much more than he was volunteering. But they had no hard evidence, no witnesses, no motive, and nothing more to hold him on than guilt by association.

Shortly after one in the morning, one of the investigators noticed the unusual bloodstains on Charlie's shoes. At 1:30 in the morning the police asked him to accompany them to the station house on East Twenty-first Street. He didn't have to go. He wasn't under arrest. Strangely, he willingly consented.

Once there, the questioning continued. The cops asked if they could borrow Yukl's shoes. He consented. And the questions continued until dawn. Still, none of his responses implicated him in the murder.

During the questioning at Yukl's apartment, it hadn't taken the detectives long to deduce Yukl's involvement in the case. Of all the tenants in the building, only Charlie knew the woman. He had found the body. And, in a strange and demented way, he almost seemed to be welcoming their questions. Still, there wasn't enough to hang him with the crime. There was only the barest circumstantial evidence, no motive, and no witness.

And so the questions kept coming. Important ques-

tions, silly questions, questions designed to build rapport, and questions aimed at antagonizing the man,
questions planned to throw him off balance, to make
him slip and reveal a little bit of what really happened.

The first story of the Reynolds murder was out in
the early Tuesday edition of the *New York Times*
while the cops were still talking to Yukl. It was buried
in the back pages of the paper—a small, four-inch
item slipped in next to the Times' Theater Directory
announcing such shows as *Cactus Flower*, *Cabaret*, and
Fiddler On The Roof. Suzanne Reynolds was identified as a singer whose "body was found by a friend,
Charles Yukl." The Times story was already dated by
the time it hit the stands: the police had long since
abandoned the thought of Yukl as anyone's friend.

Dawn failed to stop the endless coffee and cigarettes, or the questions. It just seemed to light the
squad room a little better. At 6:45 A.M., one of the
detectives suddenly noticed stains on Yukl's trousers.
"What's that?" asked the detective. "It's some soap, I
think," Yukl answered. "Do you mind if I look at the
stain closer?" the cop probed. Yukl looked down, and
silently dropped his trousers and handed them to the
detective.

It was an ugly sight. Immediately the officers noticed brown stains on his jockey shorts. When Yukl
agreed to remove them as well, they saw the same
stains on his genitals. He was now a formal suspect.
"Mr. Yukl," began one of the detectives, "I want to
advise you of your rights. You have the right to remain silent . . ."

Yukl chose to talk. He also submitted to having skin
scrapings and samples of pubic hair taken from his legs
and genitals. His trousers were returned and the questioning continued.

Ten blocks away at 520 First Avenue, the body of

Suzanne Reynolds lay on a stainless steel refrigerated tray at the office of Dr. Milton Helpern, New York City Chief Medical Examiner. It was recorded as case number 9198, and an appropriately numbered paper tag was placed on the body's right big toe.

Dr. Elliot Gross began the autopsy. Four other doctors were present, including Helpern. In New York City, when a white woman is murdered, one doctor is politically inadequate. The brass always steps in. Besides, this was a very messy case.

With the other doctors assembled, Gross wasted no time in looking at what was left of Suzanne Reynolds. Speaking into a tape recorder, he coolly inventoried the damage he could easily see: bone fractures, hemorrhages, abrasions, contusions of the face and neck, face lacerations, and multiple slash and incised wounds. The examination lasted longer than expected, but that was only because there was pressure this time to be especially thorough, to look for the true modality of the victim's demise.

Finally, Gross got to the bottom line. In this case, as in most others, there was a distinct time progression to the death: the bone fractures and face lacerations came first, followed by the contusions of the neck. The specific cause of death: asphyxiation due to strangulation. Homicidal. The body had also been sodomized.

Not far away, the press was already gathering in the lobby at the precinct. They weren't particularly concerned with the results of Dr. Gross's examination. They wanted to see an arrest. The New York City Police Department is genuinely incapable of keeping a secret. Not surprisingly, word had gotten out that there was a break in the case.

Upstairs, in the precinct squad room, Yukl had just ended a coffee break. His story was beginning to weaken, and like many criminals before him, he was becoming a victim of the clock. He was not a good liar, and it had become increasingly difficult for him to remember his lies and maintain his fabrication with each new volley of police questions. He was tired. Besides, as the late evening turned into early morning, he was discovering that it was far easier to remember the truth.

At ten A.M., Yukl decided to tell a little of it. First, he confessed that he had sodomized the body upon finding it. He told police that he had argued with Reynolds in his apartment and had chased her downstairs.

Yukl's initial disclosure broke his composure. He became agitated in his seat. He tapped his foot annoyingly. Suddenly he started to stutter and motion quickly with his hands. He raised his voice. Then, just as suddenly, he asked to see his wife.

It was a pattern well known to the police. Often a suspect will want to confess to his wife or girlfriend before the woman hears about his crime from a disinterested third party. It's usually the first real indication of a major confession in the making. Without hesitating, the police took Yukl outside the room to see his wife.

The next step, if the pattern were to repeat itself, would be for Yukl to ask to make a formal statement. An hour later, almost as if the scene had been scripted, Yukl said he wanted to talk. A second coffee break ended and an assistant district attorney was summoned to the precinct. His name was John Keenan.

Keenan wasn't just any young assistant. He was the rising star in the New York County DA's office headed by legendary DA Frank Hogan. He was the young prince of the homicide bureau and fast becoming known as the number-one criminal trial attorney in the city. He got—or was now routinely given—both the tough cases and the big ones. Either way, he was guaranteed maximum exposure.

John Keenan's style was low-key, unemotional. In the provocative art of adversarial questioning, he was always the gentleman. He was a clever strategist in the courtroom and a brilliant tactician at the crucial juncture of any investigation: the interrogation of the suspect. In his questioning he always appealed to the suspect's inner need to be respected, his need to be liked, and finally, his insatiable (and often poorly hidden) desire to be relieved of his terrible burden: the awful truth.

At 12:40 P.M., Keenan met Yukl for the first time. He gently readvised Yukl of his rights. And Yukl again waived them. Charlie began by repeating the story of the chase and the sodomy. But he was leaving out major details. There was no time frame. Actions were out of sequence. And important things were clearly out of place.

Keenan let Yukl finish his story. Then, in his carefully crafted manner, he quietly asked Charlie to tell the truth. And Yukl broke. "I'd like to make another statement if I could," he requested. Keenan sat back in his chair and listened.

"Sir," Yukl said unemotionally. "I may have denied a lot of things until I talked to my wife and Enken told me to tell the truth. You can't just hide something like this."

Yukl admitted the earlier lies and now gave Keenan and the detectives a detailed play-by-play of the vicious murder.

The formal questioning ended at 1:06 P.M. It was a gruesome tale. It was bizarre. But it was now developing into an airtight, by-the-numbers homicide case.

With Yukl's consent, Keenan dispatched two officers to drive Enken back to Twenty-eighth Street and retrieve the tie. At 1:45 they returned and Yukl identified it as the weapon of record.

There would be no more coffee breaks. Six minutes later, three homicide detectives escorted Yukl from the interrogation room, through a pack of photographers, and up to the desk in the Thirteenth Precinct. His hands were manacled behind his back. He rested his chin against his chest as Sergeant Francis McCluskey asked the routine booking questions. Minutes later, Yukl was taken in a police van to criminal court, where Judge Francis K. O'Brien ordered him held without bail, pending grand jury action. Shortly before three P.M., Charles William Yukl was officially charged with murder in the first degree. The date: October 25, 1966.

CHAPTER TWO

August 20, 1974

The roof always leaked at 118 Waverly Place. It was an old building in the heart of Greenwich Village. Even when it wasn't raining, the roof managed to leak, and it had been raining heavily the past weekend.

But it was now Tuesday, and the ceiling at Mary Smithers' place was still dripping. It was a hot, unbearably humid day, and Smithers, an English teacher and a top floor tenant in the building, had suffered the water seepage for days. Today she was fed up. After spending an hour on the phone, she finally got the building's superintendent, Mr. Johnson, to take a look.

At eleven A.M., the pair walked up the stairs from Smithers' apartment to the roof to try to find the source of the leak. Johnson checked the tar roofing papers, the seals between the old brick, the wood joiner work and the older metal stacks.

When he reached the corner of the building, Johnson happened to look down at the rooftop of the building below and suddenly began to shake and gesture wildly.

Smithers quickly came over to his corner. She screamed.

Twenty feet away, lying in a small pool of water on

the rooftop at 120 Waverly Place was the nude body of a young, badly beaten woman.

The city had been wounded again. A body had been found in the Village. Most of the six murders a day in New York City go unreported by the press, or, at the very best, unnoticed. But this murder was different. It was a young attractive white woman. It was the Village. It was messy. It was bound to get plenty of press attention.

The body was just outside the door at the top of the stairway. About twenty feet from the entrance to the fifth-floor apartment, the body was separated from a carpeted and well-furnished sun deck by only an old blue picket fence and a row of bright orange marigolds.

By the time Detective Don Baeszler arrived at the rooftop scene—shortly after noon—the horseflies had discovered the body and the thermometer was nearing 100. He was followed up the winding, creaky stairs by Dr. Farouk Presswalla, an associate New York City medical examiner.

Presswalla was a thin, Indian man in his early forties, known for his businesslike manner at the most horrifying crime scenes. His pattern never changed. He always arrived wearing a gray suit, horn-rim glasses, and a well-concealed sense of humor. Whether it was a result of his own morbidity threshold or simply of his efficiency, he never stayed more than a half hour.

At the top of the landing Presswalla stood and viewed the cadaver. He was out of breath and sweating profusely. He moved closer to the body and examined it. It was lying faceup, its blue eyes staring hopelessly into nothing. And the face had been badly beaten. The breasts were bruised. There were lacerations of the stomach, thighs and legs. Parts of skin had been ripped away and streaks of dried blood formed an ugly trail on the legs.

Presswalla made note of an unusual birthmark on the neck. Then he put his hand under the matted light brown hair and lifted the head gently. "It appears to be intact," he said to Baeszler. "The body wasn't dropped. It was brought up here."

Baeszler just shook his head. "God only knows how it got up here," he said to Patrolman Haywood Reid, one of the first cops who had responded to the location.

The police had already begun a search of the small rooftop and the apartment leading to it. They found no clothing. No pocketbook. No identification. And although the body had been cut, no weapon.

The media was there, parked in front of the building in an assortment of vans and station wagons. When they got upstairs, they discovered that the rooftop scene was too gruesome for even the evening news, so they shot their stories from a distance.

A police photographer was busy taking the necessary close-ups. Others were measuring precise distances between the body and parts of the building. Then an assistant from the medical examiner's office arrived on the roof with the morbid accessories: heavy manila rope and a large, dark gray canvas body bag.

Don Baeszler was still on the roof. As a homicide detective for fourteen years, he'd seen dozens of bodies before this one. It was the name of this most unfortunate game. But this case was already beginning to puzzle him.

In almost every murder, no matter how meticulous the criminal, there is some clue left behind. It is often a forgotten piece of evidence with no initial meaning, but if you were lucky, it ultimately proved to be the missing link in turning a thin circumstantial case into a solid conviction.

Baeszler couldn't find the clue. Besides, the condition of the body didn't fit any established pattern of homicide investigation. It was always a process of elimination.

Was the woman a victim of a mugging, or a robbery, or a rape? Did she live in the apartment building and stumble upon a burglar who then killed her to cover up his lesser crime? In each of these cases the body is almost always clothed. And a quick check revealed that the woman did not live in the building. All the tenants were present and accounted for.

This was not an average murder by New York standards. Excluding the reasonable, Baeszler could only pursue two remaining possibilities: the woman was either killed by a spurned lover, or perhaps worst of all, this was not an isolated occurrence. The woman may have been murdered by a psychopathic sex killer on his way to killing others.

It was nearing one P.M. Presswalla was through with his initial cursory examination. It was time to move the body.

Suddenly Baeszler had an idea. They had looked for clues everywhere except two places: the rooftop under the body, and the back of the body itself. They lifted it up. Nothing on the tarpaper. Just a wet rooftop.

The attendants started to slide the canvas bag over the body.

"Wait a minute," Baeszler shouted. "I'm not through yet." Presswalla looked up. "Detective," he said in his usual monotone, "I think we're finished up here." The attendants stood waiting for their orders.

Baeszler was now acting on pure instinct, hoping for a lucky break, for the clue that would keep him up nights until it all made sense. "I want you to turn the body over on its stomach." The attendants complied.

Presswalla saw it first. Then Baeszler moved in for a look. There, on the back of this dead woman, were the most peculiar markings. On the left side and distinctly etched into her skin was a neat 2½ by 4-inch rectangle. Inside it were three small circles. It was as if someone, or something, had branded her.

"I don't know what it means," Baeszler said, calling over the officer with the camera. "But I want this photographed. And I want it measured."

A few blocks away, at 155 Leonard Street, I was laboring away, locked in my office with a handful of FBI agents and forensic technicians. I had spent hours interviewing key witnesses, trying to plug some gaping holes in a massive four-and-a-half-month-long murder case that had just ended in a hung jury. A new trial had been scheduled for the day after Labor Day.

I was one of those young assistant district attorneys engaged in the noble crusade of making the streets safe for New Yorkers. But the crusade was no longer giving even the appearance of being noble. Older and more capable DA's before me had already left the office, convinced that the mission had turned into a terrible and impossible burden, that the rate of random murders in New York City had turned the once-safe streets into the world's largest arena for Russian roulette—a playground of strangers made intimate in hundreds of isolated moments of sheer madness and death.

The attorneys who had abandoned this prosecutorial ship—many for private practice—had also jettisoned the vision of solving crimes and administering justice. They had felt they were only managing criminal cases and watching helplessly as justice evaporated into the streets. Their idea of excelling had been painfully redefined. Now, excelling meant merely surviving; their concept of winning was to cope effectively with an impossible set of circumstances.

Somehow I was still possessed with a traditional vision of justice. In fact, I was almost obsessed by it.

It was not an abnormal obsession. The New York County District Attorney's Office of Frank Hogan was unique. We weren't order takers. We didn't wait for the police to bring cases to us. We aggressively went after them, developing them from the initial investigative stages, through presentation to the grand jury, up to the final prosecution.

We were known as Hogan's Hooligans. This wasn't just another DA's office. It was the finishing school for criminal trial practice, a graduate school for trial lawyers. And for those homicide attorneys who stuck around, it was simply the hottest action in town.

Once every seven days, each assistant D.A. in the homicide bureau had his turn on "the chart"—a system that placed you on twenty-four-hour call with the city's homicide detectives. When they rolled on a case, you rolled. This process enabled the district attorney's office to be in charge of the homicide investigations.

Naturally it inspired some antagonism between the DA's and the police. Some thought we were being presumptuous in our interpretation of our roles. We were.

It was Hogan's view, shared by his apostles, that the DA's, not the police, were the chief law enforcement officers of the community. We were the ones who had to decide ultimately whether or not to prosecute a case. The police standard for "clearing" a case was simply having probable cause that a crime had been committed by the so-called "perpetrator." Our standard was far tougher, because it had to be. For us to clear a case we had to prove the defendant's guilt beyond a reasonable doubt, supported by legally sufficient evidence. The bottom line was that the facts had to be unerring servants of the truth.

Every chance I had I volunteered to be the DA on call, to gather crucial evidence and to mount the case for the People versus some incredibly bad characters. Perhaps naively, I interpreted that as an integral part of my job in public service.

I finished questioning the witnesses in my office shortly after ten P.M. It was too late for a decent meal, so I stopped at Dave's, one of those small outdoor luncheonettes, for a carbohydrate killer: an egg cream, two hot dogs and a knish smothered with mustard. For exercise I walked twenty blocks to the West Village for my dessert, a slice of pizza and an Orange Julius at Eighth Street and Sixth Avenue.

It was shortly before eleven that night when I got home to the small apartment on Twelfth Street I shared with my wife, Patti. It was advertised as two and a half rooms, but luckily we both had a sense of humor, without which one could spend a lifetime looking for the other one and a half rooms. For $230 a month, we rented an L-shaped alcove. We were treated to a partially restricted Twelfth-floor southerly view of Sixth Avenue.

I kissed Patti, who had returned earlier in the evening from her job as a teacher at Dalton, a private school uptown on East Eighty-ninth Street. We had both survived another day.

The television set was on, and the news led with the sensational story of the rooftop body found at 120 Waverly, only five blocks away from our apartment. It was news to me.

I had just passed Waverly Place on my way to the apartment. I shook my head, "It's getting to the point where there are no sanctuaries in Manhattan," I said to Patti. "It's getting too close to home."

Sanctuary for Don Baeszler was the Thirteenth Precinct. He was a top homicide detective, a large, overweight, prematurely gray man who married the police department early in his life. Uncle Don, as his fellow detectives liked to call him, was an inveterate New York cop.

At the age of forty-three, he'd already done it all, from walking a beat and busting the usual parade of Eighth Avenue prostitutes to handling the biggest cases the city had to offer.

His city landmarks didn't include the Empire State Building, the Plaza, or the Statue of Liberty. Baeszler remembered other historic sites: the bullet impact marks still visible on the Sixth Avenue building on the West Side street where he had once killed a man during a holdup. There was 26 Jones Street, an alley off Washington Square Park, Avenue A and East Ninth Street—all the scenes of unsolved murders still on the books.

And now there was 120 Waverly Place.

It had been a very long day for Baeszler. His men had questioned everyone at the apartment house and in the adjoining building. He was approaching his seventeenth hour on duty. There was nothing more he could do until morning. As he was preparing to leave the Thirteenth precinct for the long drive to his home in Staten Island, the desk sergeant stopped him. "One more call, Don."

On the other end was a man named Benjamin Lichtenstein, a state parole officer. He had been watching the Eleven o'clock news.

"Detective Baeszler, I'm calling about the body that they found."

"What about it?"

"Well . . . they said they found it at 120 Waverly Place."

"You got it. Why?"

"Well," Lichtenstein paused. "I knew the address rang a bell so I checked our records."

"And?" Baeszler was pressing now.

"Well," he said again, "one of the tenants in that building belongs to us."

I was already in bed when the phone rang. I was used to late night phone calls and early morning trips to out of the way police precinct houses to investigate the vicious crimes of the night. More often than not, working in the homicide bureau, late night interruptions by phone indicated another body for the medical examiner—and another case for me. I picked up the phone.

"Good evening," said the deep and soothing voice on the other end. To anyone else, it was a crank caller. To me, it had to be Don Baeszler.

"Okay, big Don, whaddaya got?" I asked. The game was on.

"Not so fast, Bobby boy," Baeszler was playing with me now. He liked to play this demented version of twenty questions whenever he was on to something big. "Bobby, do you know a certain Charles Yukl?"

Yukl. A name like that is hard to forget. I knew of Yukl. When I had first come into the DA's office in 1968, I studied every past murder case I could get my hands on. The *People* v. *Charles Yukl* was a textbook case, and one of the first I had read. It was a textbook case because of its complexities, not because it was routine. That's why the case stuck with me.

"Sure. I know Yukl," I said. "Isn't he the guy who killed Suzanne Reynolds in 1966?"

"Absolutely cor-rect, Bobby," Baeszler proclaimed with appropriate emphasis. "Very good. You are now batting a thousand. Now, I'll give you the twenty point toss-up. Do you know where the esteemed Mr. Yukl lives?"

That was an easy one, I thought. "Attica. He's in prison."

"I'm so sorry," said Baeszler in his worst quiz-show-host voice. "That's incorrect." There was a long pause.

"What? He's not in Attica? Okay, he's in Walkill. He's in prison, right?"

This time Baeszler didn't play with me.

"Wrong. Charles Yukl is your neighbor."

"That's impossible. He brutally killed Suzanne Reynolds. He was convicted. How the hell did he get out?"

"He was paroled over a year ago, Bobby," came Baeszler's sober response. "They let the son of a bitch out, and I don't know why. But I *do* know that he lives at 120 Waverly Place, the same building where they found the body this morning."

"Was she strangled?" I asked.

"So far you're doing very well," Don said, returning to his soothing voice.

"One more question," I said. "Did he use something to choke her or did he use his hands? Was it ligature or manual?"

"Ligature."

We both knew what that meant.

"Okay," I said without hesitation. "Pick me up in twenty minutes."

I got out of bed and got dressed. The thought of the State of New York releasing a murderer like Yukl was enough to make me question the entire justice system in this country. There simply had to be more to the Yukl case than I presently recalled.

Shortly after midnight I went downstairs. Baeszler was in the car waiting for me.

The streets were empty as we drove over Tenth Street, past the Albert Hotel, and across Third Avenue. The conversation was no longer cute telephone banter. The time had already passed for the inevitable, defensive black humor that we always embraced in a murder case to maintain our own sanity.

"It's a strange one, Bob," Baeszler said. "I saw the body this morning. Later I went over to the morgue and looked at her again," he said. "She had the same look on her face. Even in death she reminded me of somebody. I remember a photo of Marilyn Monroe that I once saw in a magazine. It was taken when she was a teenager. She had a blank look on her face, almost a sad look in her eyes."

"She reminded you of Marilyn Monroe?" I asked.

Baeszler shook his head. "No, Bob," he said sadly. "She reminded me of Norma Jean Baker."

We turned onto Twentieth Street and parked at the back entrance to the precinct.

"Did he cut her up?" I asked.

Baeszler sighed, and nodded. "No, not really. But I'm beginning to think you really *do* know this guy."

This was no longer looking like a traditional whodunit case with its custom-built enigmas designed for pure crime connoisseurs. It was fast developing into a pathetic, and disturbing *howdunit*.

"I don't understand it. I can't figure out how Yukl got out," I said as we entered the dimly lit station house. "Did somebody goof? Was there a mistake made?"

Baeszler didn't know.

We walked upstairs to the second floor—B deck, it was called—and into the main detective office, a large 40-by-15-foot room cluttered with old green metal desks and green-enameled walls that had been steadily chipping for years. The office had been the scene of this ritual hundreds of times—while the rest of the city slept, a small group of detectives and DA's would always be at some precinct house. They would sit, stand, drink coffee . . . and wait for hours for crucial information to surface.

This night was no different. We waited for what seemed like hours for the police to retrieve certain records. But at least this time we knew what we were looking for: the 1966 files on Charles Yukl.

We were still waiting for the information when another call came in. Earlier that day an anonymous telephone call had been made to the police 911 emergency number reporting a double murder at a Harlem housing project at 211 West 151st Street. When the police arrived on the scene—Apartment 4B—they found the badly mutilated bodies of Mrs. Sherrald Dickens, twenty-eight, and her nine-year-old daughter, Sharon. Both bodies had been raped.

Twelve members of the Sixth District homicide squad had worked all day and into the night, questioning scores of people at the Harlem River houses. One of those questioned was Edward Hurdle, a ground-floor neighbor, who claimed he had gone to the Dickens' apartment to ask the mother to baby-sit. When he received no answer, he claimed he had opened the unlocked and unbolted door and found the two bodies.

Ultimately the investigation led back to Mr. Hurdle himself. The police confronted him with the suggestion that it was Hurdle's own voice on the tape that had been made of the anonymous call. Hurdle broke down, confessed the crime, and implicated a friend, Henry Jefferson, in the multiple stabbings.

The two were ready to make a statement. I was still on call. The police sent a squad car for me and I headed uptown to 119th Street. Baeszler stayed behind at the Eighteenth Precinct to wait for the Yukl files; he shoved three desks together and took a short nap.

At four A.M., I began the first session with Edward Hurdle in the cramped commanding officer's room of the Twenty-fifth Precinct. Leo Cosentino, a stenographer, and Lionel Tuckett, a homicide detective, sat in on the session. I advised brother Hurdle of his rights. He waived them, and the questioning began. He was an old-looking twenty-one-year-old, his face a hardened reflection of a much tougher life. Hurdle ha the right to remain silent, but silence had ceased being a virtue hours earlier.

The answers came slowly at first, and then Hurdle spit them out in rapid fire succession. They had gone to the apartment on a dare by Jefferson who wanted to have sex with Sherrald Dickens, a neighbor Hurdle had known since he was fourteen. When she resisted, Jefferson had stabbed her, then Hurdle joined in. Soon, neither could stop the attack.

"What did you do to the little girl?" I asked.

Hurdle got up and started pacing around the room. "Jefferson said, 'You have to stab her too.' He said, 'Go ahead.' So, you know, I had to stab her too."

Hurdle felt purged of his guilt by telling me the story. His cathartic confession was a boilerplate model for conviction.

There would almost surely be a later attempt by his attorneys to present an insanity defense. It was an absurd tactic, a last resort measure made less—or more—absurd by the fact that it sometimes worked. And it was almost always tried in cases like this one.

Anticipating this as Hurdle's only way out, I asked him a series of simple questions, his responses to which then clearly indicated beyond any and all doubt that he knew and appreciated the nature and consequences of his acts. Clearly, he told me, he knew. Yes, he knew that what he had done was wrong.

There were no more questions needed. Hurdle

had willingly cooperated in the murders, and now he had willingly cooperated in his prosecution. He had buried himself. And Jefferson would be next.

Surprisingly, he wanted to tell us everything. I took Jefferson's statement a half hour later. It was just as incriminating as Hurdle's. There were no exits for these men. They were finished. The case was neatly wrapping itself up with a bloody bow. There could be no doubt that when presented with the evidence, the jury would convict them, and Hurdle and Jefferson would go to prison for life.

I looked over at Cosentino, the stenographer. He nodded. He had gotten it all down. We had also recorded the statement on tape. I took my case folder with me and left. It was six A.M.

A police car took me home to take a quick shower and change. There was no time to sleep. My thoughts were no longer focused on the Harlem double murder but on what the brass considered a far more important case—the killing at 120 Waverly Place—and on an increasingly troubling set of possibilities.

I had left the Twenty-fifth Precinct convinced that justice would serve Hurdle and Jefferson. That the system would work. But now I wasn't so sure. If justice had indeed been served in 1966, then how did a guy like Charles Yukl get out?

CHAPTER THREE

I got back to my office at the criminal court building a little after eight that morning. On the fourth floor the complaint room had just opened, but it was already filling up with the urban refugees from the night before—the victims of a disturbing variety of crimes. The criminals—the perpetrators, as almost every New York cop has been conditioned for decades to describe them—were, with any luck, at least temporarily behind bars at the Tombs, the city's holding tank in the same massive complex. They were the usual assortment of street people, each sharing accommodations with the pimps, whores, the fighters, wife beaters, and rapists.

And here, just a few blocks away, their victims sat on immovable green painted steel seats and waited their turn for justice, New York style, in the complaint room. Littered with typists, office temps, cops, and assistant district attorneys, it was always a full house with nearly seventy people at a time crammed in. The windows in the room looked to the west, down Centre Street, but most everyone's attention was normally focused on the eight partitioned booths that faced the wall. The desks were covered with dozens of official city forms—yellow forms were for felony complaints, blue for misdemeanors, and white forms were for "violations," the term we used for things like disorderly conduct, public intoxication, and first-time prostitution arrests. Yellow was always the most popular color.

If you didn't know any better, you might suspect this was the Guadalajara bus station. Like most operations in the city of New York, we were understaffed and overcrowded. Still, you could easily detect a certain order to this disorder.

From the moment you walked into the office you seized upon the frantic rhythm of the place—the shouting, the hurried conferences between hurried attorneys, and the dispensing of gut, street advice that invariably was more humane than the "justice" that awaited many of the people in that room a few hours or days later.

It wasn't a turnstyle operation, but it did move quickly. Assistant district attorneys would move from table to table taking down information, cajoling, arguing and hand-holding their way through the nearly 150 cases that they would share each day. Inside each of the eight booths, the DAs would try to bunch types of cases together—muggings with muggings, shopliftings with shopliftings and aggravated assaults with aggravated assaults.

Murder, on the other hand, enjoyed a very special position outside the room. Before the homicide cases ever got to the complaint room they stopped two flights up. There, they were prepared by the more experienced DAs in the homicide bureau, away from the maddening crowd. There were twenty tough prosecutors in the bureau on hand to work the tough cases.

The smell of old coffee always seemed to permeate the complaint room, matched only by the combined odors of dust and the perspiration of very anxious, distraught people. It was an old, messy place. It was well lit, but the harsh fluorescent lighting only served to increase the tension and anxiety that filled the room.

The linoleum floor was pockmarked with tar craters of hundreds of discarded cigarettes that formed a relief map of despair. It was not a room that anyone came to by choice. It was not a room that anyone left without being, or at least feeling, somehow reduced. The complaint room was, without doubt, a painful place.

My sixth-floor office suffered little by comparison. The coffee was fresher, and the consolation we offered seemed a little more meaningful. Downstairs there was a strong incentive to clear many of the cases, to plead them out and lessen the court burden. In the homicide bureau our objective was to go the distance whenever we could, to keep the killers off the streets as long as possible, and, if God was really on our side, to keep them away forever.

Don Baeszler was already gone by the time I got to my desk. But Kenny Klein was waiting for me. Klein was twenty-seven, a young homicide bureau assistant a few years out of Columbia University Law School.

"Kenny, I want the Hurdle and Jefferson statements typed up right away." He nodded. "Also, call Marty Davin [another detective] and get his notes on Hurdle and Jefferson. And check with the medical examiner for his findings. When you get all that, check with the grand jury and let's get a date for them to be indicted."

Klein nodded. But he didn't bolt for the phone. Now, he had something to tell *me*.

Kenny wore a strange smile that morning, one of those looks that telegraphs possession of some information you don't really want to hear. He handed me a large manila envelope. "Baeszler dropped this off for you." Inside was a worn out dark brown file folder overflowing with papers of varying sizes and ages. It was the Yukl file, retrieved by Baeszler from the depths of police headquarters near Foley Square.

Inside were the uniformed police and detective reports from 1966, the blue sheets known as DD5 forms, original case reports, photographs, grand jury minutes, autopsy findings, probation reports. Somewhere in the heart of this bulging folder was a list of all the witnesses, experts, doctors and cops. It was a scorecard for the game played eight years earlier between Charles Yukl and The People.

The case folder was, in its most disorganized form, a remarkable assemblage of information. And somewhere, in between the yellowing pages, the carbons and the xeroxes, revealed in margin notes or in an obscure reference, I hoped to discover both the history of a madman and the madness of a system that would allow Yukl out on the streets again.

CHAPTER FOUR

The Yukl file made for good reading, especially the transcript of the hearing held to determine whether the confession Yukl had given to the police and later to Keenan was voluntary.

The police had been with Yukl for a total of eight hours prior to his making any incriminating statement—three in his apartment and five at the police precinct. At the precinct, they had him take off his shoes, then his pants, which revealed the disgusting physical evidence that convinced them he was the killer of the Reynolds woman. It was only then that the police advised him of his rights.

The key question in the hearing was whether Yukl participated in a custodial interrogation for a period of time prior to being given/read his rights. If so, his "Miranda" rights had been violated, rendering his confession to the police as well as his statements to Keenan inadmissible in court.

Ultimately, after Yukl entered a guilty plea, the court ruled that the arrest and interrogation were more or less proper. Yukl's claim that his Miranda rights had been violated was denied, but the reading of the hearing made it clear that the court could have easily gone the other way.

In the Miranda case, the U.S. Supreme Court had said, "If the interrogation continues without the presence of an attorney and a statement is taken, a heavy burden rests on the government to demonstrate that the defendant knowingly and intelligently waived his privilege against self-incrimination and his right to retained or appointed counsel."

One judge took particular note of this in relating it to the peculiar circumstances of Charles Yukl's questioning. "A man, shoeless," he wrote, "and all but naked, separated from his wife who is elsewhere in the station house, alone, except for interrogating policemen, and after having been subjected to many hours of interrogation about a murder . . . is not in a condition to make an intelligent, knowing, and voluntary waiver. . . ."

It was, fortunately, a dissenting opinion. The final appeals court vote was a narrow 4–3 victory for the prosecution.

It took me the rest of the day to get through the hundreds of pages of police, psychiatric, and probation reports, to put them in a proper order, to interpret their meaning and relevance to the current investigation, and to shed some light onto the darkness of a killer's mind.

The documents contained important details of Charles Yukl's past—his parents, his schooling, his friends, his work experience. None of the papers were in any particular order, but as a whole, they painted quite a damning picture of a man who had, either by accident or design, manipulated the system to his best advantage.

The documents also projected an unflattering picture of bureaucracy and the lack of equality under the law.

Charles Yukl was developing into an embarrassing case, considering his personal history, not to mention our own previous investigative behavior. It was all right there for everyone to read—in the file.

The psychiatric interviews were revealing in their detail. Yukl had, it seemed, a normal childhood for the first four years of his life. He was born in Baltimore, Maryland, on Valentine's Day in 1935. His parents, he later told his psychiatrists, always wanted to have a child. With his birth, his father's wish for a son seemed to be fulfilled.

His parents named him Charles Jr., in honor of his father, a Czechoslovakian immigrant who came to America to seek his fortune with his own parents in the early 1900s. Charles Sr. was a classical musician, and a very good one. He had rigorously trained in the European music school tradition, and played the trumpet and the French horn with the Baltimore and Washington, D.C., symphony orchestras. He was married to Dorothea Freitag, a musician who arranged symphony and big band music for dance concerts, ballet, and music revue shows.

Charles Jr. lived in a small house in the city, along with his parents and Marie and Louis Yukl, his grandparents. The grandparents spoke no English, and they insisted on an old world existence in the Yukl household. A strict etiquette was observed.

Meals were served at precise times. Visitors didn't come to the house without an appointment. And their entertainment was modest: on occasional Saturdays, Charles Sr. and Dorothea would dress up and go out for dinner. Sundays were almost always spent at the local Protestant church, then on to weekly student piano recitals, and early dinner at home with the family.

Charles Sr. wanted more than anything for his son to be a concert pianist. Piano lessons started for young Yukl at the age of four. Dorothea was the teacher. Every day, for two to three hours, she sat at the piano

with her son. While other children went to local Baltimore parks with their parents in the afternoons, or
played with their toys in anticipation of kindergarten,
Charles Yukl went to the Peabody Conservatory of
Music. When he returned home, the playing continued. He sat on the piano bench, his mother at his side,
and practiced.

After a few weeks, Dorothea had him reading sheet
music, a remarkable accomplishment for a child of his
age. She would play him a song—a simple piano com-
position by Chopin, Bach, or Beethoven—and then
she would ask him to play it. It wasn't easy for him to
play the pieces. He was only four years old, and his
hands and fingers were too small to reach all the keys.
He was unable to stretch his fingers the eight keys
needed to make an octave, so Dorothea made him
practice special finger exercises that would extend his
reach.

Charles Yukl came to dread the piano sessions with
his mother. Dorothea was a perfectionist who had
little patience for musical mistakes, even if they were
being made by a four-year-old. Often, she would have
him play a piece he had practiced, and then intimidate
him by playing the same piece—better.

"I could only get love from her," he later told a
court-appointed psychiatrist, "if I competed. But I
couldn't compete because she was always too good.
Only once did she ever compliment me and say, 'It
was a good job.' "

Charles was intimidated by his mother, and afraid of
his father, who was a strict disciplinarian. Though
Yukl's parents never fought in front of company, or
outside the confines of their house, their anger toward
each other was not hidden when they were alone with
their son. Loud arguments often lasted for hours.

A second son, Franz, was born to Dorothea and

Charles Sr. in 1938, and soon became the parents' favorite. Unlike Charles Jr., the younger brother, nicknamed "Tex" by his parents, was never pushed into music. The newly focused attention on Tex and the continuing pressure on Chuck to perform took their toll. By the time he was five, Yukl had developed a noticeable stutter, which only served to compound his shyness. His performance in elementary school began to suffer, but his parents didn't notice. The couple filed for divorce when Charles was seven. Dorothea moved to New York. And Charles Sr. decided to move west to California. He was awarded custody of both boys and, together with their grandparents, headed for Los Angeles.

The family—minus Dorothea—settled a few weeks later in North Hollywood, in a small house at 4225 Tujunga Avenue. Charlie was enrolled at Rio Vista Elementary School, where his shy and quiet nature was interpreted as his way of coping with the inevitable adjustment problems of moving to a new city, a new neighborhood, and a new school. His father had apparently no time—or inclination—to stay on top of Charlie's progress at school. He was absorbed in his music, his social life, and Tex.

Charles Yukl, Sr. was not only playing principal trumpet with the Los Angeles Philharmonic, he was also holding down part-time jobs with the Civic Light Opera Company and the L.A. Rams football team concert band. His love life quickly picked up, and soon after arriving in California, he met and started dating a nurse, Helen. She was a plain, short, quiet woman—and she played no musical instruments.

Helen was passive, she didn't argue, and she was properly impressed with Yukl's profession and his position in the Los Angeles music community. Charles Sr. soon married her. Helen was the exact opposite of

Dorothea. Not surprisingly, Charlie, who was almost nine, by this time, had felt somewhat responsible for his parents' divorce and began to resent Helen, the new mother in the house. He started showing his dislike for her by doing little things: his room, once clean and neat, was a mess; he often came home late for dinner.

His father usually responded by beating him. One night, the father went too far—after the beating, he locked his son inside a darkened closet in the living room. Charlie screamed and banged on the wooden door, begging his father to let him out. He thought he would die. Charles Sr. simply walked away and went to bed.

Inside the dark closet, jammed with unneeded winter clothes and a host of battered old suitcases, Charlie couldn't sleep. He had trouble even standing. He tried to make an awkward bed of the luggage, but it wouldn't support him and he kept falling to the hardwood floor. He was too afraid to sleep, thinking that if he did he would never wake up.

The next morning, after Charles Sr. had showered and dressed, he approached the door. In one swift motion, he unlocked and opened it. He found Charlie asleep, hunched over two suitcases, with his face pointing down at a small puddle of vomit.

"Get out!" he screamed. Charlie looked up, and for a moment had no idea where he was—or why he was there. Then he remembered and started to tremble.

"Please don't kill me. Please don't kill me," he mumbled.

His father became strangely quiet. He just grabbed Charlie by the shirt, yanked him out of the closet, and pushed him to the living-room floor. "You're late for school," he said, and walked out.

A few days later, Charlie went on an arson spree in

North Hollywood, setting a total of eight fires. When he was caught, his father beat him again. Officials of the school asked to speak to the parents. Only Charles Sr. met with them. Charlie was still under age, they told his father. With any luck at all, his behavior would ultimately be stricken from the permanent records. But first, the juvenile authorities in Los Angeles insisted on sending the child to see a psychiatrist.

The psychiatric sessions embarrassed and angered his father. He wouldn't talk about them, not even to his wife: he made it quite clear that whether they helped Charlie or they didn't, he didn't want to have much to do with his son.

When Charlie enrolled in Le Conte Junior High School in North Hollywood in September 1947, he hardly talked to any of his classmates. His grades continued to deteriorate. He had assumed the role of a young loner, and showed an absolute fear of women. Most of his teachers were women, and when they called on him in class, his stuttering was uncontrollable.

His first junior high school semester was an academic disaster. The only grades he could muster were C's and D's in every subject—except in music, where he managed to land a B while playing E flat alto tenor horn for the school band. He did not show much improvement in succeeding semesters. In June 1950, when he graduated, he received C's in every course except two. He had managed to earn an A in music, and another A for his toils with the school band. In typing class, however, he was considered a leader—he had mastered an incredible typing speed of 100 words a minute.

On September 11, 1950, Charlie enrolled at North Hollywood High School, and his grades worsened. He failed French and mathematics, managed a C in English, and received D's in every other subject except two—band and physical education. Even though Charlie was slight, he had natural speed. Encouraged by the school's track coach, Yukl tried out for—and made—the track team. When he came home and told his father the good news, a major disagreement erupted between them.

This time it was an argument Charlie won. Charles Sr. finally, if reluctantly, agreed to let Charlie join the team, and in just a few weeks, Yukl was one of its stars. He was undefeated in the 660 yard race, holding a winning time of 1 minute 32.9 seconds. He led the school's Blue and Gray relay team and received his first headline in the *Arcade*, the high school newspaper. His father never spoke to him about it. In May, Yukl scored well in the All City track and field finals. His father did not attend. The following year, Yukl was again a headliner for the school's Huskie Bees, leading the team in the 660 and in relays.

Charlie had virtually no social life in high school. His father would not allow him to date until he was seventeen, and then only if the girl's father served as a chaperon. Under those conditions, Charlie simply didn't go out with girls. All he had left, it seemed, was his music and his sports. When track season ended, he wanted to try another sport—tennis. A friend on the track team had a racket he could borrow.

With some money earned from a paper route, he went to a nearby sporting goods store and bought a can of white tennis balls.

When he walked in the house that night, his father spotted the balls.

"Where did you get them?" he demanded.

"I b-b-bought them at the store," Charlie answered.

"You did not," his father insisted. "You stole them!"

Charlie shook his head. He could hardly get the words out of his mouth. "N-n-n-ooo," he said. "I—I—"

"You're a liar," his father interrupted harshly. He stood up and caught Charlie by the back of the neck as Charlie tried to get away from what he thought would be a beating and another trip to the closet.

Instead, Charles Sr. marched him outside onto Tujunga Avenue and into the family car. They drove over to the store. When they arrived, Charlie was pushed inside by his father, who grilled the store clerk.

"Did you sell these to this boy?" he asked, gripping the can of balls.

"Yes sir," the clerk said. "About two hours ago."

The father didn't say a word. He left the store and headed back to the car. Not a word was spoken during the ten minute ride back to the house.

Charlie cried all the way. He had been vindicated, but some real damage had been done.

This last episode was also one of the final direct conflicts between father and son.

The next day, on the way home from track practice, Charlie passed the armed-forces recruiting station in North Hollywood. He stood in front of the building for a moment or two and stared at the colored posters in the window and at some brochures stacked on a metal stand outside the building. He walked inside. He picked up some of the brochures and stuffed them inside his school bag.

That night, while his father was in another room practicing his trumpet, Charlie made the decision. For reasons he was never able to explain adequately, he narrowed his choices down to just one branch.

The following day, after school, he missed track practice and headed straight for the recruiting station. He told them he wanted to enlist in the navy.

The recruiting officer gave Yukl the usual pitch. He

started with explanations of the navy posters on the walls, the upbeat photos that painted an overly bright, comfortable picture of enlisted life, big ships, good food, and exotic ports of call. He was quite persuasive. Besides, he told Charlie, the navy offered the boy—and thousands more like him—a future he might not otherwise have. In the rising uncertainties of postwar unemployment, the navy was giving Charlie a guaranteed job—a secure place to ride out the economic storms and learn a few skills besides.

Charlie Yukl needed no convincing. He signed up immediately, and he abandoned all concern for graduating from high school or competing with the track team. He saw the navy as a way out of the Yukl house, an escape from his father.

He wasn't looking for any of the navy's challenging jobs—which the recruiting officer had vaguely promised him—but simply for a home.

There was only one hitch. He was just seventeen, which made him underage to enlist. For the navy to make an exception, and for the processing to begin, he would need the signed consent of his parents.

When he got back to the house on Tujunga Avenue that night, Charlie waited for the right moment to slip the necessary forms to his father.

His dad had signed some forms before—some medical waivers when Charlie joined the track squad—but only reluctantly and after a heated argument.

Charlie waited until just after dinner to bring the subject up. He didn't address the issue directly. He simply produced the forms and casually attempted to deposit them on the edge of the small dining room table.

"I n-n-need you to s-sign these," he said to his father in a muffled stutter. Charlie retreated to the corner of the room, waiting for his dad to explode.

But instead of launching into the argument Charlie expected, his father only stared at the forms quietly.

He already saw Charlie as a lost cause. He was convinced that his son's emotional and psychological problems were the result of some chemical accident and had little to do with him or his ex-wife.

Charlie was a hopeless kid. For quite some time, the father had interpreted his parental responsibility as no more than the providing of food, clothing, discipline, and shelter. He didn't know what to do now—or in the future—with this boy. Charlie's failure to finish high school by joining the navy not only let his father off the hook—in a strange way it also served to support the father's belief that his kid was hopeless. Maybe the navy could do something with him that no one else could.

Helen was in the bedroom, but he didn't seek her advice. She probably would defer to him anyway. The possibility of his own failures as a parent had never been discussed. The arson spree, the bad grades, the psychiatrist, the stuttering—none were subjects to be addressed.

And he wasn't about to address them now—with his wife, his son, or anyone else.

"You want to do this?" he asked his son, unemotionally. Charlie nodded. His father now studied the forms again. Charlie stayed in the corner. After a few minutes, without saying anything further, he motioned to Charlie for a pen.

"T-t-thank you," Charlie managed.

His father didn't respond. He silently scrawled his signature to the appropriate papers. When he was finished, he put the pen down and, without looking at his son, got up from the table and went into the bedroom.

He didn't speak to Charlie that night, or for the week thereafter.

Charlie cut out of his last period high school class the next afternoon and ran all the way—probably in record time—to see the navy man at the recruiting station.

The forms and signatures were in order. The processing would begin immediately, the recruiting officer told him. He could be in the navy within a matter of weeks.

For the first time in months, Charlie Yukl smiled.

CHAPTER FIVE

The navy processing took less time than expected. The recruiting officer told Yukl that his aptitude tests indicated he would make a good hospital corpsman. He was accepted in the navy reserves, and a few weeks later was picked up by the regular navy and told to report for basic training. He said a nervous good-bye to his family, and packed a duffel bag with some clothes, a travel kit, and an extra pair of shoes. He left everything else behind. There was no kissing, hugging or emotional farewells. It was a simple good-bye.

His father got the family car out and drove him the short distance to the North Hollywood bus station. They exchanged few words. When they arrived at the terminal, Charlie got his bag out of the car. His father shook his hand, got back in the car, and left.

Fifteen minutes later, along with a few dozen other young enlistees, Charlie sat quietly on the chartered Greyhound bus and headed south for the U.S. Navy boot camp in San Diego.

Almost from the moment he arrived there in August 1952, Charlie was out of place. He didn't socialize with the other recruits. When they were given occasional passes off the base, he never went cruising for women in downtown San Diego. He stayed by himself, had no friends, and before long got himself into trouble.

On November 4 he was accused of stealing eleven dollars from the lockers of two other recruits—five dollars from one, six from another. No one knew why he did it, and Yukl never volunteered a reason. But he didn't deny his guilt. There was a disciplinary hearing, and Yukl was court-martialed. His punishment was harsh—Yukl was confined to the base at hard labor for two months, and fined fifty dollars a month for the same period.

He managed to survive the sentence and on January 19, 1953, was transferred to the U.S. Navy Hospital Corpsman School in Cambridge, Maryland. There, he performed his duties adequately for the first few months, distinguishing himself by rarely speaking to anyone, especially the women nurses. But on the night of October 15, 1953, while he was on watch, he fell asleep.

He was discovered, and court-martialed again five days later. The penalty: he was restricted to the base for one month and forfeited ten dollars in pay.

About a year later, he was transferred to the Newport, Rhode Island, naval hospital. Things weren't going well for him. He still had no social life, and as a high school dropout with a disciplinary record, he saw no future for himself in the navy. To make matters worse, he didn't get along well with his immediate superior, a chief petty officer named Pearly Hargreaves. The navy just wasn't working out for him.

One December day, as Christmas approached, he simply didn't return from a ten-day leave. When he finally returned on December 27, he was in deep trouble.

At his third, and final court-martial on January 8, 1954, the navy was less compassionate. With Hargreaves testifying against him, the presiding officer, a marine colonel named J. Allen MacInnis, confined Yukl to hard labor for forty-five days and reduced his pay grade to hospital apprentice. At the end of the forty-five-day period, Yukl was booted out of the navy and given a bad conduct discharge.

Shortly before this sad turn, his father had given up his job at the Los Angeles Philharmonic and moved with Helen and Tex to the small, peaceful community of Salem, Oregon. "I didn't like the fast pace," he later told friends. "We like it here." Yukl Sr. had been to Oregon's capital city only once before. He had passed through in 1948, on his way to Minnesota, where he had purchased a farm.

He now considered himself "semiretired," gave up the farm, and then decided to give up Los Angeles. He bought a small, unassuming two bedroom house on Twenty-fourth Street. It was light green in color, and looked like many of the other houses on the block. It had a small front yard, a small backyard and garage, and a large, wood-paneled basement, a perfect place for Yukl to practice his brass instruments and tutor students.

Soon after arriving, Charles Sr. received several offers to play with the Portland Symphony, but declined each time in favor of music teaching. Helen got a job as head nurse at Salem Memorial Hospital.

Within months, the elder Yukl was running three teaching studios in Salem. He also devoted a number of hours each week to directing musical groups throughout the Willamette Valley. "I get more satisfaction out of teaching than I ever got out of playing," he once told a reporter for the *Salem Statesman*. "The potential of young Salem musicians is tremendous. Of course, students I work with must be interested or I don't mess with them." "Yukl's family shares his love for good music," the reporter later wrote, adding that

Yukl called his students his "sons" and "daughters," and former students his "grandchildren."

The article made no mention of Charles Jr.

When the navy busted him out, Charlie was truly out on his own. Feeling helpless—and being broke—he took the last of his navy income and invested it in a one-way bus ticket from Rhode Island to Salem. He felt he had nowhere else to go. He arrived in Oregon, much to the surprise of his father, and moved into the house on Twenty-fourth Street, into a spartan room his stepmother had hurriedly fixed up for him in the dark, wood-paneled basement. He would share the room with his brother Tex.

On November 28, 1954, Yukl, nearly twenty years old, enrolled as the oldest senior at North Salem High School. The other students didn't know what to make of him. He still stuttered, and he kept to himself.

His father made no attempt to help him financially. Charlie needed money, and soon got a job at a family-style restaurant in Salem called Nohlgren's. He worked as a yard man, handling deliveries, ordering vegetables, and making sure the garbage got taken out.

Yukl wasn't back in school long before he joined the band. He played the French horn. And it wasn't long before he discovered a sophomore girl in the orchestra, a young flute player named Crystal Church.

She was a shy, overweight, depressed teenager, and she was as awkward in social situations as Charlie. The oldest of three kids, Crystal had never had a boyfriend before. The two of them spent the first few weeks of band practice eyeing each other from a distance. Then one day after rehearsals, Charlie got up the courage. He came over and talked with her. At first, Crystal blushed. She was embarrassed and didn't quite know what to do. After all, she was sixteen. He was twenty.

It didn't make sense—except that Charlie had never had a girlfriend before.

Crystal was much taller than he was. Still, Charlie acted a little cocky around her. He still looked like a sailor, she used to kid him. He had his short, near-crew-cut hair, and walked in little, quick steps, both feet pointing away from each other. Charlie would walk a few blocks with Crystal after school each day. She lived out in the country on Hyacinth Road in a large five-bedroom house. Her parents often drove her home.

But when they were sure no one was looking, Charlie and Crystal would hold hands. And when they were truly alone, Charlie never stuttered. But news travels fast in Salem high school circles, and soon Crystal found herself confronted with a new nickname by her classmates: "jailbait."

She weathered the name calling. He made her feel good about herself. He cared about her. Thanks to her, he would say, even his grades were improving. In his academic work, Charlie was now managing a steady C average. He got an A in music.

Neither Crystal nor Charlie had a car. Only Tex, Charlie's younger brother, had wheels—his motorcycle. Crystal used to call him the "motorcycle man," but they never really talked. Tex fit the image. He was a tall and angular kid, partial to jeans, plaid shirts and boots. He never said much to Crystal, and even less to Charlie. She saw Tex around school, and whenever one of her folks drove her over to Charlie's house.

For their "dates," Charlie and Crystal depended on their parents to drive one of them over to the other's house. Every once in a while, Charlie and Crystal would go to the Saturday dances at the Crystal Ballroom in Salem. Most of the kids didn't go there. They liked the new music. But Charlie hated the new dances; he preferred waltzes and fox trots.

When it was Charles Sr.'s turn to drive, Charlie turned white and clammed up. They never once spoke when they were in the car together.

Charlie only spoke to his father when he was playing with Crystal in the Silverton Community Band, directed by Charles Sr. They practiced Sousa marches and the 1812 Overture, but the joke in Salem was that Yukl's band always rehearsed. They never really played.

The real playing for Crystal and Charlie was left to their high school band, which performed at all the basketball and football games. The school had its own song, of sorts—"On, North Salem," played to the tune of "On, Wisconsin."

The two were also members of a local Salem fife and jug band, and they played at some of the high school parties. It was all good, clean fun, and still innocent. Charlie wanted to break the rules with Crystal.

But he never did. They necked only occasionally, in the family room in the basement of Crystal's house.

Part of that was due to Mr. and Mrs. Church. Crystal's parents never approved of the relationship. Her father, a pioneering Oregon newspaper publisher, would often argue with her about the merits of "that boy." Her mother, a bookkeeper for a boys reform school, would simply harass Crystal directly.

Each time he called their house and got her mother on the phone, Yukl began to stutter. He couldn't get Crystal's name out. "Hold on," her mother would say in disgust, and then call out to her daughter, "It's that idiot on the phone." Huge arguments would then ensue between child and parents, and they usually ended with Crystal crying and running from the room, sobbing, "I don't care what you say, Chuck loves me."

Crystal was, to be sure, the only woman Yukl felt

he could talk to. And he would often talk of Chicago. He'd been doing some reading, he told her, and he felt that his destiny was to go there to pursue a professional career in music. As soon as he graduated, Yukl had told Crystal, he was leaving Oregon and heading east. He wanted to go to George Williams College in Chicago. He had written away for the college bulletin, and everything looked promising. The school even offered a financial assistance program.

He was barely passing English, but he was still holding on to a 2.33 grade point average, good enough for him to graduate on June 8, 1955. Charles William Yukl, Jr., earned his high school diploma, graduating 204th in a class of 316.

Charlie wasted no time in leaving town. He had told his father about his college plans, and Yukl Sr. responded with the same lack of enthusiasm he'd felt for his son's enlistment in the navy. When he asked his dad to loan him some money, his father quietly reached down into his pants, pulled out a bill, and gave it to him. "Good luck," he said, in his angry, quiet manner, and left the living room. Charlie just stood and stared at the picture of Abraham Lincoln he was holding in his hand, and then quietly pocketed the five dollars.

It was a cool June night, and he packed quickly. Barely saying good-bye to his father and stepmother, and ignoring Tex altogether, Charlie headed over to Crystal's house for a last farewell on his way to the bus depot.

They stood on the front porch of her parents' house and talked in hushed tones. Crystal fought back the inevitable tears and tried to change the subject. She giggled nervously when she noticed that everything he was taking on his trip to Chicago was in neat, tiny rolls inside his duffle bag.

"It's a little trick I learned in the navy," he boasted sheepishly. They held hands briefly and listened for the first crickets of summer. There wasn't much to say. Soon it was time to go. She held him one last time, and he kissed her awkwardly. Then he left.

He took the bus only as far as Portland. He hitched the rest of the way to Chicago, trying to save enough money to find a place to live once he got there.

Charlie arrived in Chicago early in the morning and headed right to the college. But he hadn't done his homework. The school wasn't in session, the classes were booked for fall, and financial assistance was only offered in extremely limited cases.

With the last of his money, he rented a small room in an old wooden boarding house on Ashland Avenue, on the city's north side, and began scanning the classified ads of the *Tribune* and the *Chicago Daily News,* for a job.

The next morning he answered an ad placed by Ravenswood Hospital. Within a week, he was hired as a $115-a-week operating room orderly, working with a team of general surgeons. When the team moved their practice to Chicago's Presbyterian Hospital, Yukl went with them.

Each day, the pattern never seemed to vary. Yukl reported to work inside the old section of the hospital. He changed into a simple green smock and began the procession: wheeling the parade of hernia, colon, hip, and stomach surgery patients in to the large operating rooms.

At the hospital, he wasn't known as a loner. Charlie was known as *the* loner. He nodded occasionally to the doctors. He never spoke to the nurses. When forced to talk, he stuttered uncontrollably. One surgeon liked to describe Yukl as "a piece of furniture that moved every once in a while."

Yukl made no real friends in Chicago. At the end of his OR shift, he'd walk home, down Ashland Avenue, stopping at a nearby mom and pop grocery for some fruit and an occasional six-pack of beer. Once a week he'd go shopping. He loved clothes, especially soft V-neck sweaters and quality slacks. It was his one and only vice, he liked to tell himself. And when he wasn't working, he was modeling his new outfits.

The monotony finally began to take its toll. One winter night, alone in his boarding house room, Charlie started to drink. First it was beer, followed by vodka. Around midnight, he gathered all his loose change, went to the pay telephone in the hall, and placed a station-to-station call to Salem.

He apologized to Crystal for the late hour, but he called because he missed her. Charlie was just a little drunk, and he was overly sentimental via long distance. He told her how much he wanted to say how sorry he was that he hadn't married her. They talked for a good hour. When it was over and he was out of dimes, he went back to his room and slept. A few hours later, he awoke, still in his clothes. He had overslept for the first time since he had started his job.

The talk with Crystal, he later reasoned, was a catalyst. It forced him to think, and his conclusions were less than pleasant—his options exceedingly limited. He had come to the city to study music, to build a career with his piano and a rewarding life for himself.

He had done none of those things.

There seemed to be no future for him in Chicago. Outside of a few acquaintances at Presbyterian Hospital and at the boarding house—none of whom he socialized with—Yukl didn't know, and had made no attempt to know, anyone in the city. He had applied for a staff position at both the Bellevue Hospital of

Nursing and the private Alexian Brothers' School of Nursing in New York City, but had not been accepted.

It was 1956. He was almost twenty-two years old. He had no money saved, no friends, and no plans. The only thing he knew how to do—or wanted to do—was play the piano, so he quit his job as quietly as he had been hired, turned in his orderly's uniform, and cashed out of Presbyterian Hospital. With the last of his money, he paid the balance of his rent to his landlady. Then, still clutching the small duffel bag that brought him from Oregon, he went out to Meigs Field and bought a coach ticket on a DC-6 from Chicago to New York. It was his first plane ride.

On landing at LaGuardia Airport, he took a bus to the Manhattan terminal, and then another bus downtown, to the Lower East Side, where his mother, Dorothea Freitag, lived in the Kips Bay housing development. She was surprised, but seemed genuinely happy to see her son again. It had been fifteen years since they'd spent any time together.

Dorothea was doing very well for herself, writing dance arrangements for Broadway shows and accompanying visiting foreign dancers on the piano. She told Charlie he could stay with her, and soon after arriving, he went out to look for work.

Through Olsten's, a job agency, he landed some day work with the Credit Bureau of Greater New York City. Next he was a clerk at Pinkerton's, then an office manager for a small Wall Street firm. The typing skills he had acquired during junior high school in Los Angeles remained excellent. He still boasted a speed of nearly 100 words a minute. He wasn't able to hold on to any one position for very long, however, and continued bouncing from job to job, ending up for a brief time, as a program scheduler at the CBS Studios on West Fifty-seventh Street.

During this time, he held down a series of night piano jobs. He was hired as a player at clubs like the Red Onion in Manhattan, and at the Band Box in Union City, New Jersey, just across the Hudson River.

Yukl often performed under the stage name Yogi Freitag and was always partial to music from the late nineteenth and early twentieth century; he especially liked ragtime music, Scott Joplin songs, and show tunes. His sense of humor sometimes found its way into his choice of music; one of his favorites was "Where Did Robinson Crusoe Go with Friday on a Saturday Night?"

Often, on weekends, Charlie would travel to Bucks County, Pennsylvania, and play piano at some of the local vacation resorts. During the summer, following his arrival in New York, Yukl played piano and helped choreograph a revue, *Out of This World,* at the Bucks County Playhouse.

He liked the trips out of New York, and especially the chance to stay at places like the Logan Inn, where he had his own room and could be by himself. The trips also served to confirm what he had already begun to feel, that living again with his mother was depressing him. She was still a perfectionist, and Yukl's pattern of temporary work didn't fit into her definition of success. Little by little, she had started to pressure him again. After all, she would tell him, he was now nearly twenty-five years old. It was 1960.

After a little less than two years together, Charlie moved out. He rented a small, furnished room at the Belvedere Hotel, an old, inexpensive place for transients on the West Side.

The move out of his mother's house was another catalyst of sorts. He now wanted very much to do something else besides temp work and playing the piano. The temp work reminded him too much of a future he thought he didn't have. The piano reminded him too much of his parents—especially his mother. There was no piano at the hotel, but Charlie didn't care. He could play anytime he wanted to at any of the bars where he worked.

He had few vices back then. Occasionally, he would get drunk—by himself. And there was his passion for clothes. By the time he moved into the hotel, he had amassed quite a collection of outfits—as well as acquiring a taste for Smirnoff's.

One night Charlie started to drink. He was alone, and hit the vodka hard. At four in the morning, he picked up the phone and called Salem. Crystal knew he was drunk the minute she awoke and answered the phone. He was in New York, he told her. He was unhappy living by himself and wanted her to move east and marry him.

"But I can't," Crystal tried to tell him as soothingly as possible. She had recently married. In his predawn stupor, Charlie wished her well. Crystal couldn't help noticing that Charlie had started to stutter again. He told her he would call again soon, but they both knew it was their last conversation.

The next morning, Charlie saw an advertisement in a magazine for the New York Institute of Photography. He filled out the card and mailed it in. In a few weeks, he had enrolled as a student. He took night classes in all the basic subjects—light, film development, darkroom procedures, depth of field. It was a fascinating new job opportunity, and he was an excellent student. Soon he had filled his small $125-a-month, one-bedroom apartment with camera equipment—reflector lamps, light meters, background shades, and tripods. He bought a small Pentax 35 millimeter camera, a 4-by-5-inch professional Rollei, and a 5-by-7-inch Pentax studio camera.

It was a happy time for him. He was still very much alone, yearning for some kind of human connection, but for a time, Charlie seemed happy to live in the perpetual present, contentedly locked in the solitude of his room and the companionship of his cameras. His cameras were stable. They were precise instruments. They worked. And they didn't question his thought processes or background.

At the institute, no one cared who you were—or weren't—or where you came from. If you paid your tuition, you were compelled only to appreciate the art and to learn the science of photography. Charlie met a young woman named Enken at the school. She was foreign born, a quiet but tough lady who worked at a Manhattan insurance agency. At first, they shared an interest in photography. Soon they started dating, taking occasional bicycle rides and going to the movies together or to concerts at Lincoln Center. Enken loved the movies. She was a strong woman, but she didn't want to control Charlie. Since he kept to himself much of the time, the friction was minimal. Enken was the first woman since Crystal whom Charlie could talk to without stuttering.

One night, just after New Year's, they were on their way back from a movie, and Charlie proposed marriage. Four months later, on April 6, 1961, at the Grace Lutheran Church in Forest Hills, they were married. The ceremony was held in Queens because Enken's sister and brother-in-law lived there.

There were just a few people at the small wedding that Friday. Dorothea attended, as did some of Enken's relatives. Yukl's father was invited, but declined to come. Instead, he sent Charlie $100 and a note that simply said, "Good Luck."

That afternoon, after the wedding was over and everyone had left, Charlie and Enken returned to

Manhattan and spent their first night together as man and wife at the Barbizon Plaza Hotel. They had dinner at the hotel, and then went upstairs to go to bed. Charlie was scared. The most he had ever done was some necking with a young kid in Oregon. He paced the room. Then he drank some beer. It was clear he didn't want to consummate the marriage.

Enken undressed, got under the covers, and waited for him. Finally, Charlie came to bed. He curled up at one far corner, hoping she'd leave him alone. Slowly, and as surely as her own limited sexual experience would allow, Enken moved closer until she held him in her arms. Roughly an hour later, in the early morning of April 7, Charlie Yukl, at the age of twenty-six, nervously, awkwardly, and with fearful hesitation, finally lost his virginity.

It was a traumatic experience for him. He even thought it was painful. Enken tried to reassure him that the sex would get better. It had to.

The next morning, the couple headed for Pennsylvania Station and the train that would take them to Trenton, New Jersey. There, they boarded the bus that would finally deposit them, five hours later, at the Logan Inn in Bucks County for the rest of their weekend honeymoon. Charlie had not quite recovered from the night before. He was very nervous on the trip and kept shaking his knee and tapping his right foot in a continuous rhythm against the side of the bus.

That night after an early dinner, they retired to their rented cottage. They tried to have sex again; and again, Yukl was almost drunk before he got up the courage to get into bed.

It was the last time they were to have sex in 1961. For a few weeks, Enken tried to be openly affectionate with Charlie, but he never reciprocated, and he stayed completely away from physical contact with

Enken for the next nine months. After a while, she stopped trying. She even tried talking about it with Charlie. He refused to respond, and the subject was never again discussed.

Charles Yukl, Jr., was a very troubled young man. Although he had no real comparisons, he considered himself an inadequate husband to Enken. He went into an acute depression.

One day, Enken came home to find Charlie in the kitchen with his head in the oven. All the windows in the apartment were closed, and Yukl had the pilot light out with all the gas jets turned on. She quickly turned off the oven and opened all the windows. Then she walked Yukl around the apartment for a good five minutes. He was more embarrassed than anything else and finally confessed his feelings of inferiority and inadequacy. Enken told him it was all right, that things would get better.

Not long after, he awoke and found that he had been admitted to Roosevelt Hospital, an apparent attempted suicide. He told the doctors he had been kicked in the head and had blacked out for four hours. He remembered nothing about the incident.

Typically, he would not talk to Enken or anyone else about his sudden hospitalization.

In 1962, Charlie and Enken moved out of a small, temporary hotel apartment they had rented and into their own place on East Twenty-eighth Street. Charlie got a job as the resident manager—he got a break in the rent—and used the extra space for his growing interest in photography.

He would spend hours playing with his photo gear at his "studio." Photography was still more a hobby than a profession for Yukl. It barely paid for his film and developing costs. Occasionally, he shot composite pictures for models and would-be actresses, charging them five dollars for each shot they ordered.

The cameras seemed to have a special dual purpose for Yukl. When he was looking through the lens, he felt he could get closer to the women, that the camera somehow separated him from the reality of having to deal with his fear of women. It seemed to work. When he held the camera up to his face to focus on a model, he could talk to her. When he put the camera down he began to stutter again.

It was during this time that he started to play a little exhibitionist game. He would sometimes schedule the models for a time during which he was sure his wife wouldn't be home. Then he'd purposely set the clock in the living room back an hour.

When the model arrived at the appointed hour, the door to the apartment would be open. When the woman entered, Yukl would burst from the bathroom or kitchen partially naked and apologize for his appearance. He would then glance at the clock, and ask the woman if she wasn't an hour early.

By the summer, Yukl had had sex with his wife a total of three times. He had also graduated—momentarily—from the Broadway bars to a job as musical director for Gaslight Village, a summer music theater in Lake George, New York. He was paid $125 a week, which included housing. During the days he rehearsed with the other performers. From June through Labor Day, he helped direct, choreograph, and play piano for a number of shows and revues at the opera house there.

Each night, from nine through the early morning hours, he'd underscore the music for the parade of singers, silent movies, and ice shows that appeared at the resort. Enken never came to any of the shows. She stayed in the city.

Yukl was, in a sense, following in his mother's foot-steps. Perhaps that is why he did everything possible not to speak to her and to see her only on holidays. Besides, he was having enough trouble maintaining his own relationship at home. He feared sex. He repressed his sexuality. He refused to let Enken get close to him. Instead, he started to spend more and more time outside the house.

In the fall of 1964, Charlie began to take an unusual interest in his neighborhood. He saw a small ad on a New York City subway and called the number listed. Soon he was enrolled as a night student at John Jay College. After taking the preliminary courses—of min-imum duration—Yukl was made an auxiliary New York City policeman. A few days later, he reported for work as a volunteer reserve cop in the Thirteenth Precinct near his house. Just as he had done on the hospital floors of Chicago, Yukl stayed mainly by him-self. He wasn't considered a team player by most of the line cops.

As a result, they used Charlie mostly to work in the station house, doing some of the routine paperwork, filling out the endless number of booking forms and the often revisionist history known as official police reports. Every so often, his captain would assign him to directing traffic during peak rush hours or when there had been an auto accident. Sometimes the cops would take Yukl for an exciting ride-along, a chance to see the grit and the despair of the streets firsthand, to observe the victims and the hypes, the low-class scum and the high-class scoundrels.

During this time he also began playing the piano more, working occasional club dates and uptown bar happy hours. Yukl liked the music, and he liked the attention.

He lasted as an auxiliary cop for more than a year,

quitting the unpaid position as quietly as he had signed on when a few extra club dates opened up.

In 1965, just after he left his police duties, Yukl and Enken added a new member to their family—a large Great Dane named Bessie. Charlie used the excuse that they needed the protection, but the dog was hardly a man-eater, despite its size. The large, friendly female dog filled the apartment, which was barely large enough to hold Yukl's upright piano in the cramped living room.

Yukl was beginning to earn the major portion of his income from his piano playing, working with voice students, and teaching ragtime techniques to other players. He continued playing the club engagements, which paid for his photo hobby and supported the couple's modest social itinerary of movies and concerts.

About the time of Bessie's first birthday, in March, 1966, Yukl began placing ads in small, local community papers announcing his services as a piano and voice teacher. Soon he got some responses, and began taking on a few new voice students. They were all women. One of them was a first-timer, an aspiring singer, a cute redhead named Suzanne Reynolds.

The first song they worked on together was "Satin Doll." She knew the words and could follow the arrangement. She was also full of energy and optimism. "This is just the beginning," she said, beaming after their first session. "Just remember," she said, "we started all this together. If I make it, I'll bring you with me."

Yukl smiled an uncomfortable smile, and played on.

CHAPTER SIX

The arrest of Charles William Yukl for the murder of Suzanne Reynolds was front page news. Both the *New York Times* and the *Daily News* played up the case.

Over at the Thirteenth Precinct, where Yukl had been booked, the cops who knew the real story were too embarrassed to go for the usual post-bust publicity. The boys in blue knew, but didn't volunteer to the reporters hanging around the station house, the special irony of the situation. Charlie was more than just a little familiar with the troops at the precinct. He had worked out of the same building just a year earlier as an auxiliary cop.

Sixty blocks uptown, Dorothea Freitag didn't have to confront the press. Almost no one knew that Charles Yukl was her son—that she was the mother of an accused murderer.

Enken had called Dorothea with the terrible news as soon as she could. Together they went downtown to see what they could do. Dorothea's brother suggested an attorney to defend Charlie. Enken and Dorothea headed over to his office, at the Graybar Building on Lexington Avenue. His name was George Monaghan.

Monaghan was an imposing figure. A tall, energetic, heavy-set man, Monaghan was more than just another defense attorney. He was a former assistant district attorney, and had been both the New York City fire commissioner and its police commissioner. He later became the "czar" of harness racing for the state, before entering private practice. It was a safe bet, some said, that Monaghan not only knew the ropes, but the rope-makers. "Once you've been police commissioner," he told Enken and Dorothea, "everything else is easy."

Monaghan then heard the story the two women presented to him, and he agreed to see Charlie at the Tombs.

Later that day, Yukl was escorted to a small visitors' room and introduced to Monaghan. Monaghan told him he had been contacted by Charlie's mother and wife in order to help him, and he asked what had happened.

In a calm, polite, and straightforward manner, Yukl told him that he was aware that he had killed a woman, because the police had told him he had done so. He also told the attorney that he remained very hazy on the details. He didn't even remember the act of murder, he told Monaghan.

But Monaghan was a master of legal procedure, and was most interested in how John Keenan had been able to collect a thirty-page signed confession from Charlie. He spent the good part of the next hour asking Yukl question after question about the chronology of his interrogation by the police and his subsequent admissions.

Yukl was not hazy on specifics. He told Monaghan what happened after he had called the police, how long the police were with him at his apartment, and how long they were with him at the station house. Yukl reported to Monaghan that the police had asked him to remove his shoes and then his pants.

Monaghan was interested in pinning down when and where the police or district attorney representative had advised Yukl of his rights. What he heard convinced him that he had a strong chance for dismissal because of improper interrogation procedures. He thought he could probably go into court and get the confession thrown out. He also came away from his jail meeting impressed with his new client. The prisoner had intelligently and coherently expressed himself, and he gave Monaghan the distinct feeling that he was the unfortunate victim of an overzealous investigation.

Before he left the Tombs, word was already out that Monaghan was handling Yukl. A colleague caught him on the way out and asked the question that is inevitable in bizarre murder cases. "Well, George, do you think the guy's nuts?" Monaghan didn't hesitate to reply. "No."

Monaghan called Enken and agreed to represent Yukl, but told her the defense would not be inexpensive. It would cost at least $5,000.

Mother and daughter-in-law thought it over and two days later said yes. They felt that Monaghan was a more than competent defense attorney. Dorothea managed to come up with a $2,000 retainer, and Monaghan went to work.

When Yukl told Monaghan he wanted out of the Tombs because he thought he needed psychiatric treatment, Monaghan went back into court and got a judge to order a thirty-day psychiatric observation for his client. Charlie soon found himself in a day room on the prison ward of Bellevue Hospital, enjoying regular visits from the staff, a steady diet of institutional food—and thorazine.

On November 3, 1966, a New York grand jury indicted Yukl for first-degree murder.

For the next two months Yukl shuttled between city prisons and various psychiatric clinics. He had four major psychiatric interview sessions at Bellevue. The doctors all wanted to know, and they kept asking, whether Yukl was aware of the consequences of his actions.

In December, Yukl was transported back to the Tombs. On December 7, 1966, two of the psychiatrists who had examined him, Dr. Leonard Abrams, and Dr. Alan Holden, issued their report:

History:

This patient was born in Baltimore in 1935. Both parents were musicians: they were divorced when patient was seven years old although he cannot specify on what ground. However, from what he says, it appears that there was a great deal of incompatibility, his mother evidently the dominant of the parents. Patient has shown neurotic symptomatology since childhood. He had exhibitionistic tendencies as a young child and these have remained with him. At the age of 12, he remembers going on an "arson spree," and after setting approximately eight fires, he was sent to a psychiatrist. However, there was no further treatment or psychiatric followup. Patient describes having difficulties with his father. He spent two and a half years in the Navy, eventually given a general discharge under honorable conditions, following several minor infractions and an attitude which he describes as marginally insubordinate. This attitude related primarily to nurses with whom he was working (he was stationed in a Navy Hospital), and he admits to generalized feelings of hostility directed towards women, particularly American women. Following his discharge, he worked at miscellaneous jobs as a technician in a hospital, with a credit bureau in New York, as a private investigator, and for the Dreyfus Mutual Fund. He later went to photography school where he met his present, foreign-born wife. They later opened a photo studio which lasted some three years, during which time his wife seems to have been the main source of financial support. During this time, she maintained a job in a brokerage firm. While he worked as a photographer, his exhibitionistic tendencies rose to the surface again and he admits brief body exposures to some of the models he photographed. He denies making sexual overtures to the girls and he generally tried to pretend that his exposure was accidental. He was not successful at photography, dropped it, and concentrated on music with the help of his mother, who was his critic and teacher. Again, however, he relied on his wife very largely for financial support. In recent years, he has begun to drink more heavily, but does not consider himself an alcoholic. He claims that his wife apparently is a placid and uncomplaining type of woman, did not reprimand him for his drinking, for his lack of support, nor did his mother, whom he claims was an extremely heavy drinker herself . . . The deceased allegedly was his singing pupil.

Examination:

Patient responds in a relevant, coherent and alert manner. He appears obsequious and overeager to please in his general demeanor. He shows a mild speech defect, stuttered quite frequently during the interview. The content of various of his responses suggests that this man attempts to conceal deeply-

rooted feelings of inadequacy and frustration, as
well as feelings of resentment and suspiciousness.
The patient harbors significant doubts about his
personal, and especially about his sexual identity,
and his fear and hostility toward women (especially
American women), are on a conscious level. These
feelings most probably derive from his relationship
with his mother, who is a dominant, critical and
significant figure in his life. He demonstrated his
ambivalence towards her as well as his dependence
on her, and was constantly engaged in bids for her
attention and approval. There is considerable concern with his felt failure to achieve his goal and his
objectives and he tended to blame the women who
are close to him. At the same time, the persistent
quality of anticipation that he will some day become a famous pianist gives this hope inappropriate
precedence over his apparent concern with present
legal involvement. Indeed, during the examination,
feelings of personal responsibility and remorse appear to be lacking.

The physical and neurological examinations are
essentially negative.

Impression:

He is not in such a state of idiocy, imbecility, or
insanity as to be incapable of understanding the
charge, indictment, proceedings, or of making his
defense.''

The two doctors had thus found Charles Yukl competent to stand trial.

For the next six months, Yukl stayed in the Tombs
and waited for what everyone thought would be the
beginning of his criminal trial for murder.

He had few visitors—Enken, Dorothea, and Monaghan. Enken came regularly. Dorothea came about once every two weeks. Monaghan showed infrequently.

But Monaghan had been very busy during the period of psychiatric observation. Before Yukl's trial could begin, and despite the competency findings, Monaghan had moved in court to invalidate the confession, basing his case on the landmark 1966 Miranda rights ruling. Yukl, he argued, had not been adequately informed of his right to have an attorney present during his interrogation.

Simultaneously, Monaghan began to maneuver through the courts to free his client. Somehow he was convinced that Yukl was a short, slight, quiet defendant who was no risk to society. Bail, he told Yukl, had nothing to do with whether or not a person had committed a particular crime; it was a system designed to make sure he would show up for his trial.

Perhaps he was also confident in his ability to pull it off, to succeed where other lawyers—and defendants—had failed. In any case, Monaghan did it; he was able to convince the judge to grant Yukl bail during the appeal he filed.

Dorothea and Enken quietly raised the bond money from friends. There had been quite an outcry when Yukl was arrested. Now, just eight months later, no one seemed to notice when Yukl was released on $75,000 bail on July 19, 1967. The bond only cost his mother $7,500, and despite the incontrovertible fact that bail for murder suspects like Yukl was a rarity, his release went unreported in the press.

He returned to the apartment on Twenty-eighth Street to be with Enken. The next day he returned to the piano and began looking for work. His first job, while on bail, came quickly—temp typing work for Olsten's. He stayed at various temp jobs for the next five months.

In January 1968, State Supreme Court Justice George

Postel ruled against Monaghan. Postel agreed with the prosecutor's contention that the Yukl confession could be used as evidence. The Yukl murder trial could now begin.

Monaghan was prepared. Earlier, he had conferred with prosecutor Keenan and told him that his client would plead guilty to manslaughter if the confession ruling went against the defense.

There would be no trial. After Postel's ruling, Keenan and Monaghan conferred again. A plea bargain was in the works.

"What about manslaughter in the first degree?" Keenan asked Monaghan.

Monaghan agreed, and the deal was struck.

If Postel had ruled that the confession was admissible and the trial could begin, then why was Keenan so anxious to make a deal with Monaghan? The reason was that Keenan knew that the only real evidence against Yukl was his confession. Even with the confession, Keenan had doubts about his ability to prove premeditation in the Reynolds murder, a 1968 requirement for a first-degree murder conviction.

He also knew that Monaghan would immediately appeal Postel's ruling—no matter what charge Yukl pleaded to—and that the appeal stood a good chance of overturning Postel's ruling. If that happened, Yukl was a free man.

Under the circumstances, both sides thought they were getting a good deal.

Keenan figured that even if the appeals court found for Monaghan, the fact that Yukl had pleaded guilty would still keep him in prison since there would be no need to use the confession against him. Keenan felt he was doing his job in keeping Yukl inside for at least ten years.

Monaghan was also able to justify the manslaughter

arrangement. He was able to get Yukl a much smaller sentence. (In 1968, if Yukl had been convicted of first-degree murder, he would have been sentenced to life imprisonment, ineligible for parole until he had first served twenty-six years in prison.)

After Keenan and Monaghan shook hands, Monaghan called Yukl. On January 29, 1968, Yukl went back to the Tombs. Three days later, on February 1, Yukl was brought into Judge Postel's courtroom. He was asked by Keenan if he had murdered Suzanne Reynolds.

"Yes sir," he said in his calm, polite way. "I did strangle Miss Suzanne Reynolds." The guilty plea was entered, and sentencing was set for March 5.

Eight days after his February court appearance, Yukl was back in the psychiatric clinic, undergoing more presentencing examinations. On February 14, his thirty-third birthday, the psychiatrists evaluated him again.

This defendant was somewhat compliant and subservient in manner [one doctor wrote in his synopsis of dynamic clinical findings].

His full scale IQ was 108. He may be classified as of high average intelligence. He may have a somewhat higher potential, but scores are lowered by a need to yield almost instantaneous answers, and a hesitancy to use introspection or to weigh alternatives.

His general personality characteristics show evidence of chronic maladjustment. The trends are somewhat mixed but hysterical features are prominent. This is evidenced in rather pronounced repression and a tendency to interpret such repressed material on terms of his own with some disregard of appropriateness; there is also a good deal of blandness, especially in emotionally charged situations. To a lesser degree, there are also compulsive features and a need to exercise controls, probably to cover his own needs to be controlled. He may also be described as schizoid to the extent that his interpersonal relationships are somewhat remote and detached. He appears not to have reached any stable sense of identification and consequently his psychosexual adjustment lacks mature orientation. In stress situations, he is apt to block, or to be momentarily immobilized, but has, it would appear, rather rapid recovery resources.

This defendant appears to have made a borderline adjustment. However, at this time, he is in good contact and able to make realistic discriminations. He might be classified as one with mixed neurotic trends, among which the hysterical appears to be predominant.

One of the psychiatric reports was especially revealing. It was filed on February 26, 1968, and submitted to Judge George Postel just prior to Yukl's scheduled March 5 sentencing for the Reynolds murder. Two psychiatrists, Emmanuel Mossinger and Matthew Levine, examined Yukl. It was a long session. Their notes:

Examination of this defendant indicates that he is WITHOUT PSYCHOSIS. Intelligence is high average, IQ 106.

The defendant was reared by his father and paternal grandmother at the age of five years when his parents separated. He left home at the age of 17 and shortly thereafter joined the U.S. Navy.

He believes that his childhood was not entirely happy, as he was very high-strung and nervous and, at times, shy. In his adolescent life period, he felt discontented since he was unable to accomplish anything that would indicate he was superior. The father was described as a stubborn and self-righteous man with whom the defendant had poor relations. At the age of twelve, the defendant was arrested for arson and saw a psychiatrist on three different occasions. Defendant was examined in 1967 at Bellevue Psychiatric Hospital, in regard to the alleged instant offense. A xerox copy of the hospital's report to the court stated that he was suffering from a "character disorder with neurotic features."

The defendant is a pianist and believes that he was moderately successful as a music teacher. There is no drug history. There is a moderate excessive use of alcoholic beverages but he denied frequent intoxication. However, he claimed that he was intoxicated at the time of the alleged instant offense. He described himself as a friendly person, who, however, could be bad-tempered.

The defendant stated that he received an unfavorable discharge from the U.S. Navy after serving more than two years. He claims that the discharge was eventually cleared to a general discharge under honorable conditions. He had been placed in the medical department and admittedly made a bad adjustment. He admitted that his difficulty was working under orders of female nurses which he finds very difficult to do. However, he denied that he disliked females, in general.

He was married at the age of twenty-five, his wife being six years his junior. He claimed that he had frequent and regular sex with her the first year of their marriage and then, since he never had any pleasure, he lost interest and their sexual relationships were very sparse. He was always a heavy masturbator which increased after marriage. He denied homosexual experiences. In a modified way, he is an exhibitionist. For example, knowing that a female student was about to come for her lesson, he would manage to be taking a shower and then to go to the door and open it for her while making profuse apologies as to his state of nakedness. He admitted that he was a very nervous person who was overly sensitive, restless, moody, and very compulsive. There were no abnormalities in his thought processes elicited.

Concerning the alleged instant offense, defendant described in detail a sudden impulse which he still does not understand. He stated that he had been drinking vodka excessively the day of the offense. Apparently, a female student who came to him for singing lessons had been doing very poorly and he had intended to dismiss her on the next day of the instant offense. He admitted placing a necktie around her neck and pulling it and then dragging the body to an empty apartment in the building and then slashing the body with a razorblade. He also claimed that he did not have any recollection of placing the necktie around her neck for six weeks after the incident and had no recollection of taking the body to another apartment and then slashing it.

The defendant gives the following explanation to help understand his behavior: His mother is a fine piano concertist and she had been his teacher for several years. She was erratic in that on one day she praised his playing a piece of music on the piano and on the very next day that he played the very same piece of music, she found fault with him and criticized him severely. He realizes that he suppressed his feelings of insecurity and anger which had been stored up in him throughout the years as a result of his mother's treatment. He further wonders whether or not his excessive drinking the day of the alleged instant offense released his anger which he turned upon the deceased female.

Again, the doctors had found him competent to stand trial, although now that was purely academic.

Postel sentenced Yukl to a minimum term of "not less than seven years and six months and not more than 15 years." Keenan was surprised at the light term. He had assumed that due to the heinous nature of the murder to which Yukl confessed, Postel would mete out a ten-to-twenty-year sentence. In fact, he was so sure that Postel would go heavy on the manslaughter charge that he simply had not made any recommendation to the judge. It was a tragic assumption.

"I didn't give him the maximum," the judge later told a reporter, "because the prosecutor didn't insist upon it. The DA must have been aware that when there is a plea and discussion before the plea, then the maximum sentence would not be given."

Still, on the day of sentencing, Keenan raced back to his office and filed a memorandum to be sent to the parole board when Yukl became eligible for release. In red pencil, he wrote "recommend against parole . . . severity of crime and leniency of sentence." He had District Attorney Frank Hogan sign the memo.

Perhaps the most bizarre development of all was that even though Yukl had pleaded guilty and had been sentenced, he was set free again—this time Monaghan was able to muscle $100,000 bail pending the outcome of his appeal of Postel's confession ruling.

"If I thought he was a killer," Monaghan later said, "I probably would have taken a different course. The psychiatric reports said he was sane. It was my duty to defend him to the best of my ability and I did."

Yukl stayed at Gaslight Village a few weeks after

Labor Day. In early October 1968, he returned to the city and went back to work at some local bars and clubs. While he was away, Enken told him that she had found them a better place to live, in the Village. The address was 120 Waverly Place. It was a quiet, modest apartment, and both Charlie and Enken liked the place.

While in New York, Yukl also found some work as a pianist with a musical company that had to go down south to play dinner theaters. He rehearsed often with the group in New York before they traveled, and became friendly with one of the players, Terry Selbert.

The cast immediately took a liking to Yogi Freitag—his stage name—and accepted him as one of their own. But Yogi didn't exactly fit in with the other members of the troupe in manner or dress. He was a 1950's dresser ten years too late. He wore plaid pants and striped shirts. He was, in the words of the 1950's, square. But he was quiet, well mannered, and if someone asked him to do something, he willingly complied.

The Saga of Roaring Gulch, an original light musical farce, opened in Charlotte, North Carolina in February. The group was in Charlotte for just over a month and then took the spoof on westerns to Hendersonville and on to Nashville.

Yogi always flew back to New York on Sunday evenings and returned to the show on Tuesdays. No one in the cast ever questioned the commute.

One day Selbert, considered the unofficial company manager, decided to ask Yogi why he traveled so frequently. "Plagiarism," Yogi said.

"What?"

"Plagiarism," Yogi said. "Some people are trying to steal some music I wrote and I've got to see some lawyers."

The story was believable. After all, Yogi had a habit

of writing and rewriting songs. After almost every performance, he could be found sitting alone at the piano, composing. During the run of the show, he composed seven different songs for the production, tunes like "Code of the West" and "Hanging Tree."

When he was in a good mood, he'd often do things that were totally out of his apparent character. One time, the cast was changing planes in Atlanta and had a three hour layover. They were hungry and went to an airport restaurant that boasted "international cuisine." Yogi liked to drink, but he especially liked to eat. He had already had a few drinks when it was time to survey the menu. He started to laugh. Then he called over the manager. "I see here on the menu that you have five international dishes. Is that right?"

"Yes, that is correct," the manager said.

"Well," Yogi offered, "if I order all five and eat all five, can all my friends get their dinners for free?"

It was quite a challenge for an airport restaurant manager. He offered a compromise. "Tell you what," he said. "I won't pay for their dinners, but if you can eat it all, you get yours for free."

For the next ninety minutes, Yogi ordered and ate, and ate again. A number of people started crowding around the table, rooting for him. As soon as he finished one dish, another would arrive. Surprisingly, he made it through all the dinners and won the challenge. He got the free meals—and was sick for two days afterward.

But the bold eating display earned him full membership rights in the cast. Often, on the road, he'd score extra personality points by writing spur-of-the-moment ballads, changing the words of well-known tunes to poke fun at the members of the cast. It was his way of expressing himself, and many of the tunes he wrote were about Nancy, one of the cast members. Yogi was quite taken with her. She had long, black hair, and she played the heroine in the show.

Late one night, Yogi called Selbert down to the theater after the show. He'd been drinking. "I want you to listen to this," he said. For the next hour and a half, Selbert watched and listened as Yogi performed one of the more beautiful ballads he'd ever heard. The music was soft and the lyrics were enchanting—it was a song written about Nancy, and what Yogi felt for her.

But Nancy didn't feel the same way about Yogi. She spent time with him only when they were part of the theater group.

Still, Yogi didn't get the message. He kept asking her out, and she kept politely declining. One night in Charlotte, after the show, Nancy again refused his offers, and Yogi started to stutter, then yelled at her. "You're a c-c-c-cunt, you're a whore," he shouted. He started to move toward her, and she ran out of the theater.

Nancy went to Selbert and told him the story. A few minutes later, Yogi called and wanted to see him. When they met, Terry noticed Yogi was unusually agitated. He was perspiring and had apparently been drinking. When Terry casually brought up Nancy's name, Yogi nearly exploded. He pounded his fist into a nearby table. "She's a c-c-cunt," he repeated. "I bet she's been laying everyone on the road."

Terry was taken aback at Yogi's personality reversal, at his display of anger. "Yogi," Selbert tried to assure him, "you're wrong. Nancy just isn't that type of girl and you know it. She may play a dance hall girl, but that's just a character. There are other girls in the cast you could say that about, but not Nancy."

Yogi had already drifted to thoughts of another female. One of the women who worked at the dinner theater had a young niece—a girl about seventeen and barely out of high school—who liked to hang around the actors. Yogi was attracted to her and asked Terry to fix them up.

Selbert agreed, hoping it would calm things down between Yogi and Nancy at the theater. When he asked the girl, she told Terry she wasn't interested in Yogi, but she knew someone else who might be.

The someone turned out to be her younger sister.

The next day Yogi met her, and for the following two days all he could talk about was going out with her. Terry spoke with the girls, and a double date was planned. The sisters lied to their mother and said they were going to a friend's house. Instead they met Terry and Yogi at an expensive Charlotte restaurant. When Yogi arrived he appeared nervous. He began to stutter and talk loudly as they all made small talk and looked at the menus. He was carrying a large bottle of Southern Comfort in a brown paper bag, and proceeded to take the bag out from under the table and drink from the bottle throughout dinner.

No one stayed up late that night. Yogi was totally drunk before dessert. Terry and the two young girls drove him back to the theater and put him to bed.

The next morning, Yogi remembered nothing of the night before. The cast did the show as usual, and that night, he began drinking again.

Terry found him in the theater with another bottle half finished. Yogi was in a talkative mood.

"You know that plagiarism case I told you about?" he asked.

Selbert nodded.

"Well, it wasn't really plagiarism. I'll tell you the truth," he slurred, "but you can't tell any of the other guys, okay?"

"It'll be our secret," Terry said.

Even in his near-drunken state, Yogi was able to concoct a coherent fairy tale: He had been down and out in New York. One night, he was walking in the Bowery and passed a vacant storefront. He looked in, and he could see a man was lying facedown on the floor.

"I went in to see if he was all right, but the guy was dead. I called the police," he continued, "and I waited there for them to arrive. But when the cops got there, they took me to the station and tried to get me up on charges. That's why I gotta keep going back to New York—to get this thing over with."

"You mean a trial?" Terry asked.

"No," Yogi replied quickly. "It's not up to that yet. I don't really think there'll be a problem. You know, the truth always wins out, right?"

"Right."

A few days later, Yogi disappeared from the show. He had returned to New York, and became Charles Yukl once again. Shortly after arriving, he went back to Olsten's, his old employment agency, and secured temporary work as an office manager and typist.

The clerks at Olsten's were surprised to see him back and one of them asked Yukl why he was still doing temp work. He shifted nervously and said, "I think I'll be moving out of town soon."

Fourteen months after pleading guilty, Yukl had nearly set a city record for staying out of prison on a murder charge to which he had already confessed. Attorney Monaghan had performed well for his client in delaying the sentence. But now, all appeals and motions had been exhausted.

On a rainy morning in April, 1969, Monaghan called Yukl and told him it was time. Monaghan drove by the apartment and picked Charlie up for the short ride to their appointment with the district attorney. A few minutes later, Yukl turned himself in to the authorities and began serving his prison term at New York's Ossining State Correctional Facility, formerly Sing Sing.

CHAPTER SEVEN

Sing Sing was a tough prison, where violence was a way of life—and a way to survive. Yukl didn't stay there very long.

He often complained to prison officials that he needed continuing psychological help, and that if the other prisoners discovered he had murdered a woman, they would kill him.

They could tolerate a barroom killing involving two men. But child molesters, rapists, and women killers were the least-tolerated prisoners at Sing Sing. He told Enken he needed protection.

At her urging, Yukl found it, with the piano. There was an old battered upright piano in a prison recreation room, and it was out of tune. But it was still a piano. Yukl started playing again. It was a skill that other prisoners wanted to learn, and soon Yukl was able to "buy" some personal safety by performing Scott Joplin tunes for his cellmates. He also taught a few of them some basic chords, and each Sunday he'd play assorted hymns at the Protestant chapel service.

Yukl spent nearly a year and a half at Sing Sing. For the first nine months of his stay there, he worked in the shoe shop of the maximum security prison. Then he became chief clerk in the Sing Sing stockhouse.

Enken came up to see him every weekend. She took the train. Once a month, Dorothea would visit. Dorothea didn't drive, and she didn't like the train. When she visited, she'd come up with Enken on the bus.

In 1971, Yukl was transferred to New York's Walkill correctional facility. Life was easier there. It was a minimum security prison, with no outside perimeter walls and few locked bars. There were rooms, not cells, and Yukl had one all to himself, complete with a real bed, a desk, a chair, and more space than he had ever seen in Sing Sing. He was, to say the least, a model prisoner.

Yukl's behavior was exemplary at Walkill, and the prison administration began to take notice. The warden, Harold Butler, a jovial and mild-tempered man, took a special interest in Charlie.

Butler had worked for nearly forty years as a corrections officer, and had performed every imaginable job within the prison system. Prisoners like Charles Yukl were rare birds.

As soon as Yukl got to Walkill, he went before the assignment committee. It was standard procedure. They reviewed his record, his history, and then they made a decision regarding the inmate's best interest. The service unit supervisor, a counselor, the educational director, the vocational director, and Butler sat on the committee.

They asked Charlie about his interests, his previous work experiences, his family relationships and what he planned to do when he was released. Charlie told them he had been a professional photographer.

In fact, Yukl said all the right things. He said that it was an unfortunate situation. He didn't know how he had gotten into difficulties. But, he said, he was there to clean his slate and to do whatever he could to help himself go back into the street and live a normal life. He projected a healthy attitude.

Butler called for Yukl's file. He studied his record. Prior to his manslaughter conviction, he had no previous arrests. Butler was a percentage warden—most manslaughter cases are accidental homicides between friends or family members, and the crimes are not likely to be repeated.

Yukl established an impeccable reputation in the facility. He seemed to have intelligence and ability, and, Butler thought, he just might be able to be rehabilitated.

Shortly after his arrival at Walkill, Yukl worked in the mimeograph and photography shops. Charlie was put in the prison's mimeograph room to edit all of the institutional pamphlets that were issued to the inmates. Butler felt it was a good time to bring them up to date. So Charlie reedited the pamphlets and rewrote most of them.

By prison standards, he did a fantastic job. The mimeograph shop was adjacent to Walkill's photo lab, a run-down room with obsolete equipment. When Yukl finished the booklets, he went to Butler and said, "Why don't you let me go in there and bring your photography department up to date? It's terrible," he told him. "It's in awful shape. Your equipment is antiquated. You're doing lousy work."

"Could you do any better?" Butler asked.

"I think I could," Yukl said, "but you gotta get some new equipment."

Butler quickly had Yukl switched to the photo department and asked Charlie to bring him a list of the materials he thought were required to fix up the photo unit.

Two days later, Yukl brought him a detailed, typewritten three-page list.

Butler was initially shocked at the projected cost, but he liked the idea. The funds were somehow found. Yukl threw out everything Walkill had in the photo department and bought all new equipment, new cameras, new developing paraphernalia. The big Yukl expansion plan was to go from black-and-white to color. Butler gave the go-ahead to that plan as well.

As soon as Yukl had set up the photo lab, he went to the warden again. "Why don't you permit other inmates to have their pictures taken in plain, white shirts and send them home?" he asked. "People who haven't seen guys in a long time would probably like to see them in something other than the prison uniform."

"That's a pretty good idea, Chuck," Butler said, "but how are we going to pay for it?"

Together, the pair worked out a system through which inmates could buy chips in the prison commissary—one chip per picture. They would turn them in to Yukl and he would photograph them. Prisoners were only charged what the film actually cost.

The program was a huge success. And Yukl's lab work was extraordinary. He processed and printed all the color work himself.

Word leaked out to other prisons about the photography program. When corrections officials asked Butler about it, he proudly replied, "Hey, we've got a guy that's terrific. He has a degree in photography. This guy is really good. In fact, he's good at anything he touches."

Butler only later discovered that Yukl was a good musician. When he mentioned that Walkill needed a choir leader, Charlie immediately volunteered to help. And help he did. His reputation among fellow inmates and guards was soon enhanced by his arranging musical shows at the prison. A group of black inmates who sang spirituals wanted to make a record. They were able to find a small company willing to come up from New York City and cut the record. Charles Yukl did most of the musical arrangements and set up the recording date.

He also formed a small musical group. Three nights a week, when he got off work from the lab, he got together with four other prisoners and jammed from six to nine P.M. in the prison's band room. One convict played sax, another trumpet. A third played the guitar. The fourth prisoner handled percussion, and Charlie led them all on the piano. Yukl was not a born musical leader, but he had a distinct advantage with this ad hoc group of musician-prisoners. He could read music, and they couldn't.

The band rehearsals were disorganized sessions. Little by little the prisoners' musicianship improved—although they still couldn't read a note of music—and Yukl got them up and running in tune and rhythm on one appropriately titled piece: "Exodus."

By Christmas of 1972, the band expanded their repertoire and played a half-dozen seasonal songs—such as "Silent Night"—for the Walkill prison's Christmas show, which Yukl wrote and helped choreograph.

Despite the rosy behavior, Butler could not ignore the nature of Yukl's crime. He thought Charlie needed a lot of psychotherapy. At the very least, some counseling sessions.

On Sundays, the prison offered a psychiatric counseling program, thanks largely to a number of moonlighting doctors from Matteawan and Poughkeepsie State hospitals who were paid by Walkill to meet with inmates.

First, Butler involved Charlie directly in the private sessions. Then, Butler suggested to Charlie that since Enken was visiting him each week, it might be a good idea if she joined him during the sessions. And she did, on a number of occasions. Soon Yukl was receiving more psychiatric counseling than any man Butler had ever seen in his corrections career. But Butler didn't interfere—he thought Yukl was being helped. Still, one thing bothered him. Whether or not his impression of Enken Yukl was justified, from the moment Butler met her, Enken seemed a puzzling and frightening enigma.

"There was something about her when I was in her presence that made my back crawl," Butler told his wife. "I don't know what it is, but there's something about that lady that bothers me. I'm worried about her. She is a cold, cold person. There's just something . . ."

Butler often spent time with Enken alone. They'd talk about Charlie, his future and what he planned to do. She appeared to be genuinely concerned, but Butler was suspicious. He had never had that feeling with other inmate wives. But Butler just couldn't pinpoint his feelings. All he could say to his wife was, "There's something about that woman that upsets me. I'm worried about Charlie. But I don't know what it is."

Yukl's behavior remained perfect. Butler admitted he liked Yukl and wanted to help him. Yukl had the warden's trust, and almost unrestricted access to his office. Once Butler even let him go down to a nearby state university campus and speak to a group of students in a sociology class. It was highly irregular.

The rest of the prison population resented the arrangement, and began to resent Yukl. Some envied him simply because he had the warden's ear. Others envied his musicianship. Many thought he was obsequious. "If I could have an institution full of Yukls," Butler would often say, "I'd never have any problems.

"I've seen thousands of inmates, and if we're supposed to release anyone, then this was the right guy," said Butler. "There wasn't a mark on his record. He did everything, and more than was asked of him. And you have to figure that his case, like most manslaughters, was a once-in-a-lifetime crime. Such murderers rarely kill again.

"He was soft-spoken, polite," Butler recalled, "he was in contact with female employees here, and there was never any hint of a problem. He must have been a con artist because he must have realized he had a serious problem and kept quiet about it.

"We thought Yukl was a classic version of the rehabilitation system working at its best," Butler continued. "He didn't get a harsh sentence, he became a model inmate who seemed to have learned his lesson. But I guess underneath it all he was a con man. He certainly fooled me and it's giving me a lot of sleepless nights."

Unlike New Jersey and four other states, New York has no special prison program for sex offenders. Inmates can, however, request psychiatric counseling. During the last eighteen months of his sentence, Mr. Yukl met twenty-three times with Dr. Emmanuel E. Feuer, a state psychiatrist.

Dr. Feuer thought Yukl talked easily about his past. "After some weeks of treatment, it was clear that he hated women who reminded him of his mother," Dr. Feuer said. "He resented the pressure she put on him. She was a strict disciplinarian who wanted him to succeed as a pianist."

Dr. Feuer said he believed that Yukl "understood his problem" and would be able to deal with it, but in early 1973, despite what seemed to be great progress in his therapy sessions, Yukl told prison officials he felt he still had some serious psychological problems. He wanted more professional help, and Dr. Feuer was again assigned to meet with him. For the next two months, Feuer met with Yukl once a week. Charlie seemed to respond well to Freudian analysis, and at one of their last sessions, Feuer asked him, "Do you think this could ever happen again?"

Yukl said, "No."

The year 1973 was a watershed year for Charlie. Having served two-thirds of his minimum sentence, he was now eligible for parole. No one was more aware of the date with the parole board than Yukl.

The monthly parole board sessions at Walkill were excruciatingly short. There were approximately forty men who were waiting for their cases to be heard. Each member of the board was given ten or more case folders to read in the hour before the prisoners, one by one, entered the room. This meant that each prisoner's case would be reviewed in depth by only one member of the board—and the "depth" averaged just under six minutes. Six minutes to study an inmate. Six minutes to understand him, his crime, and his subsequent prison behavior. Six minutes to determine a man's history and to direct his future. Six minutes to freedom, or six minutes back to hell.

When appearing at a session of the New York State Parole Board, a prisoner has painfully little time to argue his case. One commissioner normally handles the interview—usually the one man (of three) who has actually scanned the prisoner's case file. Traditionally, the other two members of the board go along with his judgment.

On a warm spring day in April, Yukl reported to Butler's office. There wasn't enough space at the prison for a separate board room, so the three-man interviewing group, a guard, and a stenographer met in the warden's office around a small conference table. The light from the large Gothic windows lit the room well.

Yukl patiently waited for his turn before the board, passing the time in his cell. He didn't have to wait long. He was escorted into the conference room shortly before noon wearing slacks and his best V-neck sweater.

Both Dr. Feuer and Butler had been supportive of his parole petition. So had Dr. Vytautas Damijonaitis, Walkill's attending psychiatrist. "He functioned quite well and seemed to improve under treatment," said Damijonaitis, who wrote Yukl's preparole psychiatric report after a forty-five-minute interview with him. (He later insisted that the report was only a statement about Yukl's medical condition and was not intended to recommend either release or continuation of sentence.)

When he entered the board room, Yukl had the distinct impression that someone had spoken to these men in his behalf. Dr. Feuer had, indeed, told some prison officials that in his opinion Yukl was no longer mentally ill.

The board was more polite—and casual in conversational style—than Yukl had imagined. Only one of the men had read his file, but he had informed the other members of Yukl's perfect behavior record as well as the final psychiatric report, written by Damijonaitis. They had, it seemed, chosen to ignore the strongly worded letter in the Yukl file from Manhattan DA Frank Hogan adamantly arguing against parole.

"Mr. Yukl," one of the men explained, "if your parole was based solely on your institutional record, although it is excellent, we would not let you go. But we realize you've had some psychotherapy."

Yukl nodded. "Yes, I have had quite a lot of it here, and I want to thank you—"

"Mr. Yukl . . ."

"Yoookle," Charlie corrected his pronunciation.

"I'm sorry, Mr. Yukl." The board member paused. "Why do you think you should be paroled?"

"Well," Charlie began, doing his best not to stutter, "I would like to have the opportunity to go out into society and start over again."

Another member asked a trick question. "Do you listen to the doctors, or your conscience?"

"The doctors have helped me to listen to my conscience," Yukl answered, "and to recognize the difference between right and wrong."

That seemed to satisfy everyone. Once again, Charles Yukl had said all the right things, and he convinced the board that they were his new comrades in conscience.

The session ended in less than five minutes.

A few weeks later, Charlie got the good news—he had been paroled. On June 19, 1973, after serving five years and four months in city and state prisons, Charles Yukl walked out of Walkill a free man.

CHAPTER EIGHT

Enken rented a car and drove up to Walkill to get Charlie the day he was released. It was nearly noon by the time he walked out of prison and began the drive home. Ninety minutes later the couple made their first stop in Manhattan—Fortieth Street and Eighth Avenue.

Ben Lichtenstein, a parole officer, was waiting for Yukl there. Charlie made a distinct impression on Lichtenstein when he entered his office. He bowed and asked meekly if he could come in. They spoke for an hour, and Lichtenstein explained to Yukl the rules of the parole game. They would see each other once each week for the next three months. There would be no associations with known criminals. No weapons. No drugs. And no alcohol to excess.

Yukl wasn't alone in his parole. In rejoining the city's population, he became one of an estimated ten thousand convicted killers who had been freed and were living in the city after having served from three months probation to 30 years behind bars. A majority of the parolees survived on the outside.

Yukl asked Lichtenstein about the possibility of continuing his psychiatric counseling. Lichtenstein said he wasn't in a position to recommend anyone but that there were dozens of qualified, inexpensive counseling services throughout the city.

As soon as Charlie got home to Waverly Place he headed straight for the most familiar piece of furniture in the house—the piano. Over the next two days, he put together a song and routine sheet. Some of the songs were ragtime, others were from *Mame:* "Don't Bring Lulu," "Big Spender," and one called "My Name Is Morgan but It Ain't J.P." By the time he was finished, there were forty-four song-and-dialogue sets in the routine. He saved his most recent favorite "Side by Side" by Stephen Sondeim for last, and played it all the way through.

The next day, again through Olsten's, Yukl went looking for work. He typed up a clean, two-page, single spaced résumé that spoke in euphemisms of his prison experiences. He wrote that he preferred "employment in a position which entails working with adolescents, young adults, and/or 'criminal' offenders, i.e. any position dedicated to 'correction' and/or guidance of persons with 'adjustment' or 'social' problems."

Yukl then launched into a long, rambling essay about prisons, which he labeled a "personal concept." "I believe that, too many times, we attempt to 'push' a pre-determined value system upon a person for whom the values have no meaning. Therefore, I feel that guidance and correction must take into consideration the value structure of the environment from which the individual comes, his ability to cope with that value system, and his ability to realize the maximum of his potential within that social structure."

Yukl was a master of hedging the truth, noting that in 1972 he had received a "degree" in music. (This was a lie. While he was in prison he had paid $100 and received the phony diploma from a made-to-order diploma mill.) He then added courses at New York

University which he claimed he had taken to earn
credit toward a Master's degree: Criminology, Adolescent Psychology, General Psychology, Ed. Psychology,
Juvenile Delinquency, Social Stratification, Marriage
and the Family, General Sociology, and Advanced
Sociology.

Last, and most revealing, Yukl listed his "experience within correctional field," stating that he had
taught music and sociology at Sing Sing for eighteen
months. Never mentioning the minor detail that he
had been a prisoner, Yukl claimed he had been employed at Walkill for three years and had "worked
with inmates, drug-related problems and otherwise,
held cell sessions, the purpose being to ameliorate the
individual's adjustment to incarceration and provide a
'socially acceptable' mode of ventilation of hostilities,
such hostilities being one of the predominant dysfunctions of incarceration. Also taught Music, Psychology,
and Sociology."

All Olsten's knew was that Charlie Yukl could type.
And based on his typing ability alone, they sent him to
do some temp work at the Manhattan engineering
firm of Greeley and Hansen. Yukl reported for work
at the firm's downtown offices at 233 Broadway
promptly at eight A.M. the next morning and filled out
the company's standard application for employment.
Three days later, on August 13 he began as a reception secretary. His salary: $670 a month.

Still, Yukl harbored some strange feelings of resentment toward the prison officials at Walkill. He was
paroled and working now, but still bitter at having lost
out on a chance for a civilian job at the facility.

On October 31, 1973, after hearing a WCBS-TV
news editorial on the condition of New York's prisons,
Yukl sat down at the electric IBM typewriter at work

and composed a long and rambling nineteen-page "paper." He promptly sent a copy to the editorial department at the television station, with copies to Peter Preiser, New York's commissioner of corrections, and to his old friend, Warden Harold Butler. None of the three replied.

The essay was called "An Endorsement of Mediocrity," and it was Yukl's attack on the system which he felt kept him from landing that job:

"Should New York State, whose motto is Excelsior, endorse, much less tolerate, a condition existing in our state "correctional facilities" which promotes, encourages, and reinforces mediocrity? [Yukl asked.]

It is the purpose of the following pages to present examples as to how the Correction Officers' Union, in reality, obstructs correction, encourages mediocrity and siphons off tax dollars for "non-production" and "dis-service" to the community.

The following will support the opinion that this union, rather than concentrating upon their obligations to society by assisting the inmate in receiving a positive benefit from incarceration, is more concerned with achieving a power status and formulating administrative policy while conveniently disregarding the educational and experiential requirements necessary to function in that capacity.

The following are a few examples as to how this seniority system, and the union in general, obstructs correction:

During the day, when inmates are up, working, etc., it cannot be disputed that experienced correctional officers are required to supervise these inmates. The most important time for inmate supervision is during the 8 A.M. to 4 P.M. shift. Other shifts, i.e. 4

P.M. to midnite and midnite to 8 A.M., are generally
considered as being "easy duty" tours, i.e. tours
where nothing much is happening. Correction officers, knowing this, naturally try for assignment to
these shifts. After all, as one correction officer once
said, "Why work if I don't have to?" As a result of
the seniority system the "experienced" officers who
are really needed during the daylight hours are
assigned to the night shifts while the new, inexperi-
enced personnel attempt to fulfill daytime responsi-
bilities. Just the opposite of what it should be.

Consider a situation where a sincere, dedicated,
and experienced individual is assigned to a position
where he would indeed be functional. His knowledge of inmates, correction experience, etc., would
be an asset to that position. Somehow, this individual is assigned to a position in which he can do
something FOR the institution and the inmate. Is it
not a "sad state of affairs" when, because of union
intervention, this individual, not having the necessary seniority for that position, is subsequently removed and reassigned? Isn't it even sadder when
another person, obviously less qualified, interested,
etc., IS assigned to that position? THIS COULD
ONLY HAPPEN UNDER THE SENIORITY SYS-
TEM.

The above examples involve correction personnel.
The following applies to the inmate, which has even
more serious consequences and implications since
inmates are the ones we are presumably rehabili-
tating.

Then came a poorly disguised autobiographical note:

I personally knew an inmate, experienced in photo/
offset, who was assigned to the photography unit at

one of our "correctional" facilities. This man, undisputably, was qualified in that field. When he first went to his assignment he noticed how badly ill-equipped, underproductive, and sub-standard "his" department was. There was no emphasis upon production and the quality control left much to be desired. Due to the retirement of the supervisor there was no qualified supervisory personnel available. This inmate, being interested in his work (even as an inmate) took an active part in making "his" department functional. He requested permission of the superintendent and deputy superintendent to:

1. purchase new equipment
2. begin new programs
3. upgrade the quality
4. increase production

Such permission was readily granted and the inmate began 'a crusade' to create a department which would be functional not only for the state and the inmate but for society as well. Accentuation was placed upon providing the opportunity for another "vocational training" program in the photo/offset field. Within one year the photographic unit at that institution improved 500% (improvement percentage quoted from statement of correction official). The department was becoming functional and its potential even more noticeable. Then . . . the union stepped in again. The job of supervisor could, most certainly, not be left to an inmate . . . no matter how qualified or interested, responsible, etc., he was. It must be filled by a 'correction' officer . . . not even a qualified civilian. The position, therefore, went up for bid. Three persons bid for the job. Two were apparently interested in learning the field and upgrading the unit. The third person had spent most of his tour of duty working in the laundry and mess hall. This person knew absolutely nothing about photography, offset, and related disciplines. Because of the correction officers' union and its seniority system this "laundry expert" was assigned as supervisor in the photography unit. In other words, this department is now being supervised by an individual not having the slightest idea of what he is supervising. He is, in effect, being paid out of tax dollars for NOT doing something. The most serious part of this situation is yet to come. The inmate, qualified in the field, took it upon himself to attempt to train this correction officer. Most of us assume that inmates are sent to prison to BE trained . . . not to train correction officers. At any rate, textbooks were purchased, many at the inmate's expense, in the hope that this officer would take an active interest and learn the field. This was optimistic since this officer apparently was only interested in doing only what he had to. To quote this officer: "The mark of a good supervisor is that he surround himself with good men." He conveniently forgets that a "good" supervisor should be able to do whatever he asks of his subordinates. This made no difference to the union, however. Comments directed at the new supervisor by the union included: "What's the matter with you . . . taking orders from an inmate" . . . "I wouldn't put up with an inmate running me . . . you're the boss . . . you're the officer . . . you're running that department . . . not that inmate." The obvious fact that this officer just had no idea of what he was doing was overlooked by the union. One would think that this union would be interested in the effective running of their institution. Their attitude in this situation obviously contradicts such an interest. Eventually the inmate came up for parole. Every effort was made by administrative personnel to employ this inmate in a civilian capacity as supervisor of the photo unit. Briefs were presented, letters written, etc. Everyone agreed (on paper) that this was an excellent idea, even Albany. What a wonderful opportunity to show society that New York State *does* have faith in its own corrective process and *will* employ an ex-inmate in a responsible position. But . . . thanks to this correction officers' union, and their seniority system, our "laundry expert" is still supervisor of that department and the inmate since paroled. The union fought the administration on the grounds that putting this inmate in that position would mean the ultimate loss of a correction officer position. They did not consider the loss to the institution or the state which would be the obvious result of a department not working up to its potential. They did not consider the loss to other inmates who might be interested in learning a vocation yet cannot do so in this field because they must work for an officer having nothing to offer in that field. The one and only concern of the officers' union in this matter was *JOB SECURITY* . . . NOT PRODUCTIVITY. This was frustrating for the inmate. To take an active interest in the institution while incarcerated is unusual in itself. To attempt to train a correction officer is almost unheard of. Then, for the icing on the cake, to have all his (the inmate's) efforts go up in smoke because the union was more concerned with power and economics than with meaningful job performance must have been the ultimate in frustration. How does this inmate feel about correction as a result of this?

*   *   *

Yukl was upset about having been denied the prison photography job. He wanted a job, but didn't quite know how to go about getting one. He started scanning the newspapers, looking for job listings. One day, while he was looking through the classified section of the *Village Voice*, he noticed something else—an ad for the Fifth Avenue Center for Psychotherapy.

When he walked into the downtown office, he was listed by the receptionist as a "self-referral" and was asked to wait. Behind the receptionist there were a few dozen offices—more like small cubicles. Inside each were a table, two chairs and a small lamp. No couch. No window. When it was his turn, Yukl was directed to one of the cubicles where he met William Player, who was to become his therapist. Player was a young, preppie-looking, bespectacled psychology graduate who had joined the center just a few months earlier.

As he did with Lichtenstein, Yukl came in and bowed. It startled Player, made him feel uncomfortable. He asked Yukl to sit. For the next fifty minutes, Yukl gave Player a capsule summary of his life, his anger toward his father, his fear and repression of sex.

"I want to help you, Mr. Yukl," Player told him. "If I can help you accept and articulate some of your rage and deal with some of the repression, then we'll do just fine." The sessions would not be overly expensive, Player explained. Fees were based on the patient's income, in Yukl's case, they would be about thirteen dollars a visit.

Yukl wanted to meet more than once a week. He seemed determined to get to the bottom of his problems. He appeared to be genuinely interested in investigating his killing impulses, his fantasies, and the nightmares that still haunted him. "I really want to find out," he told Player, "what I've done."

When he got home from the first session, Charlie wrote to his father, told him he had been paroled, and asked him for some help in paying Monaghan's bill as well as some anticipated psychotherapy charges. A week later he got a letter back from Salem.

His father responded to his son's request in a short and less than positive way. He told Yukl that he had just bought a small outboard boat and trailer. "So I just don't have any extra money. Don't worry about things," he wrote Charlie, "just pray to God."

CHAPTER NINE

Yukl was soon paying Player twenty dollars a session at the center, and he started seeing him more frequently through the summer. "I want to gain insight into myself and knock out my problems," he told Player as he began to unload his sad personal history, his sexual problems, and his fears of being rejected by women and by society in general.

"I feel a great urging for other women, although I've been married for twelve years," he said in one of the early sessions. "At first, my wife treated me with patient understanding. But she is German. She wants sex all the time. I don't. So I have sex with her once every two weeks, just to satisfy her."

The discussions stayed on sex. "My dad would never talk about sex with me. Every time I asked him, I got slapped." Yukl was angry at his father, Player noted, and still felt rebellious toward the elder Yukl.

When the sessions began to shift toward discussion of his mother, Charlie reacted differently. "She's a fine person, a good musician," he said. "But she's perfectionistic."

"Perfectionistic?" Player asked.

"Yes. Perfectionistic. You know," Yukl tried to explain. "When it came to music I could never please her. Her approval of me varied from one day to the next. Still," he added, "I'm proud of her. She's single and independent."

He talked little of his stepmother. "My wife and mother stuck by me when I was in jail, and that helped."

"Are you working now?" Player asked.

Yukl told him he'd be starting a new job soon, but he also wanted to go "back" to college. "I want to get a masters in sociology or criminology at NYU."

It seemed an ambitious goal, but Player was supportive. "I applied for a job as a parole officer," Yukl proudly told Player. "And I was even offered a job at the prison. But I had a record. It wouldn't have worked."

Player talked with him about Lichtenstein. "Oh, he's a dream." Yukl smiled. "I'm happy to have him. I feel very relaxed around him."

Two days later, Yukl was back to see Player again. He wanted to talk about women and black people. "I think my wife is heavy because of me," he suggested. "She weighs a hundred and sixty-five pounds." They talked about the concept of inner and outer beauty.

"We're snappy with each other. My wife and I just don't get along."

"Why?" Player asked, taking it all down in illegible doctor scrawl.

"Well," Yukl said, "I keep trying to prove my masculinity. But it doesn't work. I also have trouble making decisions. It's very difficult."

"What effect did the murder have on you as a person, Charles?"

"I . . . I think it was a good experience." He paused. "Yes, I really think it helped me to take a good look at myself. It woke me up."

It was an answer he had used before, for the prison

psychiatrists upstate. But now that he was out, he continued, with more candor. "At that time I hated women. I found them crude. The woman I killed had no talent. In fact," he argued, "I was even teaching her without getting paid. I wanted to be needed, Dr. Player. And I saw that woman as a symbol. In destroying her I wanted to destroy the kind of women I hated."

The next week, Yukl responded to an ad in the classified section of the *Times* for a job at an engineering firm near Wall Street. On the application for Greeley and Hansen, he claimed to have earned a bachelor's degree in sociology. Under the section marked "postgraduate work," Yukl again lied and wrote that he was currently attending NYU, studying criminology. His objective, he wrote, was to find "employment in a position which entails working with adolescents, young adults, and/or 'criminal' offenders. . . ." Though the job, as office manager for an engineering firm, hardly offered him that type of employment, he was hired.

At the same time Yukl enrolled at Hunter College night school. His first courses were Child Psychology and Deviant Behavior and Social Control. He took the courses, he told Player at their next session in August, because he honestly wanted to know more about his problems. "I want to know where I'm coming from intellectually as well as emotionally."

They joked about Player being around in August, the most dreaded month for therapy patients in New York City. It's the thirty day period, usually extending through Labor Day, when all the psychiatrists and psychotherapists take their vacations. It is also a period during which the suicide/homicide rates increase dramatically. Yukl said he felt lucky that Player was in town. He needed to talk.

It appeared to be a good sign. He told Player that he was feeling better about himself since he started taking the courses. "Even the sex has improved with my wife," he boasted. He also hinted that his relationship with his mother was improving. "We're communicating more," he reported. "But she always calls me when she's drunk. We talk for about two hours, and then I use walking the dog as an excuse to get off the phone."

The next session with Player in August saw Yukl in a depressed mood. He had received a 92 on one of his Deviant Behavior papers, and had argued with the professor. "I got him to raise it to a ninety-six," he told Player. "It's a major problem area for me," he said. "I need all A's to cover my feelings of inadequacy."

The following week Yukl walked in beaming. He was working full-time now at Greeley and Hansen. He was typing 100 words a minute, taking twelve credits of college work.

"Are there people at work you like?" Player asked.

"Oh, yes," said Yukl. There was one colleague in particular, Irwin Klein. Klein was an engineer with the firm, and was one of the few people at the company who was overtly friendly to Yukl. Yukl first came to Greeley and Hansen as a part-time worker. He was such a good typist however, that Klein soon recommended that the company hire him full-time. Charlie was a nice guy, Klein told his superiors, and gave the impression that he could get along with just about anyone. In fact, when Greeley and Hansen hired him, they didn't even bother to check out his references.

Every lunch hour, Klein and Yukl would take out a small plastic chess set, open a folding board, and play. On the weekends, Klein and his wife sometimes socialized with the Yukls. The foursome would go bowling or stay at home and play Monopoly.

With Klein, it was just a game, but Charlie always wanted to win. The competition was essential. Klein beat Yukl at bowling, and averaged 160 a game. But Yukl kept records of all their chess games, and delighted in reminding Klein that he had won 55 percent of all the matches.

Yukl told Klein all sorts of stories about his past. One week he told him he had an advanced degree in criminology; the next week he forgot he had a degree and told Klein he had done some time in jail as a make-believe prisoner working on his college thesis. When Yukl signed up for additional courses at John Jay College, a New York City school known for educating policemen, Klein began to believe the stories a little more.

Yukl always boasted to Klein that he was going to get something over on somebody. One night, when they were playing Monopoly at Charlie's place, he pointed with pride at his Great Dane. "Bessie's her name," he announced to Klein. "But that's not all. I listed her as a deduction on my tax return."

Every once in a while, Yukl would reveal more information about himself to Irwin—his photography background, his piano playing. When the Kleins invited Charlie to a party at their house in Bayside, Queens, Yukl saw they had a piano, and sat down to play. "It's broken, Charlie. Sorry," Klein said. Yukl stayed at the piano, fixed it, and played Scott Joplin tunes all night long.

When the firm needed pictures taken for new employee applications, Charlie volunteered. The next morning, he appeared at work with his camera, tripod, and film. He took excellent head shots. "You ought to try to get some fashion work," an employee told him.

THE PIANO TEACHER 119

"Work with models. There's good money there." Yukl said he'd check into it.

"We go out together every few days," Yukl told Player. "I even like Irwin's wife."

Player felt it was time to go back to some deep emotional investigation of the Suzanne Reynolds murder.

"I felt no remorse for that girl," Charlie admitted. "Only for me and my wife. I killed her because I wanted to get back at my mother and father. In fact, I think I did somebody a favor."

"You did?" Player asked. "Who?"

"People in the musical profession," Yukl laughed. When he stopped laughing, he said, "I also did somebody a favor by getting me out of the way." He didn't elaborate.

On August 17, Yukl came to Player with the news that he and Enken had gotten a kitten, a new playmate for Bessie. "Now that's something I feel *good* about," he said. "But here's a question for you," he said to the therapist. "Why is it that when company comes over I'm wide awake, and when I'm alone with my wife I'm always sleepy?"

"Does it have anything to do with sex?"

"Yes. I do everything I can to avoid her sexual demands. I abstain to foil her," he said, half smiling. "If I think back," he said, trying to self-analyze, "I think that sex was something for which I was punished abruptly and promptly."

In his notes for their August 25 session, Player wrote "achievement orientation versus play. Yukl doesn't want to play." They talked about how Yukl spent his time. "People want just to relax at work," Yukl claimed. "They don't want to work hard. But relaxation for me is like sex—it only wastes time."

"But don't you ever relax?"

"Not really. I feel like I have a police state over myself. It's a self-imposed totalitarian rigidity."

"Surely you must do something other than work," Player challenged.

"Yeah. I let Enken make those decisions. Sometimes we ride our bikes. But she handles the money and I get an allowance each week. You know what we did last week? We went to see a hard-core porno film with a friend of hers."

"Which one?"

"*The Harrod Experiment*. It made me nauseous."

Player thought he was beginning to understand Mr. Yukl and came to enjoy their sessions. He found Yukl an argumentative sort, the kind of person who liked to challenge authority and provoke people. But, Player didn't consider Yukl a serious paranoid, and thought he could help Yukl deal with his current problems.

Sometimes their discussions would focus on books Yukl was reading. One day, Yukl brought in a copy of *The Fountainhead* by Ayn Rand, and claimed it was his favorite book. "It's got a lot to say," he said, offering the book to Player. They talked about the Libertarian party, another new Yukl interest. Then the conversation centered on Charlie's Great Dane. "I had him neutered yesterday," he reported. Before Player had a chance to respond, Yukl interrupted. "I still have an urge for other women. But I'm afraid of being rejected. Maybe," he asked, "I don't want my wife's understanding? Maybe I want to be *made* to perform?"

"Are you saying you want some direction?" Player asked.

"No. To me," Yukl answered, "direction means permission. Wait. There's something else I want to discuss. You know, I'm now feeling concern about castrating the poor dog."

The fifty-minute weekly sessions with Player continued through the fall. And Yukl maintained a certain consistency: he said he felt attracted to other women but felt unable to deal with his urges.

On October 27, he began the regular session with Player with a piece of news. "I've decided to try an experiment," he said.

"What kind?"

"It's part of school," he said. "I'm doing a special project I initiated myself. I call it 'studying urban social acceptance.' "

CHAPTER TEN

At the end of October and in early November, Charles Yukl could often be found in the early evenings outside Washington Square park in Greenwich Village, standing with his Great Dane and handing out questionnaires. Using the guise of his Hunter College graduate thesis, he would stop women who were walking by and ask them to take one of the single-page surveys.

There was no class assignment. There was no graduate thesis. And this was not an authorized independent class project.

For two or three hours a night, Yukl became a regular in the park, handing out the papers. The questions followed no particular pattern, except that they were deliberately provocative. And they were directed only at women. He asked questions about homosexuality and if the respondent accepted it in society. Questions about blacks, minorities, and a number of questions about personal sexual preferences. Yukl made a point of attaching a self-addressed, stamped envelope to each questionnaire, which he labeled at the top of the page as anonymous. Still, at the bottom of the page, he listed his name and phone number if the woman wanted to be interviewed.

At Hunter, he was doing well, not only in his grades,

but in interacting with the other students, most of whom were considerably younger than Yukl.

On October 27, Yukl was in a particularly good mood when he met Player. "Progress has been made," he announced.

"My wife went to Monticello for a few days last week," he told him. "And you know what I did? I took out one of the students."

"And?" Player asked.

"It was nothing. We just had lunch. We talked about school."

"You didn't feel anxiety?"

"Yes. I did. But I controlled it. I liked it. When I got home, there was a letter from my father," he said, his mood suddenly growing somber. "Getting a letter from my father is like getting a statement from Con Edison."

"What did he say?"

"Nothing. I don't want to talk about it."

"Don't you ever think of just writing to him?" Player asked.

"No. It would be useless."

"Why don't you try it. Let him know how well you're doing in New York."

Yukl promised Player he would.

During one of the Yukl-Player sessions, Ben Lichtenstein arrived at Yukl's apartment. He knew Charlie wouldn't be home. He wanted to chat with Enken. She was surprised to see him, but asked Lichtenstein in. "I'm very satisfied with my husband's adjustments," she told him.

"And I'm satisfied with our relationship together." It was a short meeting.

At their regular parole office meetings, Yukl always brought Lichtenstein his pay stubs, talked about his job, his progress, his photography and piano playing. And his therapy sessions.

On the surface, everything was going great.

And on November 19, Yukl finally got up the courage to write to his father in Oregon.

"I did it," he told Player. "I wrote my dad and asked him for money. It'll be good," he said, "whether he calls me a fool or gives me the money. At least I stood up for myself."

The next week Yukl and Enken had a small party. He complained that he felt old, that the party made him afraid he might be losing control. He smoked marijuana for the first time that night. He didn't like the experience.

He told Player that his meetings with Lichtenstein were working out well and had been reduced from weekly to monthly. "I like Ben," he said. His class project was working out just fine. He had handed out hundreds of questionnaires. They were being answered and mailed back to him.

Player noted the apparent progress, but never asked Yukl to tell him about his class project in detail.

"Happy New Year! It really is going to be a new year for me. A great one," Yukl said to Player at their first session of 1974. Yukl told him he was firmly committed to finishing school. "I borrowed five hundred dollars from the bank for tuition."

Again, he had enrolled in sociology and psychology classes.

"I think Christmas was the turning point with my wife," he told Player. "We both are beginning to understand each other."

"In what way?" the therapist asked.

"Well, we both knew what we wanted for Christmas. She gave me a razor, a pair of pants, a gold tie clip, and an electric drill. I gave her a coat, a diamond pendant, and an electric razor."

Yukl still hadn't had sex with his wife for months, he confessed to Player, "but I'm not having bad dreams anymore, either."

On January 12, their next session, Yukl decided to talk about politics. Watergate had been dominating the headlines, and the subject was almost unavoidable.

"I got into an argument at the office," he told Player. It wasn't with his friend Klein, but with another co-worker.

"They're all pro-Nixon people. You know what I think?" he asked the therapist. "Whether it's the tango or the chacha, Nixon's still dancing. And we all have to dance to his tune. It's just terrible."

Player seized the moment to discuss the differences between compliance and oppositionalism. "Charlie, do you think you're trapped into dancing to other people's tunes?"

"Yes, but I'm changing." He began to smile. "You remember those questionnaires I handed out? Well, a lot of the women who filled them out . . . they're calling me. They want to be interviewed! I'm really having a debate with myself. Do you think I should have sex with these women?"

Player was clearly surprised. Yukl had never mentioned the idea of personal interviews.

"I want to make the first move with these women," Yukl kept speaking. "What do you think?"

Player wrote down some more notes, then looked up. "Charles, I want you to think this over very carefully. Are you checking out your own controls about acting out your hostility toward women?"

"I think so."

"You can't just think it. I'm sure you don't want to

play brinksmanship, especially considering your prior history."

Player was now truly beginning to worry. This was the first time Yukl had openly expressed an interest in sex.

"Yes. You're right," Yukl seemed almost eagerly to agree. "It's something I should be thinking about. I wouldn't want to do anything bad." Yukl promised Player he would put thoughts of going out with these women on hold.

A week later, he made no mention of the possible interviews. Instead he was back to politics. "I went to a political rally for Koch last week," he reported.

"By yourself?" Player was anxious to know.

"Yeah. But there was this girl with a terrific body who I met there. She wants me to take her to Long Island for a dog show."

Surprisingly, the woman had an apartment in the same building as Ben Lichtenstein, the parole officer. Yukl had decided not to tell either Lichtenstein or Player about the weird coincidence. But he thought about it. Even now.

"How do you feel about that?" Player asked.

"About what?" Yukl looked up, momentarily confused.

"About the girl with the great body."

Yukl looked upset. "I don't know. Why is all this shit necessary? I mean, she came over to the house a few days ago. She's taller than I am and that bothers me. She's got a master's degree from Harvard in chemistry."

"And that bothers you, too?"

"A little," Yukl admitted. "I know now that I want to get involved with a lot of women, but lately I've been having that dream, and that bothers me the most."

Player had never heard of the dream. He asked Yukl to elaborate.

"Four or five months before I killed that woman, I had a dream of exactly the way the murder would happen," he confided. "I would wake up from the dream and say, 'What a jerk you are . . . you'll even go to jail.' You know what else? I even dreamed that I'd get seven-and-a-half to fifteen years."

This was a significant revelation, especially since Yukl was claiming to be having the dream again.

"What do you think the dream means, Charles?" Player asked. (Yukl's answer was crucial, Player reasoned, whether he had in fact had the dream or had made it up.)

"I've given it a lot of thought," he said. "It sort of sounds like from the beginning getting punished was part of my plan. Perhaps," he suggested, "you even set up a punishment to allow yourself to commit the act."

"Is that what you feel you're doing now?"

Yukl shook his head no.

"Are you sure?"

"No."

Player paused and looked long and hard at Yukl. "Charles, until you *are* sure," Player cautioned, "I think we should talk about this area much more."

Yukl nodded his head. "I agree."

The sessions continued, uneventfully for patient or therapist, through the end of January and early February.

On February 8, Yukl told Player he was having a problem. For the first time since he had left prison, Yukl had begun to stutter in the classroom when addressed by a woman.

Player made note of this development, but did not think it serious. At Player's suggestion, Yukl began looking for a speech therapist. At about the same time, Lichtenstein, noting Yukl's apparent progress, told him that his parole visits would be dramatically reduced to just two times a year.

The stuttering got worse in class in March. But Yukl told Player "the best thing about my psychology class is that it's blowing away my rigidities. The professor is a woman." While he still admitted to having desires for some of his fellow students, he now told Player he was identifying more with the woman professor. "I'm seeing myself more in an assistant professor role. Besides," he added, "Enken is so narrow. I don't really want to be with her. I'm growing away from her. I'm recognizing my needs for the first time."

On April 6, Yukl got his midterm grades back from Hunter. All B's. He was angry. "I can't study when Enken is around," he told Player. "I like to be alone. You know, I just realized that my wife knows more about me than I will ever know about her."

"Then why are you still in this marriage?" Player asked. He had asked the question a number of times before during their meetings, but Yukl had always changed the subject.

This time he decided to answer.

"Security. An obligation," he muttered.

"What kind of security?" Player pursued.

Yukl sighed and looked down at the floor. "Just someone to do the laundry."

Player broached the subject of a special session in which Yukl would bring Enken. Much to Player's surprise, Yukl reacted eagerly to the idea.

A week later, Charles and Enken sat down with Player. Yukl repeated some of his earlier feelings, of confinement, of distance from his wife. He began to stutter, to hesitate at the beginning of every thought and in the middle of almost every sentence. Enken sat on the couch. Yukl sat rigid and upright in a chair.

"Have you done anything to intensify contact in your relationship?" Player asked.

Yukl withdrew into silence. "I'm just afraid."

"Afraid of what?"

"Afraid of being swallowed up."

A few days later, Enken came in by herself. Player found her a quiet, inflexible woman, who, when pressed, gave pat answers, offered no reasonable solutions, and volunteered nothing about her relationship with Charles.

Player wrote in his notes "she says absolutely nothing new. Her sense of what's happening in the relationship is identical with his."

When Yukl came in for his regularly scheduled appointment two days later, he was all smiles. "Your session with Enken went very well," he thanked Player. "She's at home, doing my typing for my schoolwork."

"What else?" Player queried. "What about the relationship?"

"Oh," Yukl said, lowering his voice. "Well, we had sex three times this week. I did it after your session with her because I felt sorry for her."

It was not the response Player had been hoping for. He also did not believe Yukl had sex with his wife, whether he felt sorry for her or not. Player noted that Yukl seemed more nervous than usual.

The next night, Yukl was back with his Great Dane at Washington Square Park, handing out more questionnaires.

This time, there were more than the usual number of takers. It was a warm spring night, and lots of people were out on the streets.

One of them was Ellen Pahl.

In 1974, Pahl was one of the great minor theater characters of the city: one of the passionate women

who was always busy, always organizing, always net-
working with actors, directors, and producers to get
projects done.

In the spring and summer of 1974, Pahl headed a
performing group called Friends of the Family. It was
a satirical review group—lots of music, political and
social material, almost all of which was written by
Pahl.

Like many of the city's small theater groups, hers
was headquartered downtown in the Village—at NYU,
with offices at the university's student center. The
building also housed a big hall, where the group
rehearsed.

As Pahl left the building with a close friend and
headed into the park, she saw a man standing with a
large Great Dane.

"Yogi! Yogi!" the friend shouted across the street.
Yukl turned around. "It's Terry Selbert!"

Yukl bounded across the asphalt, pulled by the Great
Dane. He was happy to see an old friend.

"What a surprise," Selbert began. "I haven't seen
you in years."

"You neither," Yukl answered.

Terry introduced Yukl to Pahl. "Ellen, you really
ought to get to know this guy," he advised. "He's a
great piano player."

"And teacher too," Yukl added.

The three stopped and talked for a good twenty
minutes on the corner. Ellen invited Yukl to see a
show she was rehearsing. As they left to catch their
subway, Ellen asked Terry how long he had known
Yogi.

"We go back to dinner theater in the south. He was
the assistant musical director and a very interesting
guy. But we didn't have him the whole summer," he

said quite casually. "In the middle he had to leave to go to prison."

"To prison? What for?"

"I don't know exactly," Selbert shrugged. "All I know is that somewhere along the line, someone was killed, and Yogi was thought to be involved. He had to go and leave and begin his sentence, I think . . . something like that. But we were all sure it had to be an accident. I mean, can you imagine a guy like that killing someone?"

A few days later, Yukl went over to NYU and saw the revue. Afterward, he and Terry and Ellen went back to Terry's apartment for a small party. They talked at great length about the music business. Yukl told Pahl that he worked with a number of students and was always looking for more work. He also boasted that he was a good sound technician. Ellen asked him for a favor, and he readily agreed; the next day he transferred some old, big, reel-to-reel tapes she had onto regular cassettes.

He called her a few days later and asked if she could recommend him as a vocal coach for the people she worked with. "I really think I can help them," he told her. "Besides," he boasted, "I've got some great connections in the business. I can help you showcase these people. Tell you what," he said. "I won't even charge them a nickel."

He also informed Pahl that he was about to begin playing at a small club in New Jersey and that Ellen's people could work with him and use the club dates to try out some of their material.

One of the first women Ellen sent to him was an up-and-coming singer named Jeanne Crain. He began writing material for her, and they started working together. But Yukl was really interested in two other women. One, Brenda Gardner, was a regular in Pahl's revue. But she turned down his work offers, because they also included requests for dates.

"He gives me the heebie-jeebies," Gardner reported to Pahl. The two of them laughed. "They can't all be winners," she said.

The other was an aspiring young actress and singer named Melanie Chartoff. She was a terrific singer and had a great range. Her only problem was that she had yet to be discovered. She was practicing a nightclub showcase act and often met with Yukl to work on her song routines. Like the other girls, Chartoff never seemed to consider Charlie's behavior bizarre.

If Charlie was a little strange, well, then, everyone was a little strange in show business, she surmised. Emotions existed and throve in the extremes; shrill outbursts or quiet, moody depressions were the status quo when you asked someone to be vulnerable, exposed, and in front of an unforgiving audience.

Chartoff never paid much attention to Charlie. He would call her and ask her to dinner. She always found a polite way to decline.

One day, Ellen got a call from a friend who needed some singing help. Maybe Yogi could help her out. After all, he was free.

CHAPTER ELEVEN

Nancy Pauley was very much like the other women who knew Yukl. She liked him when she first met him in the early summer of 1974; he seemed deferential to women, willing to work and spend long hours with them, and he was a pianist who didn't mind playing other people's music. Pahl had told Nancy only that Yukl was looking for somebody to do club dates on weekends in New Jersey. Nancy didn't really know if he worked anywhere. All she knew was that Ellen knew Yukl and that he played the piano.

For their initial interview, Pauley came to Yukl's apartment at 120 Waverly. She brought along her eight-year-old daughter Liz. From the moment they first shook hands and looked at each other, Yukl seemed nervous. His behavior was slightly erratic, and he began to talk very fast. Pauley chose to ignore the mannerism. Yukl seemed very knowledgeable about Max Morath, a well-known ragtime pianist and a favorite of Pauley's. He talked about channel 13—New York's public television station—and how they were about to do a special on Morath.

"If we get lucky," he suggested, "maybe we could get a spot on the show." It sounded good.

Yukl talked briefly to Nancy about Liz, and they

133

discussed the possibility of his teaching her how to play the piano.

"Do you teach kids?" she asked him.

"Oh yes," he stuttered. "I have a number of children students."

It was time to get Liz home, so they agreed on a second meeting a few days later.

This time Yukl came to Pauley's apartment on the West Side. Nancy had a piano, and while Yukl was there, a neighbor of hers dropped in. Within minutes, the piano playing had stopped and the three of them were sitting in the living room talking.

Yukl's conversation was jumpy. He would dart from one subject to another, never lingering long enough on one topic to pursue it to a conversational resolution. He was chock full of loaded questions. In the middle of talking about the current nightclub scene, he suddenly blurted out, "What do you think of homosexuals?"

Nancy paused. "Well," she answered, "I'm very sympathetic to homosexuals because I don't know any little kid who ever wanted to grow up and be a homosexual. It's really a misfortune the way society treats them and everything else. . . ." She looked over to him, to try to gauge his response to her answer. He simply sat in his chair and quietly pondered the subject. Then he looked up.

"Boy, what did you think about Attica?" he asked.

For the next few minutes the trio attacked the subject of the prison riots that had occurred a year earlier in upstate New York.

"Yeah," Yukl casually submitted, "I've done undercover work for corrections."

Nancy didn't quite understand. "You did what?"

"You know," he hesitated. "The department of corrections. I did some work for them recently. That

Attica stuff was a real mess," he continued. "And I know where all the bodies are hidden. There's going to be a big exposé, and I've got all the inside dope. I'll tell you something," he confided, "I've got direct channels through to the Governor. I know a lot about the prison system. And now," he said, smiling for the first time, "I'm a student at NYU."

Nancy nodded a vague acknowledgment. In the theater, she surmised, you meet a lot of flaky people. She agreed to meet Yukl the third time at his apartment back on Waverly. Yukl left her some sheet music to study—some songs he was working on with another woman. When Yukl left, Nancy rationalized his behavior as "unique."

A few days later, he called and they made an appointment. Pauley had never won any punctuality contests. When she got off the subway, she glanced at her watch. It was after six o'clock. Once again, she was going to be late. When Pauley got to the apartment on Waverly, it was 6:15. She noticed for the first time that the name on the door didn't match the apartment number. She knew him as Yogi Freitag, but the name on the apartment bell said Yukl.

Most security-conscious N.Y. landlords require guests at their building to ring a bell to a specific apartment; then a buzzer releases the lock on the main door to the building. Pauley rang the bell a couple of times. No answer. She pushed on the main door. It had been locked the first time she had visited Yukl. But this time it just opened, as many apartment building doors capriciously do, and Pauley walked in.

It was a five-story walk-up, and she began her trek to the top. When she got to the apartment, she noticed a note on the door. It was almost illegible. She had to read it three times before she could decipher it: "Gone to get some milk," had been scrawled across the top. "Be right back 15 minutes. Make yourself comfortable." There was a postscript. "The dog is a pussycat. Not to worry."

She took the note off the door, turned the knob, entered the small living room. She walked through a small hallway, and noticed Yukl's passive Great Dane resting on the floor. The bathroom and the kitchen were close to each other, a peculiarity Pauley noticed before she sat down on a chair in the living room.

She opened a large, fat bag she had brought with her. It was stuffed with sheet music, her makeup kit, phone book, checkbook, and assorted necessities. She looked at the sheet music Yukl had given her. Once again, in her rush, she hadn't fully prepared for their session. For a minute or two she studied the pages.

Uncomfortable sitting in this strange apartment alone, Nancy began to study the room. There was a mantelpiece in the center, with bookcases on either side. There were two windows that looked out onto Waverly. There was a large contour couch along a side wall and a little dressing alcove. The dog stayed right there at the front door. The one thing Pauley couldn't help noticing, something that seemed strangely out of place, was the large clock sitting on the coffee table.

But it wasn't the clock that caught her attention. It was the *time*. She had been due at six. The clock on the table said it was only 5:40. Then she looked up on the mantel and noticed a second large clock. It also said twenty minutes to six.

She couldn't figure it out. How could two clocks have the exact same wrong time? Pauley shrugged at this consistent inconsistency and got up from the chair. She went over to the window and looked out over Waverly. Maybe she could spot Yukl walking back home.

Suddenly she heard something move behind her.

She turned around and inhaled quickly at the sight. Yukl was naked, running out of the bathroom, racing across the floor toward his bedroom.

He was only two to three feet away when he stopped suddenly and looked at Nancy. He tried to act surprised. But he simply stood there, dripping wet, and stared at her. Nancy was taken aback, but her reaction was surprisingly calm. "Oh," she said, "you're here."

Yukl just stared at her. Then, he stammered, "You're not supposed to be here. I thought you weren't coming till six."

"No," Nancy hesitated. "I . . . I think your clocks are wrong."

Yukl kept staring. He remained standing. "Oh . . . I ha-ha-had thought I had the t-t-time to t-t-take a shower before you g-g-got here."

"Well, I thought you were at the store because of the note on the door," she said.

"Oh, did I leave the note there? I put that there earlier for a student who was coming for a lesson earlier in the day. It was much earlier. I guess I forgot to take it off."

But at that instant Nancy knew that she had somehow been set up, that this bizarre display was deliberate. She had always thought of Yukl as innocuous. Strangely, as he stood naked before her, he gave her a look that broadcast a sudden, unstoppable strength. She immediately thought that if she were indeed an actress, now was the time to perform.

Yukl didn't say anything. He simply made a gesture toward his penis, a sort of visual acknowledgement to his nudity.

Pauley saw the move.

"Oh listen," Nancy giggled nervously as she sought to control the situation. "I'm a big girl. I've been in

show business and I've shared a lot of dressing rooms
with a lot of guys."

Yukl just stood there. Motionless.

"Look," Pauley continued. "Why don't you go throw
a robe on? By the way," she added, "I'm sorry. I
don't have all my lyrics done. I know I was late . . ."

Nancy knew she was in trouble. She had always
prided herself on her intuition. What she felt was not
that Yukl had intended to rape her. She felt he had
come out of that bathroom to *kill* her. It was the look
on his face that told her she had become an unfortunate participant in a psychotic episode.

The key to her survival, she thought, was to go
along with his craziness and not to react in a shocked
or scared way. That was what he seemed to want.

A number of thoughts raced through her mind. Foremost was her failure to tell anyone of her singing
appointment. Nobody knew she was with Yukl. Nobody was going to miss her for days. Should she fight
him? Pauley feared if she struggled with him and
screamed and fought, nobody would hear her, even if
she broke all the windows. It's amazing how much
information one can process in an instant of fear,
especially when, as in Nancy's case, there is no mistak-
ing what was going on.

Yukl went into his bedroom and put on a knit shirt
and some slacks. He was watching her all the time. If
she tried to run for the door, he would easily get there
first.

Pauley sat down on the couch. He came back out,
walked around the coffee table, and sat down next to
her. Nancy's big music bag was between them.

"Look," he began. "I'm up, I'm really up. I've
taken a number of pills, okay?"

Pauley nodded. All she was thinking about was how
to get out of there.

Yukl continued to talk quickly. He tried to steer the conversation towards death. "Isn't it amazing," he said to her, "that you can live a life and end it just like that?"

Nancy nodded cautiously. She kept thinking about the time she had talked to Ellen Pahl after meeting Yukl. "There's something about him," she had told Ellen. "Yeah, Nancy," Pahl said. "There's something in his background. Something to do with the death of a girl. No one really knows."

Yukl now started to tell Nancy about a detective that had come to see him "because some woman had complained about him." Pauley acted very curious and asked him why.

He told her that at NYU they were doing a sexual study through his job. "It was part of this thing," he explained, "for me to send out these letters—you know questionnaires. Nancy, you know how people are—there are a lot of prudes around."

"Yes, I know," she said.

He tried to ask her some of the questions.

"Let's get back to the music, Yogi."

"But I did the questionnaires because I knew the questions to ask," he said, not listening. "I've been drawing on all my knowledge and expertise. Want a drink?" he suddenly asked.

"No thanks."

Yukl jumped up from the couch and went over and poured himself two water glass tumblers full of scotch and drank them both in quick succession. Then he came back to the couch and sat down. His talking seemed to accelerate now. "Tell me," he said excitedly, "what did you think when you saw me come out of the bathroom nude?"

"Yogi," she said tactfully, "you are a very attractive person. But I think I mentioned to you that this guy

I'm seeing is getting kind of serious and I wouldn't want to do anything to jeopardize that." She thought quickly. This was her chance to protect herself. She wasn't a good liar, but she was a better actress. "Besides," she said, "he's coming up to meet me in a little while to take me to dinner."

Yukl seemed to accept that. For the next fifteen minutes, he rambled on about a variety of unconnected subjects. He was still sitting there on the couch, effectively pinning Pauley against the wall, with only her bag between them.

Finally, near eight o'clock, Nancy made a point of glancing at her watch. "Yogi"—she smiled—"we've got to do some work, right?"

She got him up to the piano. There was a phonograph between the two living-room windows, and she turned it on. For the next ten minutes, the would-be killer and his would-be victim played the records and sang along.

The effect of the pills was beginning to wear off. Yukl was coming down. By the time he finished playing the third song, he was down. The mad look on his face had somehow evaporated. He suddenly looked exhausted.

"I'm really kind of sorry." He sighed.

Nancy got up.

"Are you kidding me?" She laughed, just beginning to tremble with relief. "Don't think anything about it." Then, without realizing it, she started to ramble nervously.

"What do you think I should do with my hair?" she heard herself ask, as she picked up her bag and headed for the door. Yukl never answered. He just sat on the piano bench.

Nancy looked back. He was still sitting there. She

reached the front door. This time she didn't look back. She opened it and left the apartment.

She started to shake before she reached the street. As soon as she got outside the building, she started walking. Faster and faster. She walked for miles. At about eleven P.M. she looked at a street sign. She was way uptown on the West Side, somewhere in the mid-eighties. She hailed a cab and went home to Washington Heights.

It took her two days before she could even allude to what had happened. She went to see a friend of hers—a local political district leader. She told the man about what did—and did not—happen. He just shook his head. He wrote down Freitag's name, but said that there was little he could do. He told Nancy that he used to work for a judge, that he would give the name to the judge and see what he could do.

"I got these really bad vibes from this guy," she told him.

"Yes," he said, "but you can't bust a guy on vibes."

After all, he cautioned her, the police could do nothing. There had been no overt criminal act.

She left the meeting still determined to do something about Freitag. But within a few days, the incident had been all but forgotten by Pauley. She wrote it off as just another New York experience, a lesson to be learned. She had been lucky, and the best medicine, she decided, would be not to think of it ever again.

CHAPTER TWELVE

Soon afterwards, Yukl decided to do more than just hand out questionnaires and wait for the mail. He wanted more women like Nancy Pauley to come to his house. A few days after the incident with Nancy, Yukl sat down at the typewriter and pounded out eight lines of copy. During his lunch hour, he went down to the offices of *Show Business*, a weekly New York theatrical newspaper, and gave them an ad.

The ad was printed in the next week's issue. It appeared on page 15 of the magazine's July 4, 1974, issue, at the top of the "Casting News" section and directly above a legitimate ad from the William Morris Agency. The Morris advertisement sought comedians, and encouraged unknowns to send photos and résumés. Yukl's 2-by-4-inch ad was far more enticing. It promised something tangible. A real movie was about to be made.

"NON-UNION FILM," it proclaimed. "Actresses, ages 17 to 25 are being interviewed on Fri., July 5 and Sat., July 6 and 13 for both principal and extra parts in a motion picture which will be filmed in New York in early August. They are looking for non-SAG, non-Equity, college types only."

Yukl didn't want photos or résumés. He wanted

direct, personal contact. At the end of the ad, he didn't ask for mail or phone calls. And he didn't use his real name.

"Contact Mr. Williamson at 120 Waverly Place NY Studio 4-F from 10 A.M. to 7 P.M. only."

Deborah Falcone was an avid reader of the trade magazines—the *Hollywood Reporter, Variety, Backstage,* and *Show Business.* And she always scoured the classified ads each week, hoping there might be a chance for her to audition somewhere.

Show Business comes out each Thursday, and Falcone bought a copy from the corner newsstand near her Greenwich Village apartment. She quickly spotted Yukl's ad. She was twenty-four but looked younger. She thought she fit the bill and decided she'd audition.

Falcone was new to New York, and to acting. She had gone to college at Wagner, a small liberal arts school on Staten Island. After graduation, she had moved to New Jersey, where she taught school for two years in the small town of Floren Park. But Falcone always loved the theater and soon decided to attend graduate school in New York.

On Saturday, July 6, Deborah Falcone responded to the ad. She lived on Thirteenth Street in the Village, and since it was a nice afternoon, she decided to walk to Waverly Place. When she got to the building, there was a handwritten sign on the main entrance door referring to the audition. "Just buzz the buzzer and come up to the fourth floor," it said.

Falcone did. When she reached Yukl's door, it was ajar. Inside were at least twenty people, almost all of them women. The small apartment was jammed. People were sitting on the couch, the kitchen chairs, the floor. At first, she almost thought it was a party. The

mood inside was festive, and it took her a few minutes
to realize who was the leader of the audition.

"Mr. Williamson?" Falcone presumed.

"Oh," the man answered. "Mr. Williamson isn't
here. But my name is Charlie Yukl."

Yukl was dressed casually, in khaki pants and an
Izod pullover. He told the group his wife was out,
working at her receptionist job at a nearby doctor's
office. Then he began speaking about the project. He
said he was getting his Ph.D. in Psychology at NYU,
and that he had decided a way of doing his thesis was
to do a movie about women. He then handed out
some literature about the film, two mimeographed
pages of typewritten notes. Specifically, he told the
women that his film was going to be about his patients, people with whom he had done therapy.

One by one, Yukl had the actresses stand up, tell
the group a little something about themselves. They
talked about their goals as actresses.

Then, Yukl handed out some more papers. This
time, the typewritten notes concerned improvisational
material on children. "Let's talk about our childhoods,"
he suggested. And, as each woman began to speak,
Yukl would interrupt.

"Was it a happy childhood?" he would ask.

Invariably, each answer would be yes.

"That's not true!" he would challenge.

The other actresses thought he was just being intentionally provocative, and they played along. After all,
this was an audition. But Yukl was searching for a
personal admission from each actress, a sort of confirmation that his was not the only traumatic childhood.

"Your parents didn't love you, did they?" he would
ask.

"Did you feel you got along with your father?"

"Did the other kids love you?"

The questions kept coming.

Deborah Falcone looked across the room and recognized an actress friend who had also responded to the ad.

It was Judy Carlin.

Carlin was also new to acting. A petite brunette, she was sitting with some of the other actors on the floor, listening to Yukl.

In fact, it was Carlin's first summer in New York. She'd moved to the city from Philadelphia to give acting a try. It was only her second week in Manhattan when she saw the *Show Business* ad and found herself at Waverly Place.

She had been the first to arrive that Saturday morning.

Carlin had just turned twenty-two. And her first impression was that Charles Yukl was a very nice man. Her second impression was that Yukl seemed like an established type. The apartment was crammed full of stereo equipment, camera gear—in her mind he seemed to have all the possessions of a stable man. He had offered her something to drink, and then told her that the film would be a series of improvisational skits, that there would be five principal characters and the rest would be extras.

"Would you be willing to do some nudity?" he asked her.

"No," she quickly said. Yukl didn't pursue the subject. Other hopefuls were arriving at the apartment.

One of the new arrivals was a young woman named Karin Schlegel. Some of the girls recognized her from school.

Of all the people in the room, Schlegel was clearly the most shy, the most nervous, the most withdrawn.

When it came time for her to speak, however, she managed quite well. She had been told in acting school that to be a successful actor, you had to remove your-self from your own personality. This was her first audition, and whether or not she got the part, she had been able to stand up, speak clearly, and come out of her shell.

Carlin and Falcone were both impressed that Yukl was talking about a film that paid money instead of screen credit. He was quoting figures of $200-a-day for each actress. For a nonunion film, that was a lot of money.

One of the women asked, "Where is the money coming from?"

Yukl confidently responded that he had received a grant from the Department of Health, Education and Welfare. "They're subsidizing this particular study in conjunction with my thesis and a film."

Everyone, including Falcone, accepted his statement. There seemed no reason to doubt him. For one thing, Yukl seemed very bright, he spoke well, and came across with a certain sophistication. Another reason no one appeared to have second thoughts was that, after all, almost everyone in the apartment that day was young—between seventeen and twenty-five—and they were, with few exceptions, new to New York and acting. It all seemed legitimate.

Falcone stayed there with the group almost three hours. When she left, she gave Yukl her picture and resume. The next day, Falcone's roommate received a call. It was Yukl. "Tell Deborah," he told her, "that I've decided to use her in my movie. She's got the part."

Then he called Judy Carlin and told her the same thing.

Finally, he placed a call to Karin Schlegel. "You've got a part in the movie," he said.

Schlegel was so excited she took a deep breath

before saying a very subdued "thank you." It would be her first real acting job. She couldn't wait to tell her friends, and her acting teacher, Ed Kovens.

Kovens was one of the better known teachers at the Lee Strasberg Theatrical Institute, a small private acting school on Thirteenth Street. Like many of the other members of the staff, he was an actor, and taught at the Institute to supplement his income. Kovens had been teaching for five years when Karin registered for one of his classes. She was not an outstanding student, and Kovens often worried that she would never get anywhere beyond her class. He regarded Schlegel as one of those young, nonaggressive, nonassertive women who was living a life of obscurity, who had survived by embracing a belief that the key to coping lay in not being visible.

And yet this woman was in an acting class. It always intrigued Kovens that Schlegel had suddenly decided to take a chance, and was using his acting class as the acid test.

Still, he didn't think she would make it.

But when he walked into the classroom to teach his first July session, a smiling Karin jumped up from one of the tacky orange plastic chairs in the room and walked over to him. "Guess what?" she said, beaming. "I got a job . . . I'm going to be in a movie!"

CHAPTER THIRTEEN

Karin Schlegel was born in New York City, at Presbyterian Hospital, the first child of Alfred and Irene, in 1949. She was an Rh baby, almost died just after birth, and had jaundice and a poor blood supply. Despite her small size and weak condition, however, she survived.

Survival was an integral part of the Schlegel family history. Both Alfred and Irene had managed to escape Hitler's Germany at the right time, emigrating from Hamburg with renewed hope and the plan to start their life over—and to have their own family. They rented a small "starter" apartment on the East Side of Manhattan, at Eighty-first Street in Yorkville. But living in Manhattan, even in the postwar years, was too expensive.

With some money the Schlegels had managed to save, they put a down payment on a small plot of land across the Hudson River in Cresskill, New Jersey. And there they started to build their American dream house.

The house was finished in 1951, when Karin was almost two years old. They waited to christen Karin at Lutheran Emmanuel Church on Eighty-seventh Street, then moved across the river to begin their new suburban life.

Cresskill was a new development. Most of the roads were in place; most of the houses and the people were yet to arrive. It was, in a very real sense, a brave new world of opportunity for Alfred, Irene and Karin. After spending money for the house, the Schlegels didn't have much left over to pay for the rest of the American dream. They lived a quiet, spartan life in the small New Jersey community. Alfred would travel over the George Washington Bridge every morning to commute to work at his job in the city. Irene would stay home with Karin. In 1952 a second child, Denise, was born.

Karin was an extremely quiet child, who delighted in nature. She was always seen near the house, carrying a bunch of flowers, which she would often bring to the small Bryant School in Cresskill.

The Schlegels were a strong churchgoing family, with little extra cash to spend on frivolous diversions. Alfred and Irene accounted for every penny in their struggle to live the American dream. But every so often, the family would save enough to enjoy a small vacation. Karin's first view of the Atlantic Ocean came when she was three, when the Schlegels rented a small place in Beach Haven, New Jersey.

A few years later the family traveled again. Irene's father treated them to a trip home—to Germany—in 1958. The family stayed in Hamburg for three months, and in that time both Karin and Denise learned to speak German.

Karin and Denise were two very different children. Karin was a quiet, shy youngster and Denise was a more difficult younger sister—a loud, rambunctious misbehaver who sought all of her parents' time and attention.

Most of the time, Denise got that attention. The

more demanding Denise became, the more removed Karin seemed. "Karin is one of those children who just doesn't make waves," one of her teachers told Irene. It was considered a sign of character and strength and to a noticeable degree, it was.

In junior high school, each child retained her distinct character. Denise had discipline problems. Karin got good grades. Denise would talk back to her teachers. Karin quietly answered when called upon. Karin had an absolutely miserable time in high school. She had no friends, spent time with no one outside of class. On Friday and Saturday nights she never had a date.

Irene was the first to notice that Karin seemed more at home with her relatives in Europe than with her peers in the U.S. Karin always wanted to go back there. When she was sixteen, she took the summer off and stayed three months in Germany.

Karin's senior year in high school was spent sitting in class, or sitting in her room at home on Heatherhill Road with Shu Shu, the small family dog, counting the long and often painful minutes until her graduation.

Karin was not the kind of teenager to stand out in a crowd of her peers. She was a plain, shy student, who gave the appearance of being more frail than she actually was. Karin was a quiet thinker. Like her classmates, she often wondered about her future, but always seemed to maintain a grasp on what was really possible for her.

It was only when she confronted the old-world German ways of her parents that she began to lose perspective. Before she had even gone to high school, Karin had told her parents that she wanted to be a dancer, and before long the drive to be a ballerina had become an obsession. Karin enrolled in a local dancing school, but in class, her energy would dissipate quickly, and she had trouble on the bar. She refused to be talked out of it. "You have weak bones, Karin," her mother would tell her. "You can't even go on the toe. It's taking away time that you can better spend with your friends." Irene's argument was futile. The more her mother tried to discourage her, the more Karin went to class.

Her sister Denise was an excellent piano player, and she was getting more than her share of attention. Karin wanted something to excel at too. But it would not be ballet. After a few weeks, the dance teacher had a talk with Karin, who was finally willing to admit defeat.

Her departure from the dance world only focused Karin's determination in a different direction: she announced to her parents that she was interested in becoming an actress.

Ballet was tolerable in the Schlegel home. It was a respectable profession with a proud artistic tradition. But when Karin mentioned the acting world, a big family fight erupted. In Alfred's view there was nothing ennobling about acting, and he doubted that it even was a profession. "Why not go to a college that has a theater program?" Irene suggested.

Karin didn't want to go to college. She wanted to go to the Lee Strasberg Institute, the private acting school in New York.

"No, you will not go," Irene said, firmly standing her ground. "You will go to college."

It was probably their most emotionally exhausting family fight, and finally Irene and Alfred prevailed. Reluctantly, Karin registered at Concordia College in Bronxville, New York, a small two-year college.

For Karin, it was a blessing in disguise, a surprise confirmation that there was, indeed, life after high school. For the first time in her life she was on her

own, away from immediate family pressures. And for
the first time in her life, Karin began to blossom.

Irene and Alfred felt the normal sense of parental
loss when Karin left home to go to school. After all,
their old world values did not include a girl's living on
her own before marriage and family. The three would
often fight when Karin came home on occasional visits
from college. Irene seemed more tolerant of her daughter's new life, but Karin confided in her less and less,
especially about her social life.

For Karin, life alone was a brave new world. One
which she openly embraced. To her own surprise, she
began to have a good time. She had friends. She had
dates. And she even had a few boyfriends.

Karin's newfound happiness and her independent
attitude were as much a surprise to her parents as to
Karin herself. The rebelliousness most children display
in high school had been delayed with Karin. Alfred
and Irene were treated to an extra dose of it with
Karin in college.

It was a difficult adjustment for them to make. Part
of Karin's behavior could easily be attributed to her
earlier home environment—a bastion of conservative
European values smack in the heart of suburban New
Jersey. Karin had done in childhood what her parents
had expected of her. But now she was beginning to
change. Her grades were not up to her usual excellent
standard. She sometimes cut her classes, or was late.
She went out drinking with her friends, and she had
occasional flirtations with marijuana. Karin Schlegel
was having a good time.

Two years later, when she graduated, Karin had had
enough with higher education. Irene suggested some
postgraduate work, but Karin would not even discuss
the matter.

"Okay," Irene countered, with the traditional parental negotiating tool. "Then you'll need a job to support yourself."

Karin eagerly agreed. She got a job, almost immediately, with a public relations firm. But it didn't last long. "I don't like these people," she told one of her friends. "They are all phonies."

Someone told her of an opening at McGraw-Hill in Manhattan. She interviewed, and got a job as an editorial assistant for an architectural trade magazine. She liked the work.

The job at McGraw-Hill didn't pay well. But the salary was sufficient for Karin to save some money. She was still living at home and commuted from New Jersey every morning.

While at McGraw-Hill, she met a woman named Charlotte Schwartz. Charlotte was older than Karin, she had a child from a previous marriage, and quickly took Schlegel under her wing. They would often spend time together after work, before it was time for Karin to catch the late bus back to New Jersey. Charlotte encouraged Karin to break free of the parental reins. Every so often, she would arrange a blind date for Karin, then talk her into having enough courage to go through with it.

She was having a positive effect on Karin, who now had a confidante and a friend. Slowly, Karin became willing to take some risks, explore some new ground. On some nights, she didn't come home to Cresskill. She had started to date a doctor. Her parents worried, of course, but Irene secretly approved. Soon, she had saved enough money to move across the river. But Manhattan rents were too high for her to live by herself in Manhattan. So she moved in with Charlotte, who had a small place in Flushing, Queens.

From the moment she got to New York, Karin began to talk about acting again. Her visits to New

Jersey were reduced to every-other-weekend excursions to see her family.

Karin wouldn't talk much about her social life with her mother. The subject was never even discussed with Alfred. But what was discussed—heatedly—was her continued desire for acting. This passion made absolutely no sense to her parents.

"Stick with the magazine," Alfred argued. "Something good will come of it."

Karin was more determined than ever to go to acting school, to become an actress in New York. Her parents tried, but she couldn't be talked out of it. In early 1974, Karin quit McGraw-Hill.

"Why?" Irene still asked, even though Karin had already submitted her resignation. "Why did you give up such a good career?"

"Because it's getting in the way," Karin said.

"Of what?" But Irene knew.

"It's getting in the way of my acting."

Within two weeks, Karin had landed an actor's job—waitressing days at the Savarin Coffee Shop in Pennsylvania Station. At night she was a student at the Strasberg Institute. Each winter morning, she would leave Charlotte's Flushing apartment and walk the six windy blocks to the subway. The ritual was the same every day. Precisely at seven A.M., Karin left, headed for the regular coffee crowd of angry and confused commuters at Savarin. She wore her coat, her boots, her pullover hat, and she carried a fabric shopping bag chock full of the things she needed for class—small props to use that night during acting improvisations.

"She never takes the bus?" Charlotte's sister would ask.

"No, that's Karin. She's determined to do certain things on her own. I won't walk in this weather. But Karin will."

Charlotte knew her wispy friend. Karin would, and often did, walk in the most inclement weather, her featherweight body leaning forward against the wind as she headed for the subway station.

Payday for Karin was Thursday. She called home on one of those Thursdays and told Irene that she was going to take Friday off "and do something for myself. It will be a shopping day," she announced proudly. She would often tell her mother things like that.

On Friday morning, the phone rang at the Schlegel home in Cresskill. On the other end was a woman in Harlem.

"Do you know a Karin Schlegel?" she asked cautiously.

"Yes . . . yes, I do," Irene replied nervously, thinking the worst. "She is my daughter."

"Well, I just found this pocketbook on the cement at a high school playground up here. All that was in there were some identification cards of your daughter's," she told her.

"Oh my God," Irene sighed. The woman told her that she would leave the pocketbook at an uptown store to be picked up. Irene thanked her, hung up, and immediately called Charlotte Schwartz. "What happened to Karin, Charlotte?" she asked, on the verge of tears. "Is she okay?"

"She's fine, Irene. She's at work."

"But I just got this call. They found her pocketbook."

"Oh," Charlotte said in a subdued tone. "I know."

"You know what?" Irene demanded, raising her voice.

"I'm sorry, Mrs. Schlegel," Charlotte said, "but Karin told me not to tell you."

She then told Irene what had happened. Karin had been on her way home from work the night before, riding on a nearly empty subway car on the way to

Queens when two young toughs jumped her and got
her purse.

"They didn't hurt her," Charlotte assured Irene.
"They just wanted the money. I talked to her. She's
fine," she said, although she wasn't so sure about her
friend. She then promised that Karin would call her
mother as soon as she got home.

Charlotte called Karin at the coffee shop and told
her about the pocketbook. "Great," Karin said. "I'll
go up there and get it."

Schlegel's resilience often surprised Charlotte. On
the surface she seemed so frail, so vulnerable. But she
always recovered from bad news well, and surprisingly
fast.

Karin had the ability to shrug off rejection, something Charlotte had yet to master. Karin and Charlotte
used to talk about their emotional wounds and their
futures. When the subject turned to acting, Schlegel
would always defend her decision to pursue the
profession.

"It's my own decision," she'd tell Charlotte. "I'm
self-supporting. I've saved my own money, and I'm
responsible for my own conduct. I'm also very realistic
about my chances," she'd tell her girlfriend. "No matter what happens, I'm going to remain realistic. I'm
never going to forget the price of tomatoes."

Then the subject would change—to men. Charlotte
saw herself as Karin's big sister, not to mention match-
maker. She was always suggesting men she knew as
possible dates or pointing out the regular menagerie of
eligibles at the Lion's Head, a local Village bar popular with the Village literary crowd. Most of the time,
Karin didn't seem to appreciate her friend's advice.

Karin's defensiveness was not directed at her friend.
It was more like a dress rehearsal for later perfor-
mances in Cresskill. Her trips to New Jersey almost

always disintegrated into heated family fights. But they also had the effect of convincing Karin that she could, and must, make it on her own.

The coffee shop, the acting classes, and a little bit of spending money were helping Karin get stronger, feel more independent. She was gaining confidence in herself as a woman and, slowly, as an actress.

As soon as she had saved enough money, Karin started scouring the want ads, talking to friends in acting class and at the coffee shop—she was looking for her own apartment in the city. Manhattan rents were astronomical, but Schlegel was convinced she could find a little something she could afford.

She was right. The actors' grapevine worked one day in early 1974. Karin heard of a place in the Village. The rent was reasonable. And, the place certainly was little. It was in a five-story walk-up building on Minetta Lane in the Village. It wasn't a pretty street, but it had character. The building was a turn-of-the-century, how-did-this-escape-condemnation masterpiece, featuring a huge, red wooden door. Karin moved in to an apartment on the second floor.

Everything in the place was contained within one small room—bedroom, living room, a tiny cooking area, tiny bathroom, and a partial closet. The bed in the living room was covered up and made to look like a sofa. There was a small, wood-burning fireplace.

"It's something right out of O'Henry," joked one of her friends upon first seeing it.

"Yeah," Karin acknowledged with a smile, "but it's home."

The first person Karin invited over to dinner was Charlotte Schwartz.

They had had a brief argument a few weeks earlier when Karin was leaving Queens. Charlotte had disapproved of one of the men Karin was dating. Charlotte didn't think he was treating Karin with the proper respect. Karin did everything for him, and Charlotte thought he was doing nothing for her in return.

In fact, it had been the fight about Karin's taste in men that had precipitated Schlegel's looking for her own apartment.

The dinner offer was Karin's attempt to say she was sorry. Schwartz's eager acceptance was her confirmation that the feeling was mutual.

When they were both living together in Queens, they were often entertained by a male friend of Charlotte's whom she affectionately called her "gourmet gay." His favorite dish—which he loved to make for the girls—was chicken cooked with rosemary and mushrooms.

On this cold, winter night in early 1974, Karin duplicated his recipe perfectly. For dessert, she offered her friend a selection of Stella d'Oro Italian cookies to which she had added a generous portion of butter and honey.

Karin then poured another round of white wine, and the pair lifted their glasses.

"A toast." Karin giggled.

"Okay," Charlotte quickly agreed. "What shall we toast?" she asked.

"A toast to my new apartment?"

"No," Charlotte quickly countered. "A toast to the future, to you getting an acting job that pays and . . ."

Charlotte stopped briefly, and smiled mischievously at her friend. "A toast to the rest of 1974," she proclaimed. "This will be the year you meet Mr. Right."

CHAPTER FOURTEEN

Enken Yukl was despondent. In early February, Bessie, the Great Dane, died. Charlie knew just what to do.

He took the bus over to Collier Kennels in New Jersey and bought a 16 month-old Great Dane for $300. It was reddish brown in color, and he took it home to his wife. They named it Sir Reginald.

The dog was young and a little hyperactive. Charlie hired an obedience trainer to come to the apartment and work with the animal, but the trainer wasn't successful. The dog, Yukl was told, was very friendly, but had a tendency to become too nervous.

"So you see," he related to Player at their next session, "with the exception of the dog, things are calm, they're stable, and I'm really working things out."

A month later, Yukl added another alley cat to his family; he called it Pinky. And when Bill Player's Siamese cat had kittens, he gave one—called Kim—to Yukl.

What Yukl hadn't told Player was that he was, in fact, having more of the "bad" dreams almost every night.

In the daytime, he had been approaching women

again on the streets, claiming to be an advertising photographer.

Since January, he had been typing phony letters at Greeley and Hansen from various advertising agencies, then using the office xerox machine to make dozens of copies, which he collated into small packets of fraudulent letters. He would give these packets to the women as proof of his claims. One, which Yukl claimed he mailed to John Filor, of Filor-Forde Artists on East Fifty-fifth Street, concerned a supposed Jantzen sportswear print ad to be shot in Jamaica.

"Should you receive any inquiries from your models concerning the above," Yukl instructed, "kindly advise them as follows:"

Since the client is not a local one, and because a job such as the one contemplated requires considerable financial responsibility, cost, planning, etc., I have requested a 50% deposit from the client prior to making any definite commitment to any agency. I have also requested a purchase order clarifying such things as living expenses, travel, etc. After selecting the models I felt would be suited for this job, the appropriate head sheets, comps, etc., were left with the client for their consideration. Taking everything into consideration I felt, and still feel, this is the soundest way of handling the matter.

As soon as I receive the necessary authorization and the above is complied with I will, of course, get back to you and make the proper arrangements. The client has assured me that they will advise me at least four weeks prior to the scheduled date of departure of their decision regarding the above so we all should have adequate time to plan accordingly.

Your courtesy and assistance was, and is, appreciated.

Very truly yours,
Charles Yukl Jr.

Other letters were addressed to Sears, Roebuck and, a few days later, to Grey Advertising.

Letters like these were, in fact, never mailed, but Yukl would keep them on hand for anyone who had answered the *Show Business* ad.

By June, he had "hired" a half-dozen young women to do one print ad or another, but nothing ever materialized. The ad brought the women to the apartment, and he skillfully used the letters to keep the women on hold while he waited for nonexistent approvals or funding for one of his fantasy projects.

In fact, Yukl developed his own bizarre mailing list of women to whom he would send the xerox copies of his letters to officials, and even xeroxes of their "responses" to him. On paper his control of bureaucratic language was effective, and bought him extra credibility and time.

One of those on the mailing list was Karin Schlegel, who was still waiting patiently for the promised Yukl movie to happen. She had only recently met him, but already she had a small collection of Yukl's letters, which she kept in a manila folder, hoping to get the one that said that the project was actually a "go."

In the meantime, she continued working hard at her acting. Together with Nancy Weems, another student, she rehearsed twice, and sometimes three times a week, on selected scenes from famous plays.

Under Ed Kovens' direction, a student was taken seriously if he worked beyond the regular assignments and developed his own material to perform in class. In fact, it was hard to stay in the class if you weren't willing to work on two of your own scenes a month. Students were required to perform their work. Once each week, one of the students would get up from the orange plastic chairs on Thirteenth Street and do a scene.

Karin had worked with Weems on one scene from *The Children's Hour*, on a segment of *Bird Bath*, and on some scenes from unpublished plays. They worked well together. They would alternate between Weems's house on West Forty-third Street and Schlegel's apartment on Minetta Lane. Karin talked often of her continuing group "rehearsal" sessions with Yukl and of how she, along with the other women, were waiting for the green light on one of his projects.

Weems was curious about Yukl. "What exactly do you do there?" she asked.

"Well, we do lots of things," Karin would say. "Lots of improvisational stuff—nonverbal communication, some role identification, you know, things like that."

Karin handed Nancy a sheaf of mimeographed pages from her Yukl file. "What do you think?" she asked.

Weems studied the papers and looked closely at Yukl's name and signature at the bottom of one of the letters.

"How do you pronounce that?"

"Yookle," Karin said.

"Strange name."

"Yeah," Karin agreed. "His parents are foreign, I think. But tell me, Nancy, what do you think? The guy hired me and some other people to do this educational film. Everyone else thinks it's okay. We're even getting some money for it."

"Well, it *is* something to put on your résumé, something to get started with. And you've got a part, right?"

Karin nodded.

"Then do it," Weems advised.

"Thanks. Now I want to ask you something else, Nancy," Schlegel continued.

Karin then told Weems of a decision she had just made two days before. "I went up to Cornell Medical Center and met with one of the doctors there. They're going to reconstruct my chin."

Nancy looked at her friend. She had very pretty skin and big eyes. But she did have a weak chin and Weems knew it could be a modeling problem. "You got a good doctor?" she asked.

"Oh yes," Karin quickly answered. "He's very good So what do you think?"

"Couldn't hurt." Weems smiled reassuringly. "In this business, every little bit helps."

That's one reason Karin stayed with the Yukl group.

There were eight regulars—all women—who would meet at Yukl's place once, and sometimes twice a week. And they were, like Karin, all waiting to have their chance. They believed. Charlie kept talking about making a film for the government—a film on human emotions—for the Department of Health, Education and Welfare.

In mid-July, the pace of Yukl's letter writing increased. He sent the girls copies of one he wrote to a fictitious government official:

Charles Wm. Yukl Jr.
120 Waverly Place
New York, N.Y. 10011
July 18, 1974

New York State Dept. of Labor
Research & Statistics
2 World Trade Center
New York, N.Y.

To Whom It May Concern:

Would you send the writer any statistical information you might have concerning:

1. The percentage of married women competing in the labor market (women without children)
2. The *percentage of married women, with children under the age of 5, competing in the labor market*
3. The percentage of married women, with children 6–12, competing in the labor market
4. Any available information concerning the *attitudes of women with children towards their employment*
6. Any available information concerning employment practices as applicable to married women

If at all possible I would appreciate the most recent information available and, if there is any charge for this service, kindly advise and same will be forwarded.

Many thanks,
Charles Yukl Jr.

CWY:ej
cc: Prof. M. Silver
    Christine
    file

Then, after waiting a few days, he typed up a fictitious response to another letter on a different, elite-type typewriter:

July 23, 1974
Mr. Charles W. Yukl, Jr.
120 Waverly Place
New York, NY 10011

Dear Mr. Yukl:

We are in receipt of your letter of July 17, 1974.

Please be advised that the project you referred to is no longer an in-film project being considered by this agency. I suggest you contact HEW direct and enquire as to whether the funding for the in-film project has been redirected to the federal level.

I am certain they will be able to direct you further.

> Very Truly yours,
> G. Blumenthal
> chief
> In-film programs
> The State Education Dept.
> Albany, NY.

At the bottom of the letter, Yukl typed a note to the women:

Received the above letter from N.Y. State which is frustrating and discouraging. I can't get a straight answer or commitment from any one department and am somewhat confused. At any rate, am writing HEW as well as trying Dennis's suggestion of obtaining private funding and going to Videotape. I would like to use all of you in this project since it is very important to me and I want it done well, but, at the same time I most certainly don't want to hang anyone up if something else comes along which is immediate and guaranteed. I do intend to keep on this thing since I've put a hellava lot into it and I can only say that when this comes through I'll be the first to call you all. In the mean time look out for your own interests and don't give up anything important. I don't know how long this is going to take. I'll be home on *Saturday*, *August 10th* if any-

one wants to stop by with some constructive ideas.
Maybe I'll hear from HEW by then . . . I hope.

Chuck

When each of the girls got her copy of Blumenthal's
letter, not one thought it odd that the non-existent
Blumenthal saw fit to draw one of those insidious
"have a nice day" smiling faces beneath his signature.

The letter did not contain the most uplifting news,
but it was written with a purpose. Charlie wanted to
show the girls he was determined to overcome government red tape and systematic lethargy.

He decided to wait two weeks before writing the
third letter.

In the meantime, Yukl needed a real letter written
on his behalf. Based on the progress he had noticed in
Yukl's attitude, Benjamin Lichtenstein asked Charlie
if Player could write him a letter confirming Yukl's
therapeutic progress. Yukl asked Player, and he agreed
to write Lichtenstein. Player agreed to supply the letter. Player remained optimistic about Yukl. He saw
his capacity "to relate with human qualities" as growing. And so he wrote to Lichtenstein that he felt
Charlie was benefiting from the therapeutic experience in a very successful manner.

At their next meeting, Lichtenstein gave Yukl the
good news about his reporting schedule. Charlie bowed,
as usual, and thanked him. He was not due back for
another month.

That night, Yukl had another one of his "rehearsals." Judith Carlin was still one of the members of the
group, and she had been working hard at the sessions,
hoping that Yukl would want her to be in his film
when the funding came through. Yukl liked her. He
wanted to do everything for her. She was a young,
attractive brunette who was actually shorter than he

was. He liked that. He wanted her to know that he cared for her. After each rehearsal, he would always send her home in a cab to the Chelsea Hotel, where she was living. "You don't have to do this, Charlie," she would mildly protest.

"You've got to be safe in this city," he would caution her, "and that neighborhood isn't the safest."

One night Carlin casually mentioned that she really liked Diet Pepsi. The next week, Charlie's entire refrigerator was full of little Diet Pepsi bottles.

Another woman in the group, Lynn Plakoff, had grown suspicious of Yukl. The letters looked legitimate, but nothing seemed to be happening, she told Carlin.

"I talked to my mother," she said to Judy. "She's into psychology and she's got questions about this guy."

Carlin had a great idea. "Hey, why don't we bring your mother to one of the sessions? She can give us an objective opinion. Plus, if we bring her to the rehearsals, she can ask the right questions and we'll find out if Charlie is for real."

The next week, they did just that. Plakoff's mother asked all sorts of questions, and Yukl seemed to have all the appropriate answers. A few of them didn't seem to make sense from an organizational point of view, and Plakoff's mother suggested some alternatives in terms of streamlining the movie's shooting schedule.

"Terrific ideas," Yukl shot back. "I think you've really added something here. If you'd like, perhaps you could assist me in the filming, if you don't mind . . ."

The woman beamed. Yukl had won her over. Now she too was participating in the non-film.

At the end of the session, Charlie approached Carlin. He was excited about his new recruit, and also eager to ask something. "I'd like to take you to dinner," he said, and mentioned the Russian Tea Room, Sardi's, the Sign of the Dove, and the Plaza Hotel. He told her he had a boat and invited her on a cruise.

Carlin wasn't attracted to him. She just wanted work, and besides, she was trying to practice the fragile and often impossible actor's art of never mixing business with pleasure. She politely declined.

At the next session, Yukl's attitude toward her had changed. He was confrontational with everyone, and especially with her. "Tonight I want to talk about the existence of God," Yukl began. He singled Carlin out. "Do you believe in Him?"

Carlin started to answer. Yukl cut her off.

"Okay, define it. What do you mean by it." His questioning of her was almost relentless.

When Carlin told him that she believed in the existence of a God but was not religious, Yukl shot back, "How can you just say that?" Then Yukl jumped to one of his favorite subjects. "Do you believe you have a soul?" he asked her. "Yes? Then do you believe the soul is real, material? Do you think it is tangible? Can you reach out and touch it? Tell me."

Carlin couldn't.

"You know why?" he asked, in a rage. "Because it all goes back to your childhood. Something traumatic must have happened."

Judy shook her head. "No, that's not true."

"Then it's because you don't remember," Yukl exclaimed.

Carlin stood her ground. "No, Charlie, I DO remember. I come from a vey middle-class background and really nothing traumatic happened to me. I'm also not very religious."

Yukl wouldn't even look at her. He quickly glanced across the room at the other women. "How many of you had unhappy childhoods?" he asked. Six of the women said they had. Only Carlin and Lynn Plakoff said they had grown up happily.

"You two are absurd," he accused. "Everyone has an unhappy childhood. You just don't want to admit it."

Yukl asked to see Carlin when the session was over.

"I don't like your work anymore," he said without any emotion. "You're going to be kicked out unless you understand what I'm trying to do."

Carlin had no idea anymore what Charlie was trying to do. Still, she managed to say, "I'm sorry I'm not performing up to your standards."

Yukl told her that he would think about her status and let her know in a day or two.

The next day, the always prompt Yukl missed a session with Dr. Player for the first time. He rescheduled for later that day, but missed the meeting again.

When the two finally did get together the following day, Player was angry with him. Charlie was extremely agitated during the session, and Player could detect a distinct personality change in his patient.

"I'm fine," Yukl protested angrily when Player asked him what had happened. Yukl didn't tell him about the letters, the group sessions, or about all the pills he was now taking—a combination of uppers and tranquilizers. He had found a doctor willing to prescribe them for "mild depression."

"You're not leveling with me, Charlie," Player claimed.

Yukl nodded. "I'm sorry I missed you yesterday," he answered. "But my schedule has become too busy. I think we can meet only every other week now," he said.

Player insisted that Yukl make room for him in his schedule, but Charlie wasn't listening. Suddenly he started explaining his most recent dream, and it was a frightening one. "A girl comes over, and I've been drinking booze, my own tie around her throat and my own genitals cut off."

"How long has this been going on?" Player asked.

Charlie hedged. "I can't remember."

This was almost the same dream Yukl had had before killing Suzanne Reynolds in 1966.

"Charlie," Player cautioned, "I want you to think about the work we have to do. I'm worried about you."

"Nothing to worry about," Yukl shot back. "We can do these sessions every other week."

"No, we can't," Player said. "To pretend to do work every other week is inadequate. I don't want the responsibility of being your therapist under those conditions. Think about it, and get back to me, okay?"

Yukl said he would. And he'd have a solid three weeks to ponder his therapy situation.

William Player was going on vacation.

The next morning, Yukl wasted no time in typing another letter, which he then promptly mailed to his women. Some of the women listed were real; others, and all of the men named, were fictitious.

Perhaps even more interesting was the reference he made in the letter to Enken:

July 30, 1974

TO: MANDY, JOANNE, KITCH, GAIL H., KAREN S., LYNN B., LYNN P., SANDY RO-SENBERG, JUDY CARLIN, DENNIS, BOBBY B., CARL, MAURY, ROBERT E., RICHARD, IRVING.
GOOD NEWS, FOR A CHANGE . . . MONEY FOR OUR PROJECT IS AVAILABLE THRU

FEDERAL ALLOCATION AND OUR PROJECT WILL BE REALIZED. I have not been officially advised in writing since approval must be received from Washington before any expenditures can be drafted; however, this is now only a matter of time. Unfortunately I cannot push a bureaucracy, they'll act on it when they get around to it. I'm not too unhappy about this for a number of reasons. First, our film will be shot locally. I'm not even suggesting a cross-cultural analysis since, if it's taking this long and this much red tape to get something going locally one can imagine the problem of leaving the country. This will enable us to work *around* you if you're involved in something else when approval comes through. In other words we can take time and really make this into something big and there is no need for you to turn down something which is completed for the February term as I mentioned, however, the time element is really not that important, just as long as it eventually gets done.

So, a very strong word of advice. While I do have a commitment that the money is available I do not have a definite commitment as to the date approval will be forthcoming. This is consistent with a highly departmentalized bureaucracy and I'm really not too concerned about it. *Please don't turn anything down*!!! There is no need to. You WILL be included in our film as soon as I get word to go ahead and you will have ample time to plan accordingly. If you're busy at the time I'll do my best to work around your schedule.

Finally, I am submitting papers, draft scripts, etc., to HEW. I would also like to submit a tape presenting a macroscopic view of the situations we propose to depict on film. I really don't need a full company for this, 4 or 5 people should do it. Therefore, if any of you are available on Saturday, August 10, around one-ish (one-ish) it would be appreciated if you could stop by. I'll have a draft script available outlining the situations and the dialogue will resemble a guided improv or psycho-drama. I felt that HEW may eventually request something like this and am trying to get the jump on them. Whether you come or not is purely up to you and if you can make it please let me know. (212)227-1229 between 10:00 and 3:00 P.M. I won't be home in the evening since I have class, however, you could leave a message with my wife (got married last Wednesday).

I'm really very happy about this, and, while the time element is still up in the air the possible reality of our project is not. I'll get back to you as soon as I have something definite regarding date, etc. Being extremely pessimistic about it I would figure around the end of the quarter.

Many thanks, Charlie Yukl

On Saturday, August 17, Charlie had heard from many of the women. He told them that the movie would start filming on the twenty-fourth. Some of the girls had called him. But he initiated two of the calls—to Judith Carlin, and Karin Schlegel.

The second call Karin received that same morning was from Charlotte Schwartz. Charlotte was in an up mood and told her friend that they had waited too long to get their summer tans. They would make up for it that day, she said. Besides, it was a hot Saturday and high time they hit the beach.

Karin was nervous about wearing her bright green

bikini, but Charlotte convinced her that it did no good to let her suit just hang in the closet.

Two hours later, Schlegel got off the train at Brighton Beach, and Charlotte was there to meet her.

Karin was smiling, eating the last of a chocolate and raspberry Dannon yogurt cup.

"I should have known." Charlotte laughed. "Your favorite flavor."

They had no sooner reached the sand when the conversation turned to Karin's plans.

"Well, I'm gonna do it," she told Charlotte.

"Do what?"

"I'm gonna have my chin done."

"You mean, plastic surgery?"

"Yep," Karin said confidently. "I've found the right doctor and it's important to me. Charlotte, you know I've got no chin. It's not helping my career."

"So." Charlotte smiled. "Tell me about this doctor. Is he cute?"

Karin giggled. "Yeah. I really like him. I'm gonna do it next week."

Charlotte asked the inevitable. "Have you told your parents yet?"

"Oh no," she said. "They just wouldn't understand."

"But Karin," Charlotte cautioned. "You aren't just 'having your chin done,' I mean, this is an operation. Like it or not, it's surgery. Your parents should know."

Karin thought about it for a moment, and then nodded. "I'm sure you're right," she said, "but it's going to be difficult. My folks aren't very good at liking my career. It took a lot to even tell them about the film I'll be doing."

Charlotte was momentarily puzzled. "What film . . . you got a film?"

"It's not a big film," Karin shrugged. "But it's a film. It's a good opportunity for me."

"What kind of a film is this?" Charlotte's question was almost rhetorical.

Karin picked right up on it. "Oh, no," she giggled. "It's not THAT kind of a movie. It's an educational film."

"What's it about?"

"Well, we're still going over the script . . . discussing it, but it's about interpersonal relationships."

"What the hell does that mean?" Charlotte shot back, concerned that her friend didn't have a firm grasp of the material.

"Oh, you know," Karin tried to explain. "It's going to be a film about how people cope with their interpersonal problems."

"Oh." Charlotte laughed sarcastically. "That really narrows it down. So what do you have to do in this film . . . I mean, what's your part?"

"Well, I'm not really sure. I do know that I've got some lines and the director tells me there may be some nudity."

That's all Charlotte needed to hear.

"Karin, I don't know anything about the movie business, but this doesn't sound kosher to me. I don't have a good feeling about this guy."

Schlegel got defensive. "How can you say that?" she argued. "You haven't even met him."

"You're right," Charlotte acknowledged. "I guess it was the nudity bit that bothered me."

"Look," Karin tried to soothe, "there's nothing to worry about. This guy is a professional. He's married. I've met his wife. I was told to go out there and start paying some dues. I'm putting my time in. I really think I'm ready to do this, and that's what I'm going to do."

No one had to convince Charlotte that Karin was determined to do the movie project, and she didn't want to precipitate another fight with Karin. She decided to change the subject. "So, you're gonna go out with Marty, huh?"

Karin nodded. "I think maybe Monday or Tuesday. He's going to call me."

Marty was a man Charlotte had met at a local bar. He was too young for her, so she set him up with Karin.

"He's real cute, although I think he's a little nuts," Charlotte cautioned. "But what the hell . . . who isn't? Besides, I know you'll both have a good time. What will you wear?"

"I think"—Karin paused to imagine her wardrobe—"I'll wear my sleeveless sundress."

"Sounds good." Charlotte was just a little nervous about Marty, although she had been the one who initiated the date. "Uh . . . be sure and wear a sweater."

"Sweater?" Karin laughed. "It's August!"

"Well," Charlotte recovered. "It sometimes gets chilly at night."

Karin looked at her watch. It was four o'clock. "I gotta head back," she said. "I'm going over to see my folks tomorrow."

"Okay," said Charlotte, a little disappointed that their time together had been all too brief. "But remember to tell them about the operation."

Karin looked at her friend knowingly and smiled. She appreciated her concern, but didn't want to commit to anything too painful. "I'll think about it."

Sunday, August 18 started out as a normal visit in Cresskill. But within minutes of entering the house, Karin knew it wouldn't be the most pleasant afternoon. Denise had been causing problems again. She was enrolled at the Manhattan School of Music, but she hadn't been doing her lessons or practicing. Irene and Alfred had just gotten a letter from the school suggesting that Denise might leave.

"We have to get Denise out of her bad mood," a friend had told them. There was a large German festival at a nearby park, and every year they picked a Miss German American. The Schlegels had entered Denise in the contest.

Karin had been in it when she was younger and had protested to her parents. Now she was protesting again. "Mom, please don't let Denise go through this. I remember what happened to me. It's so degrading. You just parade up and down, and if you don't make it, you feel like two cents. If Denise's depressed now, this will only make it worse."

It was too late. The contest was later that day. As soon as Karin arrived, Irene, Denise, and Karin went off to the Florence Shop in Bergenfield, New Jersey, to buy Denise a pretty white dress.

Denise didn't say much at the store. Irene felt awkward about buying something for just one of her daughters and insisted that Karin buy something too. But Karin couldn't find anything, and the trio returned to Cresskill to get ready for the contest.

While Denise went upstairs to change, Irene and Karin just sat on the living room couch and talked. Karin had her head in Irene's lap, and Irene was stroking her hair. "Mom, remember when we were in Germany?" Karin asked, looking up at the ceiling. "I remember the place had a very, very high ceiling. And the ceiling had lots of decorations. And each time I went to sleep I'd open my eyes and think I was a princess sleeping in her castle. Isn't that funny?"

They sat and talked for at least an hour. Karin told Irene about the educational film, but not about the surgery.

Suddenly, Denise appeared in her gown. "Look at you," Irene remarked. "How beautiful you are."

Karin got up and helped her sister with her makeup. It was time to go, and Karin had to get back to the city.

The contest was in Guttenberg, and the George Washington Bridge was on the way. They dropped Karin off.

Before she turned to go down the stairs to catch her bus, Karin looked at her sister and gave her a kiss. "I want you to win, now, okay? You can do it."

Denise smiled. Karin kissed her again, then Irene and Alfred, who was driving. Then they were all off into the Sunday bridge traffic.

An hour later, Karin was no sooner in the door on Minetta Lane when the phone rang. It was Charlie. There was great news on the project and he was taking the girls to dinner that night. She was invited.

Then Yukl called Carlin and apologized for his behavior. "You mean it was like a little psychodrama?" Carlin asked.

"Exactly," he said. "I'm glad you figured it out." He told her that she was still in the group.

"What's more important," he announced, "is that I received the funding. Last but not least," he told her, "you're going to be one of the principals, and I'm going to be taking everyone out to dinner tonight."

He asked her to join him. She accepted.

Four of the women showed up a few hours later at Trader Vic's—Judy, Lynn, a woman named Gail Hayden, and Karin Schlegel.

Yukl clearly liked the idea of hosting four women at dinner. He ordered champagne for the table and proposed a number of toasts. When the tab came—it was $190—he proudly paid it with his credit card. These were his stars, he told them, and he was their producer.

*   *   *

On Monday morning, August 19, Yukl was late for work. At nine A.M. Enken called Greeley and Hansen and told Klein that Charlie wouldn't be coming in at all that day. She claimed Yukl wasn't feeling very well.

She was right. Charlie had been having those dreams again, he had been popping pills, and he was pacing nervously around the apartment.

Enken left for work. Charlie took off his white work shirt and gray cotton tie and put them on the kitchenette table. Then he grabbed a Rheingold beer from the refrigerator and started to drink.

It was a hot morning. It was only ten o'clock, but Yukl drank heavily. At noon, he popped two tranquilizers.

The pills didn't help. He was pacing the floor. He tried calling Player, but got the answering service. Yukl had forgotten that Player was out of town. Now, it was the only time during the year that Player could get away, and reluctantly he had decided to take a trip.

Player's absence was responsible for an increased anxiety level in many of his patients, and Charlie Yukl was no exception. By one o'clock, Yukl couldn't stand the pressure. He had a six-pack, and got out his phone book. He began calling the women in his class. He desperately wanted one of them to come over. Without exception, no one was home. He popped two more pills and took a nap.

Around five, he awoke to the noise of the dog whining. He had had the dream again. Charlie was sweating, and despite his alcohol intake, he felt full of energy. He jumped up, grabbed the leash, and took Sir Reginald for a walk around Washington Square Park.

He returned home at 5:40, put the leash away, and headed back to the refrigerator. This time, he was looking for ice, not beer. He took the ice and a quart of Smirnoff vodka and poured himself a full glass. He got out the phone book again. He called Judith Carlin. No answer. He called Melanie Chartoff. She wasn't home.

He dialed Lynn Plakoff's number without success. Finally, he reached Donna Kahn. Known as "Kitch" to her friends, Donna was one of the women in Yukl's group.

"I'm shooting a print ad tonight and I need you to come over," he told her.

"Really?" she said eagerly. "What's the ad?"

Yukl told her it was for Lifebuoy soap, that he would need her to pose with a bar of soap and be partially nude.

Kahn agreed immediately. She would be at his place at eight.

Yukl got very anxious now. Enken wouldn't be home until later. She was visiting a girlfriend a few blocks away. The women were going to do their laundry together.

Charlie drank another large glass of vodka and started pacing again. He started fantasizing about having sex with Kahn, which made him even more anxious. He began to sweat, and every few minutes he would run to the bathroom and grab some kleenex to wipe off his forehead.

Suddenly the phone rang. Yukl picked it up. It was Donna. She was calling to apologize, she said. She couldn't make it that night. There had been a death in the family. Her mother had just died.

What she didn't tell Charlie was that her husband wouldn't let her go over to Yukl's apartment. They had had an argument, and her husband had won. This was New York, he told her, and you don't casually drop by on a moment's notice to have some photographs taken of you without your shirt on. He insisted that she stay home.

Yukl thanked her and hung up. He reached for the phone book. He tried Carlin and Chartoff again. No luck.

He kept going until he reached the letter S.

A few blocks away, Nancy Weems and Karin were at Schlegel's apartment, busy rehearsing a scene from *The Importance of Being Earnest.* Nancy kept looking at her watch. A new movie, starring Richard Dreyfuss, had opened, and she was anxious to see it. The next showing of *The Apprenticeship of Duddy Kravitz* would be at eight that night.

They were in the middle of rehearsal when the phone rang and interrupted their scene. Nancy went back to studying her lines as Karin picked it up.

"Hello? . . . Oh hi . . . Fine . . . Tonight? . . . Well, I don't know if I could but . . ."

Nancy looked up. Karin had cupped her palm over the mouthpiece. "It's the guy I told you about," she whispered loudly across the room. "You know . . . the guy who's doing that film."

Schlegel returned to the phone. "No, I haven't, but . . . yes, that's true. No, I don't think . . ." Another pause. Nancy Weems stopped reading her lines and tried to decipher the conversation her friend was having.

"No, no, I . . . well, I have a birthmark on my back. Well, that shouldn't be . . . well. Okay," she glanced quickly at Nancy. "All right, I'll see you."

Karin gently placed the phone back on the hook. She was smiling.

"What was that all about?" Nancy wanted to know.

"Remember the guy I told you about, the one who hired me to do that educational film? Well, that was him on the phone. He's doing a print ad for Lifebuoy soap and he wants me to pose like one of those print ads you see in women's magazines. I told him that I had this sort of birthmark on my back, but he said it didn't make any difference. He wants me to come over."

"He wants you to do this tonight?" Weems asked.

"Yeah. At nine o'clock. He said he has a deadline."

"You really want to do this?"

Yukl had offered Karin thirty-five dollars to do the shot. "I kind of need the money," Schlegel explained to Nancy. "I'm actually a little excited about this," she admitted. "And a little nervous."

"You should be in this town. Where does this guy live?"

"He lives on Waverly Place. Three blocks away."

"Have you been to his house?" Nancy started asking the routine single-girl questions.

"Yes, I have. That's where I did my auditioning after the *Show Business* ad."

"Is he married?"

"Yes."

"Have you met his wife?"

Karin was getting a little uncomfortable with Weems's interrogation. "Yes."

"Is she nice?"

"Yes."

So far, so good, Weems thought. "Okay, Karin, he seems all right, but do you get any funny vibrations at all?"

"No, I really don't."

"Yeah, but it's late. Will his wife be there?"

"Yeah, I think so."

"Well, I still don't like it," Weems cautioned. "About the only thing I can say is to tell him you have an appointment at ten. Just go in there and do it and leave."

Nancy left Schlegel's apartment at 7:40 that night for the movie. They agreed to continue their rehearsal the next afternoon at four P.M.

Karin took a shower and got dressed.

A few blocks away, Yukl continued to drink. He wasn't drunk yet—he had built up a tremendous alcohol tolerance—and he walked around his apartment, setting up his camera gear and lights.

Promptly at nine, Karin arrived at Yukl's building on Waverly. She walked up the stairs. When she got to Charlie's door, it was open. She walked in. Yukl was in the bedroom, sitting on the edge of his king-size bed. It was a small room. There was an end table, with a small clock radio and lamp. There was a photo of a black poodle on the wall facing the bed.

The bed had no headboard. The mattress was raised on top of two box frames and a metal support frame that covered part of the ugly burnt-orange shag carpet.

Sir Reginald was asleep on the living-room couch.

Karin walked into the bedroom. She was wearing a white button-down shirt and jeans.

Charlie got up and adjusted his Minolta 35 millimeter camera.

"Hi Charlie," Karin said.

"Hi" was his answer.

"What do you want me to do?" she asked.

"Go ahead," he said, "sit on the bed."

She did. Yukl put a 50 millimeter lens on the camera and loaded a roll of Kodak Ektachrome film. He adjusted his one light stand, with two 500 watt bulbs, and directed it toward Schlegel. He turned on the lights. "Good, good," he said, while she waited for further instructions. Yukl pulled out a wad of small bills from his pocket and gave them to her "It's for you," he offered.

It seemed a little strange to be paid before the photos, but Karin had never done this before. Maybe this was just the way it worked. She took the money. "Thanks."

The bottle of vodka was in the bedroom, and Yukl poured himself another stiff one. "Okay," he began with a noticeable stutter. "What I want you to do is t-t-take your sh-sh-shirt off and f-f-face the wall."

Karin started to unbutton her blouse. Yukl directed the lights. Then he went into the bathroom. When he emerged, he gave her a bar of soap to hold. She was surprised when she looked at the newly unwrapped bar. It wasn't the white Lifebuoy she expected. Instead, it was an orange cake of Dial.

Karin didn't want to appear foolish. Maybe she had misunderstood Charlie on the phone.

For the next twenty minutes, Yukl shot nearly thirty exposures of Schlegel from the back. In each shot, she was holding the bar of soap in her left hand. While her body still faced the wall, her head was turned towards the camera, five feet away.

"Okay," Yukl instructed, his stuttering increasing with every sentence. "H-h-hold it up a little higher. Now, to the l-l-left. G-g-good." He finished the shoot. He had unzipped his trousers, but Karin hadn't noticed. She put her shirt on and moved to the living room, displacing Sir Reginald on the dark green Castro convertible.

Charlie poured himself another drink and joined her. He sat in a red chair near the upright piano. They started to talk. "That was v-v-very g-g-good," he stammered as he chugged the vodka along with three tranquilizers. "I think that will work out fine."

He jumped up from the chair and went over to the

piano. There was some sheet music staring at him—a song called "I Don't Care," another called "The Old Piano Roll Blues," and a third called "Lament on Fifth Avenue." He started to play the third. "Fifth Avenue is so chic and so gay . . . its reputation's unmarred, it's just as nice as the Champs Elysées or Michigan Boulevard."

It was a terrible song. Karin was growing uncomfortable. This wasn't what she had in mind. Charlie kept playing, and singing. It was as if she wasn't even there.

"Charlie," she called over to him, trying to take Nancy's advice. "Charlie?" He suddenly heard her above his voice, and turned around. "Charlie," she said, "I've got this date at ten-thirty and I think I should be going."

"W-w-wait," he said. "I want to talk with you about something."

"What?"

"Oral sex. What do you think of it?"

Karin paused. She was in shock. "I don't know, uh, what you're getting at."

"Don't I turn you on?" Yukl asked.

"What?"

Yukl got up from the piano bench. "Don't you want to have sex with me?"

"Uh, I don't, uh, really think so. Charlie, I really must be going."

It was twenty feet from the couch to the front door across the wall-to-wall green carpet. As Karin walked to the white, wooden door, Yukl started to tremble. He raced for the kitchen table, where he had left the tie.

Karin was almost at the door when he caught her. He threw the tie over the back of her head and pulled her back.

She didn't scream. They both fell to the floor. Charlie and Karin were writhing on the floor now. She was taller than he was, and weighed more. But once again, the vodka and the pills were the triggers of his hidden strength.

The noise woke up Sir Reginald. The dog began to whimper, then bark and run nervously around the room. He thought Charlie was in trouble.

Each time Sir Reginald came near, Yukl pushed or kicked the dog away. At one point he kicked him into the wall, using the animal as a springboard to give him the leverage to wrap the tie even tighter around Karin's throat.

Karin pushed him away and managed to get the tie off. She jumped up and lunged for the doorknob, and Yukl grabbed for her shirt, ripping it. She reached the handle, and unlocked it. She pulled it. But the door didn't open. It had two locks. She had only managed to open one of them.

Charlie came up behind her and grabbed her again. This time he succeeded in getting the tie firmly around her throat. He pulled harder now, cutting off her air supply.

They were ten feet away from the door now. The glass coffee table had been knocked over, along with one of Yukl's drinks.

The dog was whining uncontrollably and running quickly from one side of the room to the other. But there were no screams from Karin, just futile attempts to punch out at Yukl, which were answered with severe blows to her head and face. Once he started hitting her, he didn't stop. He punched her forehead, fractured the bridge of her nose, and punched repeatedly at her cheeks and breasts.

She could no longer put up a fight. At 10:15, Yukl pulled hardest at the ends of the tie, and Karin Schlegel slumped to the floor, dead. It was a duplicate of the 1966 murder. Charlie sat quietly in a corner, next to the piano, oblivious to the putrid smell of fresh diarrhea. The Great Dane had become so nervous that he had defecated all over the carpet.

Yukl got up and took off all of Karin's clothes. He turned the body over and began to beat it. He ran into the bathroom and got a razor.

Just as he came out, the phone rang. It was Enken. It was 10:45. She was coming home in fifteen minutes. Charlie looked down at Karin, now lying faceup on the floor. He panicked. He had to get the body out of there.

Quickly he ran into the bedroom. In a near frenzy, he pulled the bed apart. He ripped the bedspread off and threw it on the floor. Next came the blankets and sheets. Yukl then lifted the mattress up and leaned it against the wall.

He removed both box springs and took them into the living room. Now all that was left in the bedroom was the metal bed frame, a large tripod, and a round, wooden work table Yukl kept under the bed.

He ran back into the living room. He had to work fast now. He dragged the body into the bedroom. It was hard work. It took him twelve long minutes to move Karin fifteen feet.

Then, Yukl lifted Schlegel a few inches off the floor —feet-first—and placed the body inside the bedframe on top of the table, still lying faceup.

He replaced the box springs and mattress, and then made the bed.

He only had a few minutes left. Back in the living room, he found Schlegel's black leather bag and hid it in the closet, along with his tie. Then he gathered up all her clothes, put them in a brown paper bag, and ran down the stairs to the street.

Two doors away, he found a garbage can and threw everything in it. He ran back upstairs and completed the last chore—he cleaned up Sir Reginald's mess, sprayed with Lysol, grabbed another Rheingold from the fridge, and waited.

Just before 11 P.M. Enken came home with her friend and the finished laundry. Enken went out to walk the dog, and Charlie moved to the kitchen to help his wife's guest fold the laundry. Yukl's hands were trembling, and he hoped she wouldn't notice.

She didn't. As soon as she left, Charlie went into the living room and turned on channel 2. It was about 11:30 and he said he wanted to watch "The Late Show."

Just then, Enken came back with the dog. "I'm tired," she said. "Let's go to bed."

At 11:45, Charles and Enken Yukl went into the bedroom. Enken got into the bed first. Yukl took a very long time in the bathroom, washing his hands repeatedly as if that would somehow cleanse him.

At 12:15, with Enken already sleeping, Charlie got nervously into bed. And together, husband and wife went to sleep, lying on top of the corpse of Karin Schlegel.

Every few minutes, Sir Reginald would wander into the room and start to sniff under the bed. Charlie kept kicking the dog until the animal got the message and finally left the room and slept on the living-room couch.

Charlie slept well for almost four hours.

But at 4:30, he awoke. He stared at the ceiling, and then remembered the body under him. He bolted out of bed and walked into the living room. He sat on the red chair for two hours, thinking about what he had done and how he was going to get around it.

At seven, he took the dog for a long walk, all the way to the Eighteenth Street pier on the Hudson River.

When he returned, Enken had already eaten her regular breakfast of cornflakes and milk. She left for work at 8:35.

As soon as she was gone, Yukl double-locked the front door and ran back to the bedroom. He pulled the bed apart again, finally revealing Schlegel's body. As he got closer, he noticed the foul smell.

Yukl pulled Schlegel's body off the work table and dragged it out into the living room. This time he made no attempt to stop Sir Reginald's natural curiosity. Charlie was more concerned about who was still left in the building.

It was just after nine o'clock. He slowly unlocked the door and opened it. He ran down the stairs, listening at each door. He heard nothing. He ran back up.

He called in to Greeley and Hansen and said he would be an hour late for work. He apologized and said he had overslept.

Yukl put the phone down and stared at Schlegel. There was only one way to do this.

He grabbed the body by the legs and started to pull. He had to go up one long flight of wooden stairs to the fifth floor. Schlegel weighed about 130 pounds, and the trip upstairs was a long twenty-five minute struggle for Yukl, who was hoping against hope that no one was in the building or coming to visit. He finally reached the top, opened the door to the roof, and dumped the body there. Yukl didn't notice that the work table had left some marks on Schlegel's back: small circular incisions had formed from the pressure of the body on the round holes where the folding table legs attached to the frame.

He ran back downstairs, went into the closet, and retrieved Schlegel's pocketbook, put it into a grocery bag, got dressed, and at 9:45 took the Seventh Avenue IRT subway to work. He dumped the grocery bag, along with the roll of film, into a garbage can at a construction site near his office on Church Street.

When he got to work, he explained his lateness was due to tension related to taking final examinations for his night-school psychology courses. "But those are over now," he sighed. "What a relief."

Irwin Klein was waiting for Charlie to notice. He had shaved off his beard over the weekend. Charlie looked right at him, but didn't mention anything.

"I feel especially good today," Yukl said to Klein. "I, uh, I'm feeling really lucky today." He smiled. "Bet I can beat you in chess."

CHAPTER FIFTEEN

Yukl brought his SONY transatlantic shortwave AM/FM portable radio to work with him that day.

As soon as he was at his desk, he turned it to WCBS, an all-news station. Nothing was reported, other than the usual Tuesday morning traffic jams and stock market rallies.

At 11:30, Yukl went home, ostensibly to have lunch. The body had been found. Cops were all over the place. A number of the building's tenants had been up on the roof and had seen the body.

The police asked Yukl who he was, and if he lived in the building. Yukl answered the basic questions and then went into his apartment.

On the way up the stairs, he bumped into the fifth-floor tenant Clive Kimball. Kimball was one of those who had seen the body. He was also there when Homicide Detective Don Baeszler noticed the deep, round marks on the body's back. He mentioned it to Yukl.

Charlie stayed inside his apartment for half an hour, too nervous to eat. He went back into the bedroom and again took the bed apart.

When he went back to work, he brought the table with him. He thought of leaving it on the subway, but at the last minute brought it upstairs to Greeley and Hansen.

By then, the news of the murder was out and Yukl confirmed to Irwin Klein that it had happened in the building where he lived.

"Who could have done such a thing?" Klein asked as Yukl stowed the table in back of the office copy machine.

"Must have been some nut, some real weirdo," Yukl agreed.

At that moment, Gerard Golia, an employee of the New York City Department of Highways, was working a few blocks away from Greeley and Hansen. He was on a project repaving Murray Street from Church Street to Broadway. He was looking for a temporary plug for a sewer and spotted a nearby trash can on the northeast corner of the street. There was a crumpled brown paper bag on top and he looked inside.

He saw the purse and opened it. Inside, he found the remains of a typical mugging—makeup case, lipstick, ID cards. But then he noticed something very strange. There was still money inside the wallet and another thirty dollars on top of it. In New York City, this made absolutely no sense.

Golia flagged down a cop and turned the bag over to him. Patrolman Hourican took the bag to the First Precinct, where it was vouchered and inventoried.

Back in Cresskill, Irene Schlegel was debating whether or not to call Karin and tell her that Denise had, in fact, lost the beauty pageant. She decided against it. After all, she thought, Denise was always getting all the attention, and she didn't want to rub it in. She would wait to tell Karin when she came home to visit again.

Irene's phone rang. It was a patrolman from the First Precinct in New York. "Do you know a Karin Schlegel?" the voice asked.

"Yes, she's my daughter."

"Well, Mrs. Schlegel, we've found your daughter's pocketbook."

"Oh my God." Irene sighed. "Not this mugging nonsense again."

The officer gave her his name and number. "Please have her get in touch with us to come in and pick it up."

Irene picked up the phone and dialed Karin at home. No answer. She must be at work, Irene thought. But Karin had never given her the name of the place where she worked or the phone number. There was nothing to do until Karin came home from work. There was no need to call Alfred—yet. Surely, there would be an explanation tonight when she talked to Karin, Irene thought.

Irene decided to go swimming at the Cresskill swim club. It was her way of working off tension. But before she even entered the building, her emotions took over. Irene found herself sitting under a tree, crying. She turned around, got into the car and drove home.

Back at the First Precinct, the cops thought it was strange that so much money would be in a discarded handbag, and they also tried to reach Karin. No luck. On a hunch, one of the detectives called one of his counterparts at the Thirteenth Precinct.

Within an hour, the cops had compared a photo taken of the body with an ID card from Schlegel's pocketbook. It looked like a match.

Don Baeszler went immediately to Schlegel's apartment on Minetta Lane. Inside, he found her diary, letters from Yukl, and a copy of the July 4 *Show Business*.

Irene had no sooner returned home than she tried to call Karin again. Still no answer. Then, there was a knock at the door. It was the young minister from the local Lutheran church. He was new in town, and the Schlegels hadn't attended church regularly for two years. His name was Pastor Richard Locke and he wanted to introduce himself to some of the "lost sheep."

Irene couldn't help herself. She broke down crying and poured her heart out to the newcomer, revealing her deepest worries and darkest fears.

They spoke for about forty minutes. Locke was very understanding. As he got up to leave, he said, "Mrs. Schlegel, we've made such good contact here today. I hope you will come again. After all," he said, "you are members of our church and we miss you. I have to go out of town for about two weeks, but I'll be back. You'll see," he promised. "Everything will be better then. You'll be out of your blues. I'll visit you and you'll be smiling."

She thanked him.

Nancy Weems arrived at Minetta Lane promptly at four P.M. for her rehearsal with Karin. No answer. Instinctively she felt something was wrong. Karin was the most punctual, responsible person she knew. Immediately, she called three friends from class and asked if they had seen her. They hadn't. Weems headed for work at La Poulard, a small French restaurant on Fifty-fifth Street and Second Avenue, where she was a waitress.

Irene kept trying to call Karin. At five o'clock Alfred came home. Irene told him about the pocketbook.

"I just don't understand it," she said. Then she looked at her husband. "Do me a favor. Go to Penn Station. There is some restaurant there. See if she's there."

Irene knew that Karin had her acting class at 8:30 that night, but didn't know how to reach her.

Alfred returned ninety minutes later. He had a vague look about him, and Irene pressed him for information.

"No, she's not there," he said.

"That's it?" Irene raised her voice. "What did they tell you?"

"She hasn't been in for a few days." It was seven P.M. now. Alfred tried to ignore his growing suspicions. "Could I eat dinner?" he asked his wife.

Irene called the apartment again. No answer.

"Did you go to her apartment?" she asked Alfred.

"No," he said quietly.

Irene now yelled at him. "Why did you do such a stupid thing? You were in the city. Now you go right back there and go to her apartment."

Alfred did as he was told. Finally Irene got Charlotte on the phone. When she had spoken to Charlotte about the pocketbook, Charlotte had seemed calm.

But now Charlotte was hysterical. She had seen the news. Karin had talked about Yukl and where he lived. The story mentioned the body with a swollen neck wearing contact lenses. She was sure it was Karin.

"Do you have the TV on?" Charlotte asked.

"No," Irene said. "Why should I have the TV on?" She had already begun to block certain things from her mind.

"Good," Charlotte said. "Are you alone?"

Irene wasn't. A good friend named Clara had come over to visit.

"Let me talk to Clara," Charlotte asked.

Clara got on the phone.

"Clara, my name is Charlotte," Schwartz said, beginning to shake. "I think I gotta tell you, because you're with Irene, that things don't look good. I . . ." She almost couldn't get the words out. "I . . . think Karin might be dead. They found a body on top of a roof in the Village, and it could be Karin."

"Uh-hmm," Clara responded, nodding.

"No one knows for sure, but it doesn't look good."

"Okay," Clara said. "Thanks for calling." She put the phone down and started to cry.

"What's going on?" Irene asked, almost angrily. "I just want to talk to my daughter and everyone is getting hysterical."

Alfred returned again, in even more of a daze. "Well, I went to Karin's apartment," he reported, "and for some strange reason the police were there. But I didn't want to go in."

Irene shrieked. "How stupid are you?" she yelled at him. "Go back there and find out what happened!"

Alfred dutifully got in the car and drove back to the city for the third time.

As soon as he left, Clara walked over to Irene. "It doesn't look very good," Clara said. "It looks bad."

"What looks bad?" Irene asked. "What are you talking about?"

"Look, I've got some valiums," Clara offered. "Would you like some?"

"What are you talking about?" Irene yelled. "What looks bad? Just leave me alone. Don't talk so crazy."

Irene picked up the phone and again called Karin's apartment. This time the phone was busy.

"See?" she said to Clara. "The line is busy. She's home and talking to someone on the phone."

Irene dialed five minutes later, and the phone was still busy. She kept calling every five minutes for two hours, and each time the line was busy. Finally, Irene called the operator and had her check the line.

"I'm sorry," the operator told her. "The line has been disconnected."

The phone rang, and Irene picked it up. It was Alfred.

"Irene, would you say Karin's hair is strawberry blond?"

"No way," Irene answered. "It's ash blond."

"Is she five feet six inches tall?"

"No. She's closer to five feet nine inches."

"That's very good," Alfred said.

Irene didn't understand. "What's very good?"

Alfred told her he'd call her back.

The police asked Alfred to accompany them to the morgue to identify the body of the girl they had found on the roof. But when he got there, there was no physician present, and they had to wait. Finally the cops let him go home. The identification procedure would have to wait.

When Alfred got home he wouldn't tell Irene anything about who or what he had seen in Karin's apartment. He didn't want to talk about anything.

Clara took Denise to her house for the night. "Let's go to sleep," Alfred said trying to comfort Irene. "This is all a big mix-up and we'll clear it all up tomorrow."

Late that night, at the medical examiner's office at 520 First Avenue, the autopsy began on the woman's body.

It confirmed death by strangulation. Her neck was broken, hemorrhagic fluid was in the nose and mouth; her chin was lacerated. Medical examiner case 6627 was now officially a homicide. The report was typed up.

The doctors also noticed something else. "I couldn't believe it," one doctor remarked to Don Baeszler as he emerged from the examination area. "Her hymen was intact. Twenty-three years old, and a virgin. You just don't see that anymore."

Out in Flushing, Charlotte Schwartz couldn't sleep. She was now convinced Karin was dead. But her thoughts turned to the killer. Suddenly she was possessed with a terrible thought. Karin was scheduled to have a date with Marty. Could he be the killer? She didn't know him that well. She called the police and gave them his name.

One of the cops told her that the body had been tentatively identified, and that they needed to speak to the Schlegels.

Charlotte turned on the radio, then the television. There had been no news. She called Irene Schlegel. It was 5:30 in the morning.

"Mrs. Schlegel, what's new?" she asked as calmly as she could, hoping that Irene would tell her it was all a bad dream. But no police or medical examiners had called Irene.

"What's new?" Irene repeated. "You just woke me up."

"You've been sleeping?" Charlotte couldn't believe it.

"Yes. Of course. Why shouldn't we be sleeping?"

Charlotte closed her eyes, and inhaled. "Mrs. Schlegel," she said nervously, fighting the tears, "there's a policeman who wants you to call him now."

"Now?"

"Yes." Charlotte gave Irene the man's name and number.

She woke Alfred. "Honey, some policeman wants us to call him."

Alfred called and was told they needed him to come to the morgue as soon as possible for the identification. "I'm coming with you this time," Irene insisted.

Nancy Weems was nearly hysterical at the restaurant that day. She had heard of the body being found, but not much more. One of the waitresses asked her, "Was your friend blond?"

"Yes," Weems said.

Then the phone rang. It was Nancy's friend Tony, an actor. "I gave them your name. It's so horrible."

"Karin is dead, isn't she?" she asked.

Just then two men walked into the restaurant. One of them was Don Baeszler. Weems put down the phone and started crying. "Is it true?" she asked Baeszler.

"Yes."

"Do you know who did it?"

"We think so," Baeszler said, "but Nancy, we need you to come downtown with us now to help us."

The Schlegels arrived at the morgue on Thirty-second street about eleven A.M. A police officer ushered them in. He had a brown manila folder with him. He opened it up and inside was a picture of Karin. "Is this your daughter?" he asked the Schlegels.

They both nodded. "I'm afraid that's her."

Instantaneously there was a flurry of activity around Irene as the police officer and an attendant offered her coffee.

That's when she knew. The morgue officials asked the couple which one of them wanted to identify the body. Alfred glanced quickly over at Irene. There was a pleading look in her eyes, already swelling with tears. "I'll go in," he softly volunteered.

The process was almost too quick. They went through a few doors, brought Alfred into the cold room, and opened the stainless steel drawer containing his daughter's beaten body. He leaned in and looked for a long moment. It was Karin. But the shock didn't hit him right away.

"Yes," he said quietly. "That is my daughter." He stood and looked at Karin for a full two minutes. No one in the room said anything.

The cops knew the silence was horrendous at times like these. There is nothing to do but wait for the terrible personal moments to end.

Alfred then knelt down by the body, and placed his head on the side rim of the stainless steel drawer. He prayed silently.

When he was finished, he rose, and said nothing. An attendant asked him to fill out the standard "identification of body" report.

He took out a ball point pen from his shirt pocket. Without hesitation, he filled in the blank spaces:

ALFRED SCHLEGEL, age 52, residing at 90 HEATHERHILL ROAD in CRESSKILL, NJ being duly sworn, deposes and says: that he is a FATHER of the person whose body was found at 120 WAVERLY PL. 20 AUG 74 and subsequently sent to the Office of the Chief Medical Examiner; that deponent has seen the BODY of said deceased, and has every reason to believe that the body now recorded at the Office of Chief Medical Examiner is KARIN SCHLEGEL who was last seen or heard from by deponent on 18 AUG 74. Deponent therefore prays that HIS identification of said deceased person be accepted by the Chief Medical Examiner of the City of New York.

Under occupation of deceased, Alfred listed the only known occupation that fit his description of what a job was. He wrote down "EDITOR-MAGAZINE MCGRAW HILL."

Then, in a slow, deliberate script he carefully signed the legal-sized form. And collapsed.

CHAPTER SIXTEEN

On Wednesday afternoon I got a call from the "non-security" security officer downstairs, a police detective named Mike Sepe. "There's a young woman down here to see you. She's got information about a homicide that happened to a friend of hers."

I was waiting in my office when Nancy Weems came in. She walked in quickly, shook my hand, and sat down.

She settled nervously on the long government-green vinyl couch pushed against the wall. There was nothing soft about this piece of furniture. It was greenish black in color, and the vinyl covering was pockmarked with half a dozen punchholes.

Weems was tired, and she looked drained. We had never met before, but we both knew why she was here. After meeting with Baeszler, she had come in on her own. She sat quietly, playing gently with her bleached blonde hair.

I moved my chair from behind my desk, put it beside her, and sat down. I grabbed a pad to take notes. Slowly, a bit unsure of herself, she began to tell me her story.

She was an actress, a sometimes model, and a friend of Karin Schlegel. She had been in Schlegel's apartment Monday evening rehearsing a play with her.

"I remember it well," she told me. "While we were going over a scene she got this phone call from this guy. She was very happy to hear from him and got very excited about it. While she was talking to him, she kept pointing to this letter on her desk. She pointed and whispered to me, 'That's the guy I was talking to you about.'"

There was a knock at my door. The door opened, and Don Baeszler stuck his head in. I motioned for him to come in the room. I gave Baeszler a signal that this was not the time for our usual black humor. Baeszler came prepared. He showed Nancy a copy of the letter in question, one of the many notes from Yukl to some of his girls about his nonexistent movie project. Weems identified it. And Baeszler left the room.

"Go on," I said, "tell me what happened next."

"Well," she continued, "Karin kept talking to him about some project. She was always shy and withdrawn but Monday night she was quite animated with him on the phone. All I heard was her saying, 'Yes, I can be there, nine o'clock. Okay, I'll make a note. Right. At your place. Fine.' Yeah, that's what she said." Weems paused and remembered more. "Then she wrote down his address, although I think she already knew it, and then she hung up."

She told me how she had warned Schlegel not to go to Yukl's apartment, and how Karin had assured her, then reassured her that Charlie was on the level, how he was a normal, happily married man with a nice wife and a large dog.

In retelling the story, Weems was on the verge of tears. She felt tremendous guilt and responsibility for what happened, because she had not stopped Schlegel. She had no way of knowing it then, but she kept reminding herself now that she had been Karin's last line of defense between life and death.

I had seen this reaction all too many times before in women like Nancy Weems, sitting on my couch, telling me similar tragic stories and feeling similar emotions. The operative words were always "should" and "if only," and they were always meaningless expressions in a city that was deliberately slow to forgive. It was all quite final and almost always after the fact. We had been down that road all too many times. And each time the friend needed to talk about it, to wonder out loud and to hypothesize about what was now clearly impossible.

Nancy Weems, like so many people before her, was now coming face-to-face with reality. It was now her turn to recognize the sometimes dangerous folly of a young woman living alone in New York City.

In this case, it had resulted in the ultimate nightmare.

All the horror stories Weems and Schlegel had heard about their chosen profession had now come true. At least Weems was still alive.

Weems was somehow unlike all the other friends of victims I had interviewed over the years. Remarkably, she had managed to maintain her composure as she remembered the events leading up to Karin's death. Her report was mature, accurate, and factual.

From the moment she entered my office I had been thinking about what Nancy Weems would be like on the witness stand. It is always a prosecutor's underlying fear that an important witness with important things to say in his office won't be strong enough to withstand the pressure during a trial. In every one of my homicide cases, and with just about every witness I had interviewed prior to trial, I always assumed the worst—a courtroom adversary like the celebrated criminal attorney Henry Rothblatt. My witnesses would be projected onto the imaginary stand, to be cross-examined by the very best.

Rothblatt had represented the My Lai defendant and a few of the Watergate conspirators. He was a master of strategy and trial technique. In my book, Henry Rothblatt was a great attorney—always well prepared, flamboyant in the extreme, a longtime adversary as well as a professional friend.

Weems passed my personal Rothblatt test. From this first meeting, I knew intuitively that she would be unshakable, that her testimony, although sure to be challenged, would remain untainted. I watched her carefully throughout the session, and my notepad still remained on my lap—I had written nothing on it.

I didn't want our interview to be an intimidating one. At this point, I wanted it to be informal, conversational. After all, being in a DA's office in itself is daunting.

There was another reason I decided not to take any notes. Ultimately, everything the prosecution has in its possession has to be turned over to the defense, and I didn't want any of Nancy Weems' statements to contradict any later testimony. I decided to wait until a week before the trial to take notes on Weems.

The first session was only the beginning. I did, however, note her telephone number, address, and where she could be located. I wanted to know everything about her—her background, her employment, her life before and now, everything she was doing, her perceptions about Karin Schlegel.

I was assembling this deep background on Nancy Weems for a specific purpose. Weems didn't know it yet, but she was about to become an integral part of the process of arresting Charles Yukl.

As soon as Weems left my office, a little after eleven A.M., I went upstairs to see Keenan. His office was on the eighth floor, in what used to be the "trophy room" in the Hogan days—an intimate place where the DAs known as Hogan's Hooligans proudly displayed their softball awards. It was an executive office now, full of leather couches and high-back chairs. Keenan was sitting behind his large wooden desk when I entered the room. "I've got some bad news, John," I began.

"Sit down," he soothed. "Relax."

I sat down. And leaned forward. "John, you know the nightmare that we all have. . . ."

He looked up from his desk. "What do you mean?" he asked.

It was easy to explain. It was the classic prosecutor's bad dream—that we had given a murder defendant a plea and the murderer had gotten out and repeated his crime.

Keenan listened quietly, then asked, "In what case did this happen to you? I'm sure it can't be that bad," he said. "And besides"—he laughed—"you never give any pleas anyway. Listen," he continued without pausing, "I'm sure you had good reasons to allow the plea."

"John," I shook my head. "I don't think you understand. This one was not *my* case. This is the Yukl case. You remember the Yukl case, right?"

There was no way Keenan couldn't remember the case. "Charles Yukl?" he asked, in disbelief.

I nodded.

"He got out?"

"He got out," I affirmed, "and he killed that girl in the Village yesterday."

Keenan just sat there quietly at his desk, his mouth open, staring off into space. I waited for him to say something, but he didn't.

"I'm working on the case now," I said, interrupting the silence, "and I don't have enough yet to arrest him. But he lives in the building, one flight below where the body was found. It was the same MO," I explained. "Ligature strangulation."

Keenan didn't respond.

"Is there anything you'd like me to do?" I asked. Again, nothing. "Well," I offered, "I'll keep you posted."

"Okay," he mumbled.

I got up from the chair and started to leave. "How could they let him out?" Keenan said as I walked out. Keenan had been the assistant DA who let Yukl plea-bargain six years earlier. That was a matter of public record. It would not go unnoticed by the press or the public.

He was a damn good DA. Some would argue that Keenan was the best in the office, an all-star whose decision in a murder case years earlier was now about to thrust him firmly behind the eight ball.

Keenan was normally very much in control of any situation in the bureau. But this news clearly startled him. He understood, perhaps better than any of the other attorneys, the political ramifications this development might have on his career. Even more important, Keenan understood the pivotal consequences of responsibility and public criticism.

The news I brought him had the potential to create a worst-case scenario, and Keenan was veteran enough to know that he could easily become a living example of how a careful, concerned, talented—and *responsible*—prosecuting attorney could be accused of letting someone off the hook, of essentially blowing a case.

He knew, and I knew, that in the end, all the public would really care about was that he was responsible for giving a plea to a murderer who got out and did it again. No one would bother to ask the real reasons why Keenan had let Yukl make a deal in 1968, no one consider Keenan's well-founded fears that Yukl might legally maneuver himself out of a conviction in a jury trial on the issue of the police failure to advise him of his legal rights prior to questioning.

The issue now, once we arrested Charles Yukl again, would simply be that a convicted murderer had been given a deal, he had been released, and he had killed again. There was nothing I could do to rewrite the past. But there could be no room for failure now.

Our only consolation was to arrest Yukl, make the arrest stick, and land a major conviction that would sustain itself on a probable appeal.

Don Baeszler was waiting for me in my office when I returned from Keenan. I brought him up to date on what Weems had told me. He in turn brought me up to date on the news from the street. Word on the Schelgel killing had already reached the top of police circles. Baeszler's superiors wanted an arrest made quickly and the pressure was mounting, I had expected this to happen, but not this fast.

Baeszler and I agreed we had to move quickly, but not too quickly. It was just too soon to make an arrest. Together, Don and I began to analyze where we stood in the Yukl investigation.

While we still lacked legally sufficient evidence in the case, we certainly knew our suspect. As a murderer in 1966, Yukl was a confessor, ultimately a weak psychopath who liked to talk about his crimes. He also liked to kill in the place where he lived.

The only difference between the 1966 murder and the Schelgel murder was that back then Yukl had called the police immediately. This time he was being coy, despite the fact that the police had been all over his building on Tuesday. They had knocked on all the apartment doors and had shown all the residents, including Yukl, pictures of the woman in death. Yukl had denied knowing her. He claimed his wife was with him at the time. She must be protecting him now, I thought. And just as surely, Yukl must be thinking that we would discover that he was living in the same building where the body was found.

Baeszler and I both knew we needed a plan of action to arrest Yukl. But we had to do it carefully. Yukl wasn't the ripe peach he'd been in 1966, waiting to fall from the tree and start talking. While it seemed as if he was intentionally waiting to be trapped, it also looked as if his wife was shielding him. And that created additional problems for our investigation.

A number of questions persisted about Enken. Why would she protect him? Did she truly believe in his innocence? (This seemed improbable, since she was fully aware of the 1966 case.) And if she *did* believe Yukl had killed Reynolds and/or Schlegel, what was she still doing in the apartment? Why wouldn't she be afraid that Yukl would kill her?

First and foremost, we had to develop a strategy to get an admissible statement from Yukl himself.

Nancy Weems was the answer. At that point, maybe the *only* answer. Only three people knew about the phone call Yukl made to Karin Schlegel on the night of the murder. Our ace in the hole was that Yukl thought there only were two witnesses to the call—himself and Schlegel. If we worked it right, we could startle him with this news and, at best, provoke him into the spontaneous confession I knew was inside him.

"I got a great plan to get Yukl," I told Baeszler.

He put up his hands and rolled his eyes in a characteristic way. "But remember," he said, "you're a DA and I'm a cop, and I'm telling you that the pressure is already on from the brass. They want to lock Yukl up now."

My plan was simple. We were going to play the Weems card and fake Yukl out with an incriminating phone call.

I would need the services of two detectives, Tony Sarenaro and Pete DiPascale. These cops were as-

signed to our office, and they had a specific undercover mission. They were expert "wiremen" on loan
to us for "special assignments."

During the Hogan era, they handled the wiretaps
and the bugs on virtually all organized-crime and public corruption cases. They weren't just electronic
geniuses—they also knew how to *interpret* what they
heard behind the closed doors of the mob.

To carry off the Weems strategy correctly, we would
need Sarenaro and DiPascale to wire a hotel room for
sound and videotape. Then we'd need a policewoman
to impersonate Weems, to get Yukl to admit the crime
on the phone, or, barring that, to get him to come to
her hotel room and admit it there.

"I'll take care of the wiremen," I told Baeszler.
"You deliver the policewoman."

Baeszler just laughed. "I'll deliver a policewoman
and my head will be in the commissioner's office.
They're gonna think this is a college-boy bullshit plan
hatched by some DA. It may be imaginative, Bob,"
he said, "but it won't fly. They won't buy it. They
want to know what we're going to do. They keep
asking, 'What if he kills again?' "

"Look," I said, "they've got to buy it. It's very
simple. We've got nothing against this guy other than
the fact that he was in the building and Schlegel was
going to his apartment. That's just not enough. It is
still not proof beyond a reasonable doubt," I argued.
"In a city where there are two thousand homicides a
year, she could have been killed by someone else. I
know she wasn't. You know she wasn't. But our sacro-
sanct opinions aren't enough to get this thing to trial.
In a nutshell, I would say we have shit here."

My argument wasn't with Baeszler, and we both
knew it. At that moment he looked more dejected
than I did at the notion of our lack of a case. He sat in

THE PIANO TEACHER 209

the corner, like a big teddy bear, with his head drooping over.

"Cheer up," I told him, "we're going to give something to the brass that will keep them happy. It will give them something to do and make them look good while we do the important stuff. Besides," I said, "we'll need some time to put my plan into operation."

I asked for the traditional surveillance of Yukl and another police canvas of the building. I wanted the cops to go back there, knock on all the doors again, and show everyone a picture of Schlegel—only this time one of her in life, this time a large blowup of Karin that Baeszler had found in her apartment.

The surveillance was, in effect, worthless, a makework job for some of the old-fashioned police thinkers. If Yukl was going to kill again, it wouldn't be on the streets. That wasn't his style. It would be inside, so the surveillance was really camouflage. It didn't prevent him from killing. It only prevented him from fleeing. Baeszler understood this. Yukl was not to leave New York.

It was still all quite weak. If he tried to leave, what could we arrest him for? All circumstantial cases are not necessarily weak. Some are actually stronger than those that rely on eyewitness identification. The classic circumstantial story takes place in wintertime. You go to bed at night. There's no snow on the ground. The next morning you wake up and there *is* snow on the ground. You have a pretty strong, albeit circumstantial, case that it snowed the night before. If you see footsteps in the snow, you can make an equally strong argument that someone walked in the snow.

But the problem with all circumstantial cases is that the lay public feels that if you don't have eyewitnesses, then you have a very weak case. Clever defense attorneys play on this, equating circumstantial evidence with cancer on the popularity scale. Under the law, any ambiguity in the evidence must be resolved in favor of the defendant.

In building this still-circumstantial case against Yukl, I was attempting to design a mosaic: each piece in and of itself would not point inexorably to Yukl's guilt, but taken as a whole, my mosaic would relentlessly lead to the conclusion that Yukl was the killer.

The surveillance may have been unnecessary under these conditions, but the picture showing at the apartment building had a distinct purpose. The first time around the cops had shown the residents pictures of Schlegel in death. The photos were clear enough, but the body and facial features were understandably distorted. Now we were going to give Yukl a second chance. The legal term for a killer who denies knowing his victim is called "consciousness of guilt" and may later be considered by a jury as an indication of guilt.

Yukl's consciousness of guilt was part of my mosaic, a mosiac that still included only the following: the body on the rooftop, bloodstains leading from his door to the rooftop, and her conversation with Yukl in the presence of Weems indicating her intention to go to his apartment at nine o'clock on the evening of the murder.

The law always seems to play havoc with common sense at times like this. The biggest thing I had I couldn't use. The law prevented me from using the 1966 Susan Reynolds homicide because, the law says, one previous killing, even if virtually identical to the murder at hand, is insufficient quantitatively to establish the criminal pattern the law requires.

Even if a murderer repeats his crime, under similar circumstances, the prosecution is restricted from using the first crime to establish the killer's identity, or to show to a moral certainty that both killings could only have been committed by the same person.

Under the law, one killing is simply too few. Incredibly, the law essentially places a premium on multiple killings. It was absurd to apply these legal restrictions in the Yukl case, but they would certainly be applied by the court at the request of the defense.

My hotel plan was all I had left.

Baeszler got the photos distributed to the cops, and they headed for Waverly Place. Then I asked him to check in with the NYPD's sex crimes unit. "You find a lady cop," I instructed, "who's savvy and has chutzpah, and I'll cover your ass with the brass."

Don rolled his eyes again, then smiled, as he left the office in search of our policewoman. I picked up the phone and made two calls—one to John Keenan, to tell him what I planned to do, and the other to my contact at the police department's nerve center, Lou Cottell, Chief of Detectives for the City of New York.

CHAPTER SEVENTEEN

The new police headquarters at Foley Square, a two-block walk from my office, was one of those antiseptic municipal buildings, a large, impersonal, overly bricked edifice designed, it seemed, to alienate you before you ever walked in. This was no precinct house. It was quiet and sterile, a place where New York cops were polite, well mannered, and well dressed.

Lou Cottell's office was upstairs. He fit in perfectly with the decor. He was a cop's cop, one of the most experienced detectives on the force. He had put in over thirty years to get his office and desk. He wasn't some 90-day political wonder, and he understood the importance of making arrests that would stick beyond the immediate political needs of his superiors.

Cottell was the police equivalent of Frank Hogan. He made decisions on the basis of merit. If you gave him courtesy and respect, you got it back. You also got the cooperation you needed. He had little tolerance for the arrogance of young DAs who looked upon his staff as the errand boys of their glorious investigation techniques.

Relations between the cops and the DA's office were at an all-time low. Investigators from the special prosecutor's office, still foaming at the mouth after the

Frank Serpico corruption revelations in the late 1960s, were continuing to rupture the pipeline of cooperation that existed between these two integral parts of the criminal justice system.

I had worked closely with Cottell two years before, during the investigation into the 1972 gangland murder of Joey Gallo at Umberto's clam bar in little Italy. During the course of that investigation, Cottell assigned an entire detective unit to work with me. With their invaluable help, I obtained convictions against the head of the Colombo crime family, Vincent Aloi, against Gallo bodyguards Pete "the Greek" Diapolous and Robert Bongiovi, and against other Colombo family lieutenants.

I liked Cottell. More important, we trusted each other. Lou Cottell appreciated the direct line of communication. From my perspective, Cottell was my insurance policy in this investigation. I wanted him to know everything we were doing before we did it. And I wanted his support. The phone on his desk would be ringing within hours with some police inspector out of joint over our plan and I wanted him to be on our side already.

When John Keenan and I got off the elevator on Cottell's floor, we were met by one of his assistants, an attaché-type detective who looked about as streetwise as a Proctor & Gamble product salesman from Cincinnati. But the cops all looked like that at Foley Square. They were all young turk corporate executives on the make, distinctly uncoplike in appearance and style.

The assistant led us into Cottell's office. Cottell was dressed as usual—gray suit and tie. I could never get over his office. Airplanes could land on his desk. There was a blotter, a pen set, and nothing else.

"Thanks for coming by," he began quietly and offered coffee. He knew why we were there, and I suspect he also knew that Keenan might be taking some heat, but that didn't accelerate the pace of the meeting.

That was his style. Slow and deliberate. Some thought Cottell projected a sense of battle weariness that only experience can give someone. I looked at his manner instead as an old-world civility, an unusual and uncorrupted policeman's philosophy of doing an impossible job in an impossible place. He grew up on the streets; he worked them for years. But Lou Cottell refused to be transformed by the city's rage, or its passion.

"Lou, we're working on an important case that you should know about," Keenan began. "Bob's in charge. I'll let him tell you about it."

I started to tell him about the Schlegel murder. But Cottell was already up to date on our situation. He knew we had a thin case against Yukl, and knew the special dangers of a precipitous arrest.

I then suggested my hotel plan. Cottell liked it.

"You've got my support, Robert," he said at the end of the meeting. "Whatever manpower you need, you've got it."

We shook hands. Keenan and I left.

When I got back to my office, I got the police wireman, Tony Sarenaro, on the phone. He came right down from his ninth-floor office with DiPascale.

I explained the Weems phone plan to them. They were a jovial pair, eager to help out in a major homicide case. They were professionals in search of imaginative investigations. This one was right up their alley.

"How do you want to do this?" they asked.

I told them we'd need a safe hotel.

"Where do you want to do this?"

"Anywhere you want," I said. "But try and make it centrally located."

Sarenaro had the perfect place, he said, a hotel the

pair had used before to trap some crooked cops. It was the Beverly Hotel, at Fiftieth Street and Lexington Avenue. It was a fading, unimpressive hotel and the room rates reflected its condition. Sarenaro booked two adjoining rooms for Thursday and Friday.

Meanwhile, after having canvassed the building and shown the tenants—including Yukl, who remained unfazed—photos of Schlegel in life, a contingent of three cops dressed in civilian clothes remained in front of Yukl's apartment building, sitting in an unmarked car, doing what they were told to do—watching the building. If Yukl left, they were to follow him.

Because of manpower problems, the cops assigned to the surveillance had never seen or met Charles Yukl. All they had in their possession was the old arrest photograph from 1966.

On Thursday morning, two days after the murder, when Charles Yukl left for work a little after eight A.M., two cops followed him—or at least attempted to tail him. As he walked down Waverly Place to Sixth Avenue, the cops jumped out of their car and started walking behind him from a distance. The third cop ran up ahead toward the subway station.

Yukl turned right at Sixth Avenue and headed for the Fourth Street IND subway station a few blocks away. The cops continued following as he went down the stairs and into the station. The third cop, anticipating this, was already standing by the token booth. Yukl didn't stand in line. He reached into his pocket, pulled out a token, and went through the turnstile.

The Fourth Street station is both an express and a local stop. As passengers walk down to the platform, the downtown express track is on the left. At rush hour, the place is crammed with hundreds of people doing what amounts to a balancing act, standing on the platform and trying to avoid being pushed to the tracks below.

Yukl walked down the stairs to the platform, with the cop right behind him. Suddenly, with a roar and a screech, both a local and an express train barreled into the station at the same time. The doors to the crowded trains opened and a mass of people came flying out as an equal number of combatants attempted to enter.

In the confusion, the cop lost Yukl. He took out his walkie-talkie to signal the other cops, but the underground noise turned it into a useless machine. They couldn't hear him. Even though the other two cops were now in the subway station, they couldn't even see their partner.

Which train was Yukl on? In a few seconds the doors would be closing. The cop had to make a quick choice. He knew where Yukl worked and figured he had to be on the local. As the doors were closing, he squeezed into one of the local cars.

As the other cops panicked, Charles Yukl was already on the express to Chambers Street. The cops regrouped a few minutes later. They had blown it. Before admitting their mistake to their superiors, one of them placed a phone call to Greeley and Hansen and asked to speak to Yukl. When Yukl got on the phone, he immediately hung up.

The cops had lucked out. In the end, their screw-up became irrelevant because of Yukl's consistency. After Yukl left the subway, he had simply walked the few blocks to work on Broadway.

In the meantime, Baeszler was out on the streets, trying to find the other girls mentioned in some of Yukl's letters and other papers discovered at Schlegel's apartment.

Maybe Freud was right when he said that a killer always leaves clues. That a murderer has a deep-rooted interior compulsion to get careless and an even more intense compulsion to confess.

I was convinced Charles Yukl would leave us enough clues, and soon. We would get him on Friday.

When I arrived at the Beverly Hotel the next day, I didn't like the setup. It's one thing to try to nail someone. It's quite another to invite the world to witness the event.

There were too many cops around, too much brass. Although I was glad to have Keenan there, I was concerned about having everyone else there. I was afraid they would pull the trigger too soon and arrest him before we had a solid case.

We had assembled the essential players—Sarenaro and his partner and a young policewoman, Carole Natale. If it had just been the wiremen, the policewoman, and me, it would have been an easy one-act play. But with a cast of dozens, the plan became unwieldy, and next to impossible to execute successfully.

Baeszler called from a phone booth across the street on Waverly Place and confirmed that Yukl was in the apartment with his wife. He had seen him walk the dog and return to the building.

We were ready to make the first call to Yukl. I had thoroughly rehearsed the script with Natale. She dialed. On the second ring, Enken answered the phone.

"Is Charlie there?" she asked.

"No," came a quick, short reply. "He's not home . . . Who is this?"

"I'm just a friend," Natale answered. "I just want to talk to him."

There was a short pause. "Well . . . just a minute."

A few seconds later, Enken returned to the phone. "I'm sorry," she repeated. "Charles is not home." She hung up. It was clear that Enken was covering for her husband. There was nothing to do but wait.

Suddenly the phone in the hotel room rang again. It was Baeszler. "They're leaving the apartment together," he reported. Yukl and Enken were on Waverly, walking the Great Dane.

"Donny," I told him, "under no circumstances let her go back into the apartment with him."

"How the hell am I supposed to do that?" he shot back.

"I don't know," I returned the volley. "I'm just the college-kid attorney. You're the bigshot detective. *You* figure it out!"

Baeszler followed them for a block or two, not really knowing what to do. All he knew was that he wanted to get Yukl back into the apartment alone so that Yukl would have to answer the phone when Natale called him. He also didn't want the couple to stray too far from Waverly.

Suddenly he saw his opportunity. Walking toward him were two tourists, or at least they looked like tourists. Each had a camera around his neck. They reached him as Yukl and Enken were turning a corner just ahead of him. A phone booth was to their left.

Baeszler acted quickly. He pulled out his badge. "Excuse me," he said as he grabbed one of them. "I'm a New York City detective. Give me that camera," he demanded in his theatrical best to one of the stunned out-of-towners. "This is a police action," he said, pushing them toward the phone booth. "Stay inside until I return . . . and protect yourselves."

The two had no time to ponder their situation. They meekly turned over one of the Nikons and patiently waited. Baeszler was already off and running after the Yukls. A block later he caught up a few steps behind them, at the entrance to Washington Square Park.

Yukl was walking the dog, near the curb. Enken was to his right.

Baeszler made his move. He ran up behind them and took on the persona of the tourists whom he had just relieved of the camera. Feigning a heavy European accent, he stopped the Yukls and spoke in somewhat broken English. "Excuse," he stumbled, directing his question at Yukl, and pointing to his camera. "You take my picture? I am not . . ." He purposely stumbled again and started talking to himself in thick German, ostensibly searching for the right word in English.

Enken's face lit up momentarily. It was her native tongue, and the two conversed in German for a good two minutes. Baeszler then gave Enken the camera, and she took his picture standing under the park's arch.

Just then a friend of Enken's joined them and was introduced to "Donald." Baeszler needed to separate Charlie from his wife. He asked Enken if he could treat them all to some dinner.

Enken suggested Chumley's, an old speakeasy in the heart of the West Village. Enken gave Baeszler detailed directions to the restaurant, and they agreed to meet there in fifteen minutes.

"And you." Baeszler looked at Charlie. "You join us?"

Yukl shook his head. " 'Fraid not. Gotta get the dog home and I've got work to do."

Enken and her friend headed off to the restaurant. Yukl turned the dog in the direction of Waverly. And Baeszler stayed at the park, fumbling with the camera until everyone had turned their respective corners. He then followed Yukl home, stopping on the way to return the camera to the two startled tourists, who were still waiting in the phone booth.

"New York City thanks you," he said, smiling, and removed his police business card from his wallet. "I had to use some film. Please send me the shots and bill me."

A few minutes later, Baeszler called me again. "Make the call," he said. "Yukl just went back into the apartment alone."

"Great," I said. "How'd you do it?"

There was a subdued laugh on the other end of the phone. "I'm the bigshot detective, remember? Now hurry up and get your statement."

For the second phone attempt, Officer Natale was extremely nervous. We were in a room with two twin beds. She sat on one bed, near the phone on the center nightstand table. I sat on the other bed and watched.

Yukl's phone rang six times before he picked it up.

"Hello," he said, hesitating.

"Hello," said Natale, equally nervous. "Is this Charlie?"

"Yeah."

"Charlie . . . this is Mary Costello."

There was a pause.

"Who?"

"Mary Costello," Natale said more decisively.

"Yeah?" Yukl seemed confused, as he should have been.

"Yeah . . . I'm a friend of Karin's."

"Oh yeah," Yukl acknowledged.

"You don't know me, Charlie. But I know Karin . . . and I know a few things about what happened the other night."

Yukl didn't say anything for a moment. Then he suggested, "You're just upset."

"*Very* upset," Natale insisted.

"Well." Yukl suddenly became her ally. "You're not the only one."

"Well, uh, I just feel that there's enough . . ." Natale was getting flustered. I gave her a thumbs-up sign to continue. "But I think there's enough that I know that I want to talk to you and I think you want to talk to me too."

He took the bait. "All right . . . why not?"

"Okay," Natale said, "will you come over to my hotel room?"

"Well . . . sure."

"Okay."

"Can you let me know where it is?"

"I certainly will," she said. We were rolling. "I'm at the Beverly Hotel. If you're not here in one hour, I'm going to the police with it."

"What is it you want? What exactly is your problem?"

"You come here and find out. I'll give you an hour."

"I can't come uptown. I'll have to meet you somewhere else."

"You come here. I'll give you one hour before I go to the police," Natale insisted.

"Well, fuck you," Yukl screamed. "You do what you have to do. I'm not coming that far uptown."

He hung up. Natale looked over to me.

Inspector Nicastro, Chief of Manhattan detectives, was listening on a phone extension in another room. As soon as Natale hung up, Sarenaro ran in. "This is great. You were right. It's gonna work. Get him on the phone again."

I looked over at Carole. "Go ahead. Call him again. Tell him you'll meet him anywhere he wants. We'll wire you."

She nodded and picked up the phone.

Just then, Keenan came bursting through the door

from an adjoining room. "Hold it," he said decisively. "I say we take him now."

I turned around and glanced at him. I tried to ignore him. "Carole," I continued, "just make the call."

"No," Keenan interjected. "You can't do that. They've already got him."

"What are you talking about?" I asked.

"Nicastro picked up the phone," Keenan reported, "and ordered Baeszler to arrest him."

I was enraged. "Wait," I argued. "He can't do that without our approval."

"Well," Keenan answered, "there's no sense in getting upset about it. It's already been done."

"How could he have done it?"

Keenan mumbled something.

"What? . . . How could Nicastro do that?" I repeated.

"Well . . . *I* told him it was all right to do it."

"Why'd you do that?"

"Bob, the phone call thing was a nice try but it was clear it wasn't going to work."

There was nothing to do. It became apparent that Keenan and the police brass had no faith in the plan. It was a sad moment.

Baeszler got the call in the phone booth from Nicastro. He assumed that the Natale call hadn't worked and quickly enlisted another detective to make the short walk across the street and up the stairs to read Yukl his rights.

When Yukl opened his door, Baeszler was greeted with a smile. But there was no German accent this time. He pulled out his shield. "It's all over, Charlie, you're under arrest."

He read him his rights. There seemed to be no need to handcuff Yukl, who meekly accompanied Baeszler as they headed down the stairs and into the unmarked police car for the short ride to the precinct.

Back at the hotel, I still couldn't believe what was happening. The cops were cleaning up and heading downtown. Natale was still sitting on the bed, looking more confused than ever.

I looked up at Keenan. I had to go on the record. "You realize, of course, that you approved an arrest in a case where we have no evidence."

"Don't worry," he said. "There's nothing really to worry about," he repeated. "Nothing at all. We'll get him to confess."

"But John," I had to ask, "what if he doesn't?"

CHAPTER EIGHTEEN

Nine of us sat down quietly at the long, rectangular wooden table at the Thirteenth Precinct. It was a standard oak issue, one of those big, sturdy, well-varnished but heavily stained tables that always manage to outlive generations of civil servants.

Yukl sat at the head of the table. To his left were a stenographer, Keenan, and myself. At the end of the table sat Tony Sarenaro and the other detectives—including Baeszler and Inspector Nicastro.

Baeszler sat directly to Yukl's right, an intentional placement by Keenan, the most senior man in the room. Keenan would be running the interrogation. All of us felt this made sense. Keenan did, after all, have a history with the man and was the Chief Assistant D. A.

The scene was virtually a cliché. It was a poorly ventilated room, and the cigarette smoke hung over everyone. It was well after midnight, but the thermometer never moved. It was hot, and Keenan took off his gray pin-striped jacket and folded it over the back of his wooden straight-backed chair. The others followed suit. Somehow, it would help the rhythm, enhance the pace of the questioning to follow.

Sarenaro walked over to a windowsill behind me and turned on two tape recorders—one was a backup.

Keenan acknowledged the move and looked at his watch. It was 2:16 A.M. "Mr. Yukl," he began, "I'm sure you remember me. My name is John Keenan." Yukl nodded. Of course he remembered him.

Keenan managed a strained smile. It was to be, at best, an adversarial interview with a demented soul. Rapport was everything in Keenan's search for a confirmation from Yukl of what the cops already knew was the truth.

"And Mr. Yukl, I'm going to ask you some questions about the death of Karin Schlegel. Before I ask any questions, I want to advise you first that anything you say can be used against you. Do you understand that?"

"I was read them," Yukl responded soberly, "and I asked for an attorney."

"All right. Do you want to call an attorney?"

Yukl slouched down in his seat. "I don't have one. We don't have enough funds to, uh—"

"Do you want to call the Legal Aid Society?" Keenan asked.

"I don't know who to call."

"Would you like to call the Legal Aid Society?"

"Yes," he responded quickly, sitting up, "I would."

"All right," Keenan said, "here's a Manhattan Telephone Directory, which I give to you, which is a 1973–74 Manhattan Telephone Directory. This telephone here is number 741-5825, and it's now approximately two-twenty A.M. on Saturday morning, August twenty-fourth of 1974. Why don't you call—"

"Which one of these do I call?" Yukl was confused. "I mean, there's a whole—"

"The Legal Aid Society, criminal division," Keenan cut him off gently, "is what I assume you would want to call."

Charlie found it in the book. "Beekman 3-0250," he reported.

Keenan gave him the strained smile again. "Dial it."

"They cannot—you know—put the call through as dialed."

"Excuse me?" Keenan inquired.

"You know, they say they cannot put the call through as dialed."

"You have to punch a nine on that first."

Yukl tried, but still couldn't get the phone to work.

Keenan leaned over. "Would you like me to dial it for you?"

Yukl nodded. "Would you please?"

"Yeah, sure."

"As a matter of fact, would you—'cause I never—I don't know who to call or how to do this. But I do want an attorney first."

Finally Keenan dialed the number for him. By now it was 2:25.

"All right. I'm going to call the criminal defense division of the Legal Aid Society at Fifteen Park Row and in the phone book the number's listed as 374-1737, and for the record, obviously right in front of you are, uh, microphones, and what I'm saying to you and what you're saying here is being recorded, you understand that."

"Right, uh-huh."

Not surprisingly, at that hour, there was no answer from Legal Aid. Keenan put the receiver down. "Do you want to try and dial it yourself?"

"No, if you get no answer, uh—I can't get an answer either."

"Since no one is picking up," Keenan explained, "let me finish advising you of your rights."

Yukl nodded. Keenan continued, his voice level,

never rising above that of a normal conversation. He asked Yukl his questions in a soothing tone. For this brief moment of their two lives, Keenan acted the part of the father, the priest, the friend, and perhaps most important, the analyst.

"I started to tell you that anything you say could be used against you. Do you understand that?"

"Uh-huh."

"By that, do you mean yes?"

"Yes," Yukl responded, "yes."

"You realize that you have a right to remain silent?"

"Yes."

"Do you understand that?" It was the old Miranda routine, every DA's rules of engagement, and Keenan knew better than anyone how crucial it was.

"Yes," came Yukl's repeated reply.

"Do you understand that you have a right to have a lawyer?"

"Yes."

"Do you understand that if you can't afford a lawyer, that a lawyer will be provided for you?"

"Yes."

"Now you know all those things, you've been advised of those things before, is that right?"

"Right."

"By the police, here, is that correct?"

"Yes."

But where was Keenan leading Yukl at this hour? Where could he possibly go with the questions since Yukl had already asked for an attorney?

John Keenan was known downtown as a master of the game. He used to snicker at the young, bumptious assistant DAs who flowed in and out of his office each year on their way to the nickel-and-dime cases they thought (and later wished) were much bigger. "Never browbeat a guy," he would tell them. "You'll both lose the macho contest. Make the asshole comfortable, relax the son-of-a-bitch and he'll tell you part of the truth. If he's dumb enough to think you're his friend, and especially if he's tired, he'll come clean and you can clear another case."

But the proper tactics to be used now seemed extremely well defined—and limited. Yukl had clearly asked for an attorney.

Somehow, without hesitation or consultation, Keenan decided to proceed anyway, against logic, his own advice, and well-established case law. Charlie Yukl was nervous enough, or stupid enough, to think Keenan was his friend. Sitting there, chain-smoking, in his open sport shirt and khaki slacks, Charlie Yukl was also tired. And Keenan knew it. Besides, he knew that Yukl couldn't wait to tell him everything.

In Keenan's impatience, in his zeal for the confession he knew was forthcoming, he continued with the questioning. I tried to get his attention to talk to him, but Keenan put up his hands and motioned me to wait. I felt Keenan simply had to know the rules he was breaking.

"Now, we've tried to get you a lawyer," Keenan pressed on, "and were unable to get you a lawyer. In the past, my recollection is that a Mr. George Monaghan was your lawyer. Do you wish to call Mr. Monaghan?"

It was a rhetorical question. If Charlie retained anything after his prison years, it was a good memory. Sure, Monaghan made an incredibly good deal for him in 1968, but it cost him a lot of money, and Yukl had always thought—probably mistakenly—he could have done even better for his money.

"Most certainly not," Yukl quickly fired back. Now it was Yukl who offered the strained smile.

Keenan sighed. He knew what was coming. "You don't wish to call Mr. Monaghan. All right. Now, are you willing to talk to me even though we weren't able to get a lawyer for you?"

I again tried to motion to Keenan, who ignored me. He stared right at Yukl.

Yukl paused. "Ah, that depends on what questions are asked."

I sat up in my chair. I couldn't believe I had just heard what John Keenan had just said. Nothing depended on anything anymore. I couldn't understand what the hell Keenan was doing? I felt he was losing the case right before my eyes.

Once the man had asked for a lawyer, all questioning had to stop. Yukl had asked for one, and Keenan was still proceeding with the questioning. Unfortunately, it was clear to me that even a part-time paralegal secretary could get it all thrown out on appeal. Keenan was apparently somehow disregarding this incontrovertible fact, and he continued. "Well, let me ask the questions and you tell me whether you want to answer them or not."

"That's fair," Yukl answered. If only he knew *how* fair.

"All right," Keenan commenced. He handed Yukl a picture of Schlegel. "Do you know or did you know the woman shown in this picture, Karin Schlegel—when I say do you know her, have you ever seen her, in person, so far as you know?"

"Yes."

"You have?"

"Yes."

"Ah, and when have you seen her?"

"I saw her approximately, let me see now, three weeks ago this past coming Saturday. Three weeks ago Saturday."

"Three weeks ago this past coming Saturday?"

"I'm sorry, you know, three weeks ago last Saturday."

"All right," Keenan replied, looking at the calendar.

I was no longer sitting up. When Assistant District Attorney Kenny Klein looked into the room through an outside window, he saw me sitting at the table with my head in my hands. Something was very wrong. But Keenan was the boss. It was his show, his parole, and he was handling the interrogation.

Yukl was responsive. Keenan had first maneuvered him into admitting he knew Schlegel. That she had been to his apartment. That she came there in response to an ad in *Show Business*, the ad that said to contact Mr. Williamson.

"In particular," Keenan said, "I want to show you page fifteen of the Thursday, July 4, 1974, issue of *Show Business*, which I'm going to show you. I'm leaving it [on the table] as I'm talking to you—"

"Yes."

"And up on the upper left-hand corner of the page, under the heading 'Casting News' is a little box that says 'non-union films.' Would you look at that, please, Mr. Yukl, and read it to yourself?"

Yukl nodded. "That's the ad."

"Is that the ad that you placed in the paper?"

"That's the ad that *we* placed in the paper."

We? Now the game was starting. Yukl had decided to bluff Keenan. But John wasn't buying.

"The Mr. Williamson referred to in the ad at 120 Waverly Place, is that yourself?" he asked.

"No, that's not me," Charlie attempted. "He was the one that was going to help me with this thing, and he never bothered to, you know, he never went into it, he just took off."

Keenan looked across at Baeszler and exchanged a knowing glance.

"Do you know where he lives or where he could be reached, this Mr. Williamson?"

"No, sir, I don't." Yukl was still in control.

"Do you know his first name, this Mr. Williamson?"

Yukl shifted around in his seat, trying to maintain his own rhythm and pace. Seconds whizzed by as he desperately tried to come up with something believable. All he could think of was the name of a popular black actor.

"His first name, ahh, was, let's see now, was Fred Williamson."

It was almost laughable. He knew Yukl was bluffing now. He just wanted to manipulate Charlie a little more, to trap him in the big lie, to place him at 120 Waverly with Schlegel at the right time that Monday evening.

Yukl again admitted knowing Karin. He again admitted she had been to his apartment on one occasion before the night of the murder. Now Keenan steered the conversation back to the evening in question—August 19.

Yukl offered a series of strange and often conflicting statements. He was home. He wasn't home. He worked late at the Greeley and Hansen office in the Woolworth Building. He xeroxed questionnaires for a psychology class he was taking at Hunter College.

Keenan continued. "Now, when did you work again after Monday, August the nineteenth?"

"At night?" Yukl asked.

"Uh-huh."

"I didn't."

"You haven't been back since—"

"Well, I mean I haven't been back working nights. I—I came in on my own."

"Right, I understand you've been back to work during the days. Now, what time did you leave Greeley and Hansen at 233 Broadway the night of August nineteenth? This past Monday?"

"Approximately—uh, it was approximately eight-twenty-five or eight-thirty."

"Eight-twenty-five or eight-thirty you left there?"

"I left there."

"And where did you go after you left Greeley and Hansen?"

"Then I went out to deliver my own questionnaires that I had xeroxed."

"To where?"

"I was looking for married couples," Charlie explained. "So I just stopped people on the street near Washington Square Park and said, are you, you know, are you married, are you working, and here's a return envelope, would you kindly fill out the questionnaire and send it back."

"Uh-huh. And did you stop them on the street?"

"Yeah."

"Where? What neighborhood?"

"Uh, well, it was actually around my own neighborhood."

"Uh-huh. In other words, you took the subway up from the Woolworth Building, or did you take a bus, or did you walk?"

"No, I always take the subway."

"You took the subway from the Woolworth Building back up to the Greenwich Village area?"

"Right."

"And there in the Greenwich Village are—"

"Fifth Avenue."

"Fifth Avenue. Uh, around Washington Arch, around the arch there?"

"Right."

"Okay, now, how long did you stay giving out the questionnaires near Washington Square Park on lower Fifth Avenue?"

"About an hour, an hour and a half."

"All right. So that would take us roughly up to nine-thirty or ten, is that right?"

"Around there, sir."

"Somewhere around there. Then what did you do?"

"I went home."

"All right. And when you got home, who was home?"

"No one. Enken didn't get home until about eleven with Dawn her girlfriend."

Keenan was getting closer. Yukl lit another cigarette. He was lying. Now, it was just a matter of boxing him in.

"She came home with Dawn? Dawn and Enken both came back to your apartment?"

"That's right, about eleven, eleven-ten."

Keenan played along. "And how late did Dawn stay there?"

"Ah, I don't know 'cause Enken went out with the dog, you know, immediately after, and then we went to bed." Yukl began to stutter. "So she was there maybe, oh, I'd say maybe—twenty, maybe twenty-five minutes."

Keenan couldn't get Yukl to change the girlfriend alibi, so he tried the next best thing: to reacquaint Charlie with the roof of his building. But Yukl denied having been on it. Keenan changed tactics again. This time, he went for the big question.

"Now, I don't know whether the police told you this or not. Karin Schlegel received a telephone call at her home on Minetta Lane at about six in the evening, from a man saying he was you, and that she was to go over to your house at 120 Waverly Place for a nine o'clock appointment."

Yukl shifted around again in his chair. "They told me that," he mumbled.

"They did tell you that?"

"They told me that," Charlie said louder.

"Okay," Keenan acknowledged. "Now, I just wanted to make sure you knew that. Now," he said, "did you or did you not make such a phone call?"

Yukl wasted no time in responding. "I prefer to remain silent."

"All right," Keenan proceeded. "Now, did you see Karin Schlegel at all that night?"

How could Keenan still proceed? Yukl was no attorney, but he had uttered the magic words. My head was back in my hands. I was very distressed. It was now forty-five minutes into a session that should have been stopped within the first 120 seconds. From the moment Yukl had asked for an attorney everything he was saying could be considered *tainted*.

Outside the interrogation room, Enken Yukl was waiting. She had been driven over to the Thirteenth Precinct for her turn at the oak table. Somehow, even in this weather, she was cold, and she waited on the bench with a blanket wrapped firmly around her small body.

Keenan kept up the questioning. "Did you talk to Karin Schlegel that night?"

"I prefer to remain silent."

"A detective was over to see you on Thursday night, August twenty-second, during the evening, and he showed you, as I understand it, this same picture, or perhaps another print of the same picture, but the same picture of Karin Schlegel. Is that correct?"

"That's correct."

"Did he show you such a picture?"

"Yes, he did."

"Same picture, or a print of the picture?"

"Looks like it."

"All right. And did he ask you if you knew the girl in the picture?"

"Yes, he did."

"And what did you tell him?"

"My answer was from that picture I did not know the girl. And I did not recognize her from that picture."

"All right. But tonight you do."

"I still don't think she looks like that picture."

"But you—you do recognize these letters."

"I do recognize the letters."

"And you do recognize that she did come and see you on August tenth, and that you also saw her sometime in July. Now, did you have anything to do with killing her?"

"I prefer to remain silent on that without advice of counsel."

"Now, did you use a necktie? To strangle her?"

"I prefer to remain silent."

"Now, you should know that the police interviewed a woman by the name of Nancy Pauley, who told the police that when she was seeking employment as a singer, she called your number and spoke to a man by the name of Yogi Freitag."

"That's my—that was my professional name."

"And she told the police that on the last occasion that she saw Yogi Freitag, that she, Nancy Pauley, came to Freitag's apartment at Waverly Place at about six-ten in the evening. She found a note on the door for her to come in. That you, Freitag, were out for milk, and that you'd come back. She told the police that she went into the apartment and waited for you. And after two or three minutes the bathroom door opened, and you came out in the nude and acted surprised that she was there. Do you remember that happening?"

"No, I don't."

"You don't remember that happening?"

"I don't remember Nancy Pauley."

Keenan was losing patience. It was nearly three A.M.

"Okay, you don't remember Nancy Pauley. Mr. Yukl, let me say this to you. You are taking a course in psychology—"

Yukl nodded.

"And you're not an unintelligent person. In fact, you're probably a rather intelligent person. Now you know and I know you are on parole for another killing similar to this."

"Yes."

"You know that and I know that. You know and I know that the other girl that was killed, Suzanne Reynolds, was killed much in the same manner as was Karin Schlegel. You know that and I know that. Is that right?"

"Uh, if you say so."

"Well, I'm sure that Tuesday you knew that Karin Schlegel's body had been found on the roof of your building. Is that right?"

"Tuesday, yes." Yukl paused. "Where is my wife?"

Keenan held up his hands reassuringly. "Your wife is two rooms away. She is not under arrest. She is being spoken to by detectives, and I intend to speak to her in a little while."

"She's not . . ."

"She's not what?"

"I mean, she's not under arrest or anything?"

"No, she is not under arrest."

"She's not implicated in any way?"

"She's not under arrest. Now, I was starting to talk to you about the fact that you're taking psychology and this other case." Keenan leaned closer to Yukl. "I want to ask you this, and I want to be just as frank with you as I've been since I started to chat with you. Do you feel that you're in any need of psychiatric help? Now I don't mean by that, and I don't mean to imply by that, that uh, you are psychotic, or that you don't know right from wrong, or that you don't understand what you're doing. But all human beings have certain motivations, as you're aware. Is that right?"

"That's right."

"Certain drives, certain things that stimulate them, certain things that, uh, cause them to act, perhaps to act differently than they normally act. You understand that, you know that, right?"

"Yes."

"Now, do you feel you need any help?"

It struck me that it was a perfect question for Charlie.

"I think everybody needs help."

"Do you feel you particularly, Charles Yukl, need any help in this area?"

"I prefer not to comment."

"Excuse me?"

"I prefer not to comment on that at this time."

"Now, when you were talking to the lieutenant upstairs earlier, I believe he asked you where the body was, when she was strangled in your apartment."

"I thought maybe he did."

"Do you recall telling him something to the effect that that was between you and your wife?"

"No, I said that anything that I wanted to speak to my wife about, I did not, you know, I did not want him there when I spoke to my wife. And that, you know, didn't have anything to do with his question about the relation of the body, uh, whatever body there would have been found, if any."

"Well—"

"It was in regard to your, you know, statement about making a personal decision, which I felt I did not want to make any decision without any representation, legal representation."

"Well, where was her body in your apartment?"

"I have no comment on that without representation."

"Do you deny that the body was in your apartment?"

"I have no comment without representation."

"Do you deny killing her?"

"I prefer to remain silent."

"Ah, now, you received a telephone call at home on Friday night, August twenty-third, from a woman caller, I understand. Is that correct?"

"I don't know, who was the woman caller?"

"Well—"

"To my knowledge, I don't know, I get phone calls quite a bit."

"Did you not tell a detective that you got a telephone call on Friday night—tonight, in other words, before midnight—"

"Oh, I'm sorry. Tonight's Friday night."

"Yeah, all right. It's Friday night into Saturday morning. Now, all right, take—"

"Right, yes. I had gotten a call."

"All right. It's now Saturday morning. On Friday night—"

"Yes, I did get a call. I mean, uh, I'm not sure what time it was."

"All right. Now that person that called you was a policewoman."

"Uh-huh."

It wasn't working. Keenan called in policewoman Natale and played Yukl the tape of the setup call from the Beverly Hotel. Yukl's expression didn't change. He was unimpressed.

Natale left the room and Keenan returned to flattery. "Now, Charlie, we agreed that you're not an unintelligent person. You're an intelligent person. Who did she go to see if she didn't go to see you? Who would say that he was you if it wasn't you?"

"I have—"

"Why was her body found on your roof?"

"I have no comment."

"What do you mean, you have no comment?"

"I—I have—I have nothing to say; I prefer to remain silent without the advice of legal counsel."

"Do you have anything else you wish to say?"

"No, I prefer to remain silent."

Keenan took this as his cue and walked out of the room.

Yukl was led back to another room of the precinct. I sat there, frozen in disbelief. There was nothing I could do now except wait the few moments it took to bring Enken Yukl into the room for her turn with due process.

CHAPTER NINETEEN

As if by instinct, Enken Yukl sat down in the seat her husband had just vacated. I advised her of her rights. Unlike her husband, she waived them and the questions began.

It was 3:15 in the morning. Keenan had stepped outside with Inspector Nicastro. Yukl waited in a third room, well into his second pack of cigarettes.

I felt the interview with Enken was a waste of time. Besides, I had not yet fully recovered from the Keenan-Yukl interrogation. What could Enken possibly add to the story, except extraneous, and perhaps intentionally false or misleading information?

It was Mickey Mouse time, a gratuitous intrusion— but the interview with Yukl's wife was still considered a necessary evil. Enken had always been a mystery to the police. Eight years earlier, after the Suzanne Reynolds slaying, she had managed an alibi. And now, within the first few minutes, she was managing another one. It was called laundry.

She was out doing three loads of laundry at her girlfriend Dawn's house. She claimed not to have returned to Waverly Place until eleven o'clock.

Enken came well prepared with a memory lapse.

"Who was home when you got home?" I asked.

"My husband."

"And what, if anything, did you talk about?"

"Nothing. In particular. I don't remember."

"Did you see any blood in your apartment?"

"No."

"Now did you have any conversation with your husband about Karin Schlegel?"

"No."

This was going nowhere.

I tried to be more direct. Enken admitted that she knew about the photography session but denied having been there.

"He usually tried to schedule them so that I would *not* be home," she explained.

"What was the reason for that?"

"Because I don't care for it and I would just be in the way and be uncomfortable."

I thought for a minute. "Now, quite frankly, are you aware of any sexual deviation on the part of your husband?"

"No."

"I want to tell you in the interest of fairness that we have spoken to a young lady who says she went to your apartment and your husband answered the door. When the bell rang, he told the young lady his name was Yogi Freitag. Does that name mean anything to you?"

"Yes. He used that."

"And when he answered the door he was naked. Are you aware of that?"

"No. I am not."

"Has that ever happened, to your knowledge?"

"Not that I know of, no." Enken must have known of this episode from the 1966 case.

"Does it surprise you that I tell you that happened?"

"Yes."

"Now, Mrs. Yukl, your husband was shown a photograph of Karin Schlegel here, and he now says he knows who she is."

She nodded. There was a long pause as she waited for the next question.

"How would you account for that?"

"I don't know, you would have to ask him." Enken became tense.

"Is there any reason why he would not tell the truth to the detective in front of you?"

"I don't know," she said, raising her voice. "I don't know."

"You understand that the killing of Karin Schlegel is almost exactly like the killing of Suzanne Reynolds in 1966?"

"So I have been told, yes."

"You were aware of the killing of Suzanne Reynolds?"

"Of course I was."

"And you are aware of this killing?"

"Yes."

"Did you discuss the killing of Karin Schlegel with your husband?"

"Yes."

"What did he say?"

"That he didn't do it."

"Did you ask him if he did it?"

"Yes, I did."

"Do you think it was just a coincidence that her body was found thirty-five feet, approximately, from your apartment?"

"Yes." That wasn't a big lie: it was just silly. It was the most ludicrous of responses. Enken looked up at me for a brief moment. At another time or place we both might have laughed. But at four o'clock in the morning it seemed as necessary as it was ridiculous to continue playing the game.

"I want also to tell you in the interest of fairness that your husband called Karin Schlegel that night."

"Yes. So the lieutenant has told me."

"We know she went to your apartment, and we know she was dragged from your apartment, and put on the fifth-floor landing, on the roof."

"Uh-huh."

"There's blood that tells us that."

Enken looked up again. "Yeah. So?"

"Now," I soothed, "would you like to tell us how that happened?"

"No, because I don't know."

"You have no idea how that happened?"

"No."

The questions and answers now came in rapid fire.

"Do you have a normal relationship with your husband?"

"Yes."

"Does he tell you everything?"

"I'm assuming so."

"Do you tell him everything?"

"Yes."

"Do you have a normal sexual relationship with your husband?"

This was a hard question for Enken. She stiffened. "I, uh, sort of, yes."

I was getting a little closer. "What does 'sort of' mean? I don't mean to pry, but . . ."

"I mean it's, er, er, it's, it's normal, yes."

"But what does 'sort of' mean?"

She was getting irritated. "Well, it's, er. What difference does it make?"

"Well," I explained, "it might make a lot of difference considering the fact that this is the second girl who has died very near your apartment."

"Yes, it was normal. What I consider normal."

"What do you consider normal?"

"What we had." We were going nowhere again.

"Well what did you have?"

"I really don't want to go into that."

I changed the subject. "You know, there's a trail of blood leading from the floor on which you live right up to the roof of the—where the body was found."

"No, I don't. I didn't see it."

"You didn't see it?" I asked, trying to seem surprised. "No."

"When did you first find out that this girl was dead on the roof?"

"Tuesday."

"When did your husband first tell you about it?"

"Tuesday."

"He was the one who told you?"

"Yes."

"How?"

"On the telephone."

"He called you at work?"

"Yes."

I kept at it. "Let me see . . . You say your husband got home at ten-thirty and you got back at eleven?"

"Yes."

"So if we find blood or if there is a trail of blood from your apartment up to the roof, someone else was living in your apartment and did something to the poor girl."

Enken grew silent. "I don't know."

"Mrs. Yukl," I said strongly, "you understand that we are not just talking to you."

"I realize that." She sighed.

"We're talking to you about yourself as well."

"Yes," she repeated, "I realize that."

"You want to start all over again and tell me what happened on Monday?"

"It *is* the truth," she started. "I've been telling you nothing *but* the truth. What else do you want from me?"

"Just the truth."

Enken started to cry. "I have been telling you the truth. I have witnesses where I was. My girlfriend was there, her boyfriend was there. She met me outside the building. I mean what more do you want from me?"

What I wanted from Enken I already knew I could not have. But I felt compelled to let her know the score.

"In 1966 did your husband tell you he killed Suzanne Reynolds?"

"Yes, he did."

"When did he tell you that?"

"At the station."

"Did he tell you right away?"

"No."

I waited a moment. "Did he tell you tonight that he killed Karin Schlegel?"

"No," she said softly.

"Do you understand that your husband is going to be charged with the murder of Karin Schlegel?"

"I understand that, yes."

"Do you understand that your husband is on parole?"

"Yes, I do."

"I'm telling you again, Mrs. Yukl, again in the interest of fairness, that there is no question that your husband called up Karin Schlegel and made an appointment for her at nine o'clock to photograph her for a Lifebuoy soap commercial, for a print ad, and he wanted to pay her . . ."

Enken nodded.

"Between twenty-five and thirty-five dollars. And I'm telling you in the interest of fairness that we know, not only about the conversation on the phone but that she went there. And I'm also going to tell you in the interest of fairness that the medical examiner indicates that the girl, Karin Schlegel, died at about ten o'clock at night and was found thirty-five feet from your apartment with a trail of blood from the fourth floor to where she was found. Now can you tell us anything about that?"

"No. I cannot." Enken wasn't budging.

"Do you think that it was all just a coincidence that this happened?"

"I don't know anything anymore. I am—I assumed it was coincidence. I still do, because I believe in my husband."

The biggest lie of our encounter.

I pulled out a photo of the Schlegel body.

"Now," I said, "I want you as an intelligent woman to look hard at this picture, and take into consideration all the facts that exist in this case, and consider the fact that you know, better than anybody, that your husband strangled and cut up and viciously assaulted Suzanne Reynolds. Because I tell you that this case is going to be presented to a jury and they are going to judge ultimately the innocence or guilt of your husband and perhaps any possible implication that you may have in this. Now, I ask you to purge yourself for once, finally, and tell us the truth about this girl, because the marks, the physical evidence, is immutable. It leads inexorably to the conclusion that the people inside apartment 4F at 120 Waverly Place killed Karin Schlegel."

Enken looked up. Her face turned flush. "People?"

"Do you understand what I said?"

She began to stutter for the first time. "I heard you say it, but I dis—I beg to diff-differ with you."

I would not let up. "I'm giving you one opportunity to purge yourself of this killing."

"I haven't done anything," she pleaded. "I have nothing to do with that."

This was all too much for Baeszler. He had remained silent through the interrogation, but could no longer contain himself. He began to shake his head. "Do you really, truly believe, sincerely believe, is there any doubt in your mind that your husband didn't do this?"

"I don't know." This from the woman who three minutes earlier believed in her husband.

"You don't know?"

"No. I don't know."

Now it was Baeszler's turn. "What are your feelings? Is it believable?"

"What?"

"That this occurred in your apartment, is it believable?"

"I don't know," she offered finally. "It's possible, anything is possible."

Baeszler then excused himself from the room and went outside to sit with Yukl. I continued the questions, but was making no progress.

Ten minutes later, I looked up. Keenan was standing at the window giving me a hand sign to end the interview.

"Thank you, Mrs. Yukl," I said. "End of statement." I walked out of the room.

"I just heard that he's ready to make a statement," Keenan told me.

A few minutes earlier, while waiting for his wife's interview to end, Yukl had volunteered to Don Baeszler and Sergeant Bob Goren, another detective, present during the interrogation, that he wanted to make a deal—he would confess in return for receiving psychiatric help.

Enken was ushered out of the room and briefly passed her husband, who was now on the way back in. "Did you do it?" she whispered to him.

"I . . . I don't remember," Charlie mumbled.

"Well," she said, convinced of his guilt, "I guess that settles that."

It was 4:08 in the morning as Yukl resumed his place in the interrogation room.

"Now, Mr. Yukl, as I understand it, you wanted to chat with me?" Keenan began.

"Right."

"Okay, and you wanted, you decided that you wanted to have it taped, is that right?"

"Er—yes," Yukl stumbled. "On an informal basis."

"Okay," Keenan said in a fatherly tone. "You tell us anything you want to tell us about the taping or the nontaping and anything else. You just tell us what you want to tell us."

"Well, this is—er . . ." Yukl was struggling with his words.

"You tell us anything you want to tell us," Keenan repeated.

"All right," Yukl said, and looked over at Sergeant Goren. "Well, what was your name?"

"Bob Goren."

"That's Sergeant Goren," Keenan confirmed the identification.

Yukl nodded. "Sergeant Goren. Right. Well, I had a talk with Sergeant Goren as well as the other two gentlemen."

The identification continued. "The other two gentlemen, whom you looked over at, Lieutenant Yuknes and Detective Baeszler?" Keenan asked.

"Yes. Lieutenant Yuknes and Baeszler. I'm not concerned with, er, well, let's put it this way, er, I believe that there's a double issue here that I think I have to resolve. You know, one, from the basic ethical standpoint, you know, what I am going to be capable of, you know, doing once I get back out in society again. Er, I think it's a definite, definite, er, well, I believe it's a, you know, it's a—see, a definite, so, you know, see, a medical problem."

"Now, when you say medical problem—"

"No," Yukl interrupted. "When I said medical, I meant psychological."

"With whom?"

"With me."

"Okay," Keenan said. "Go ahead."

Yukl didn't want to proceed without covering himself. "That's, you know, again I emphasize this is just an informal discussion and I do not expect to see this bounced back on me, because if it is, it will just reinforce my previous experiences. Er, while—"

"Now, when you say—go ahead, you just talk."

"Okay."

"Go ahead. I don't want to ask you anything, you just talk."

"Er, I'm—well, my—"

"Other than I'm going to ask you things to clarify things."

"That's all right," Yukl agreed. "No, that's okay. I have a double concern here. One is for my own personal benefit and then again I also have a concern for the, you know, for the basic benefit of others, and I truly believe that if I would go the way—you know, if I would tend to take the or take the, let's see now, take the, let's see now, take the, let's see now, take the criminal route."

"If you were to take the criminal route?" Keenan asked.

"Yes, if I were to take—yes."

"By the way." Keenan paused. "Let me just ask you something. You do stutter, right?"

"Oh yes, I have always stuttered."

"And I don't mean to in any way demean—" Keenan apologized.

"No, that's not derogatory, I know that," Yukl countered.

"But go ahead," Keenan continued. "So if you were to take the criminal route—"

"Er, all right, if I were to take the criminal route, all right, granted I would go back to prison. My concern is what would that accomplish other than security purposes? Er, it would do nothing for me personally because you can't get help in prisons. I've been that route. Er, I wondered if there is a way or if there is an alternative route that may be able to be taken whereas I, you know, would be able to be guaranteed the medical help that is required so that I could become, well, not become, because I am productive now in many ways, it's just that it doesn't always remain the same, you know, it's not—I was wondering whether there is an alternative route where I could be guaranteed that I would receive the medical help that I needed in a regular medical institution under licensed medical care. I'm not talking about a bunch of hoax, because they're all over the damn place. I'm, you know, number one, you know, I am mainly concerned with me because I don't like what's happening any more than anyone else does. I'm mainly concerned with my—I'm also not only concerned with me but also with the wife, you know."

"When you say the wife you mean your wife, Enken Yukl?" Keenan asked.

"Yes." Yukl nodded. "My wife."

"Is that right?"

"My wife who is, you know, she's a wonderful, wonderful person and I know that she'll stick with me no matter what happens which, when I, when I, you know, when I come out again, if I take the criminal route when I come out again, what have I got? What guarantee do I have that this, you know, that whatever is happening is not going to reoccur? Er, you could look at this from the standpoint of society where somebody else may suffer and I don't think it's necessary—you know, when I come back out, if I go back to prison just under normal criminal proceedings, you know, what the heck happens if something like this reoccurs? You know, you can always solve the case—"

"You mean the death of another girl?" Keenan asked.

"Yeah . . . The death of another person who, you know, or whatever, er, you know, I know you people can always find out who did it, but it seems an awful waste to—you know."

"All right, now," Keenan said. "You asked to talk to me?"

"Right."

"And your primary background is in music, is that right?"

It was now ten minutes into the statement session and Keenan and Yukl were still talking about the possibilities of getting psychiatric help.

But the purpose was to get Yukl's confession, and get it right. And we couldn't do it without first getting Yukl to waive his rights. He had already—and specifically—asked for a lawyer on a number of occasions that night.

I quickly scrawled a note to him. "Get him to waive

his rights. Get him to waive!" Keenan glanced down at the note. "Please listen to me, Mr. Yukl," Keenan continued. "You've asked for a lawyer."

"Right."

"Now, under the law, since you've asked for a lawyer, under the present law, what you're telling me, what you're telling us, we can't use against you and you know that, I'm sure."

"No, I *don't* know that. I'm taking you at your word."

"Under the law, under the present law today, August twenty-fourth, 1974, if you ask for a lawyer and you're in custody, and you are in custody, we can't use against you in a court what you're telling us. Now that's the law."

"All right."

"And I'm putting that down on the tape recorder. Now, what I want to know is this, before I get to the question of helping you, I got to know, do you need help?"

"Yes, I do."

"All right." Keenan moved on. "Did you kill her?"

"Yes, I did."

"When I say her I mean Karin Schlegel."

"Karin Schlegel."

"The girl in the picture?"

"Right."

"The girl in the picture that Detective Baeszler initialed a couple of hours ago."

"Right."

"All right."

"If I may add here that, you know, these statements that I am making have been made under other detectives telling me that you are a person of your word, that you are reliable—"

"I've told you—"

"I mean," Yukl almost stuttered, "you can understand my reluctance because—"

"Mr. Yukl," Keenan interrupted. But Yukl continued.

"I've spent six years in an institution where—"

"Mr. Yukl . . . Mr. *Yukl*, I prefaced everything that I told you—"

"Yes, you did."

"By telling you that under the law as it exists now, today, and I keep looking at the calendar because I want to be sure I'm accurate, August twenty-fourth, 1974, any statement that you make, having asked for your attorney, we can't use against you."

"All right."

I looked over at Keenan. What the hell was happening? I felt that Keenan had given away the store. Yukl then gave Keenan a detailed play-by-play of the events leading up to the murder, the murder itself, and the aftermath.

It was a great confession, with only one, nagging, nonnegotiable exception. It was inadmissible. And it had lasted for nearly an hour.

Keenan then changed the subject back to psychiatric care. "All right. Now, you wanted, besides talking to me, you wanted to ask something of me and I want to be perfectly fair with you, I want to know what you want."

"I want to know that I can obtain medical help," Yukl said without hesitation. "In other words, I don't want to go the route going back to prison because I don't think that's going to help me or is going to help anybody."

"Let me say this to you, Mr. Yukl, I'm not the governor of the state nor am I someone who controls the purse strings of the community. I'm the chief assistant district attorney in New York County. You indicated to me, and Sergeant Goren came upstairs and told Assistant Chief Inspector Meehan and Inspector Nicastro and me of your desire for psychiatric help."

"Right. I want to find out why this happened to make sure it won't happen again."

"I tell you," Keenan promised, "that I will do everything within my power to assure that you get psychiatric help to assist you in understanding why these motivations and drives occur, and to cure you of them. I think that I speak for Assistant Chief Inspector Meehan and Inspector Nicastro when I say they also will do the same thing." He looked at both men.

"Yes," said Meehan.

"Yes," echoed Nicastro, nodding obediently.

"And," Keenan added, "you have indicated that Legal Aid is, at least at this point, your desired counsel and I'll communicate with the Legal Aid Society and I will tell them of your desire for psychiatric help and I'll permit them, as soon as I can have these tape recordings rerecorded. I will permit the Legal Aid Society to hear these tape recordings themselves, and I don't think there's any requirement of law that I do that, but I'll do that so that they can, together with the district attorney, the courts, and the police, attempt to devise and figure out some way that you can get the proper supervision psychiatrically and that you can hopefully be cured psychiatrically."

Yukl picked up on it. "Because that's not available in the prison system."

"Well, that I don't know," Keenan said.

"But this is what we were discussing."

"That I don't know for a fact."

"But . . . I—I can tell you," Yukl argued.

"No, no," Keenan soothed. "I don't quarrel with you. I'm not trying to argue with you, I don't know whether it be the corrections system of the state of New York, any system that exists if it's run by the government can be improved . . . and can be changed to meet individuals and to meet conditions, that's why agencies exist, and I tell you that I will make every effort and do whatever I can and I will assist your lawyers in securing psychiatric help for you."

Yukl thought he was making progress. "This is what you had said because when we discussed this earlier, we were discussing that there are two routes that I can go, either I can go through the criminal route, which is go back to prison, which is—well, you know—or to go into the, take the other route, the medical route and come out ahead of the game."

"I'm saying, I'm saying to you the likelihood—and I'm not a psychiatrist—the likelihood is it's going to have to be institutionalization and psychiatric care."

The session ended at 4:59 A.M. Criminal Tape A4927 was taken from the recording machine and logged. As I left the room, I couldn't help thinking we should have burned the tape. The recorded confession was, under the circumstances, totally useless.

I went outside the interrogation room. Baeszler was already there, waiting for me, his arms folded in an uncharacteristic manner across his chest.

"You saw it, Don. You were in there. Without a legitimate confession," I said, "we've got no case."

Baeszler felt my frustration. I stood there for a moment and stared at him.

It was five A.M. I was getting ready to leave when Kenny Klein came up to me. He had walked down from a party which was already in full swing upstairs in the squad commander's office. Nicastro and a host of cops were all up there, celebrating their Yukl confession "victory."

Klein had a troubled look on his face. "What really happened in there?" he said, pointing to the interrogation room. "Everybody is upstairs patting each other on the back and you look like shit."

"The entire confession is inadmissible. It's tainted. It reeks. By the way," I quickly added, "where is Keenan?"

"He's upstairs with the rest of them," Klein said. "At the party."

"Okay," I muttered. "Let's go see the heroes."

I found Keenan a few minutes later on the second floor, standing outside the office door holding a paper cup of Scotch, still being congratulated on his performance.

When he saw me, he held out his hand in a fatherly way. "Hi," he said effusively. "C'mon in, have a drink."

I pulled away from his grasp. "I want to talk to you," I said firmly.

"Sure," he answered. "But let's stick around for a few minutes here. Then we can talk."

"No, John," I said, much louder. "I want to talk *now*. There's nothing to celebrate."

I took him by the arm and we walked into an adjacent, glass-walled office. I closed the door.

"Why did you do it?"

"Do what?" he replied.

I blew up. "John, what you did down there has tainted the case and everything else we get in the case from now on. Why did you tell him we wouldn't use anything he said against him when he was ready to tell us everything anyway? The guy was ready to waive his rights. The son-of-a-bitch was ready to make a spontaneous statement!"

"All right, all right," he tried to soothe me. "There's no judge in this city that would keep his statement out of the record."

"You mean to tell me you're going to use the statement after you told him you *wouldn't . . . couldn't*?"

"Absolutely," he said, almost laughing. "This is the case where we're gonna reverse Miranda!"

I tried to control my reaction. "John, why didn't you give him the chance to make a legally admissible statement?" I said calmly.

He didn't answer.

Then I lost it and screamed. "You gave Yukl a free pass! A goddamn free pass!"

CHAPTER TWENTY

At 10:30 the same morning—Saturday—a tired Don Baeszler took a nervous Charlie Yukl down to the Tombs for booking.

At this point Baeszler was just going through the procedural motions. He was convinced, as I was, that the case was lost and that Yukl would eventually be sprung on what the press liked to call a technicality—actually a Fifth Amendment infringement, a violation of his rights against self-incrimination. Baeszler said nothing as they entered the building.

Yukl remembered the Manhattan House of Detention—its official name—all too well. He hated the place. And apparently nothing had changed since his last visit in 1966. The building, constructed in 1838, was overcrowded, the air was foul, the windows sealed, and the ventilating fans were broken. The Tombs had always been a center of controversy. Since 1970, prison riots were commonplace, inmates often took guards hostage, set fire to bedding and furniture, smashed windows. A few months before Yukl's arrival, a suit filed by the Legal Aid Society had moved Federal Judge Morris Lasker to order the city either to improve the Tombs or to close it.

But on this hot August weekend morning, nothing

had changed at the Tombs. It was still open for business. Yukl did not relish his upcoming stay. He was fidgety in the heat, and often looked quickly around the holding room. A half hour later, as he was being photographed and fingerprinted, he decided to talk to Baeszler.

"Hey, how's my wife Enken doing?" he asked.

"Oh," Baeszler answered, "she's all right. Nothing to worry about. She's probably still with the police."

Yukl sat up quickly in his chair.

"What?" He glared at Baeszler. "What's she doing with the police?" It was the first time that anyone had seen Yukl get angry.

"There's a search warrant for your apartment," Baeszler calmly replied, "and the police are in there now."

"What are they searching for?" Yukl asked. "I *told* you guys," he insisted, "I already got rid of all the evidence."

Don Baeszler perked up immediately. He wasn't a lawyer, but he knew what had just happened. Once a defendant asks for a lawyer, all questioning must cease until he waives that right to an attorney. There's just one exception to this hard and fast rule—if he simply blurts out a spontaneous statement.

Without realizing it, Yukl had just made that spontaneous statement, and was ready to continue talking. If Baeszler played it right, and didn't turn it into a formal Q and A, this could be the ballgame.

"What are you talking about?" Baeszler asked, feigning confusion.

"You know what I mean," Yukl said, almost indignantly. "You know *exactly* what I'm talking about. I got rid of the necktie, her clothing, her pocketbook, and the table. . . ."

"Table?" Baeszler asked, continuing to play dumb.

"Yeah, *table*," Yukl said. "You know, the table that made the mark on her back."

Baeszler didn't speak another word. He knew he had what he needed, and just looked right at Yukl. A slow, demonic grin almost overcame him.

At that very moment, twenty-five miles away in Bergen County, they were burying Karin Schlegel.

The newspapers were already full of the story of Charles Yukl. PAROLED KILLER HELD IN SLAYING read the headline in that morning's *New York Daily News*. All of the stories mentioned that Yukl had been a model prisoner, incarcerated for a similar homicide, and released fourteen months ago.

None of the hundred mourners at Our Savior Lutheran Church had heard of Yukl. And no one talked about him. Instead, in a quiet ceremony officiated by Pastor Locke—he had canceled his planned trip—Denise tearfully placed a small bouquet of white flowers on her sister Karin's coffin. Irene sat next to her own sister, who had flown in from Germany. Just before the ceremony began, Irene walked up to the coffin, adding a single red rose to a spray of red roses.

Charlotte Schwartz saw the newspaper on the morning of the funeral. "I still can't believe that it's my Karin," she sobbed. "But somehow I knew that something had happened to my Karin—something terrible and final," she told a friend named Sheri. It seemed important for Charlotte to recite the events that led up to the awful discovery.

"A chill went through my body and I became incoherent, which of course didn't help her mother too much. I hadn't heard from Karin but . . . When I hung up, I, I went into the kitchen to eat something and put on the radio and there it was—a description of Karin lying naked on a rooftop in the Village. I'll never forget that picture I had of her in my mind—I let out a scream, but that scream would have had to continue my entire lifetime for it to be satisfied. The whole thing is so cruel and ridiculous. It's a nightmare," she said. "Her mother's grief is a nightmare, the whole thing gets me sick.

"The strangest thing is that Karin always wanted the spotlight. She was really becoming a good actress, and that is how she died—in the spotlight. Front page of the *Post,* and the *News,* articles in almost every paper, including *El Diario.* Everyone in New York knows the name and face of Karin Schlegel . . . when it was in the papers on the day of the funeral, it was like looking at the reviews of a famous actress on opening night.

"I loved this girl. She was innocent about life and looked at its beauty in a special, quiet way. That's why she loved acting so much: it was a chance to open up her mouth because she was very shy; she used acting to become the person she could never be—a bigmouth like you or me! I remember going for Chinese food with her and she said, 'I love the colors of Chinese food.' Who looks at colors of food? That's what she was like and I got used to it."

I was sleeping when Don Baeszler called me and told me what happened at the Tombs.

"That's very good, Don," I said. "See me first thing Monday morning."

Normally I would have jumped at this lucky opportunity. But I was concerned. Don Baeszler was a sharp, savvy cop who knew what he was doing. Cops like Baeszler know what it takes to get a conviction. And while I had never questioned his integrity, I was now worried that Baeszler might have been tempted, out of loyalty to me and a sense of outrage, to try to remedy the situation on his own.

A double negative in this case would simply not do. I was determined to avoid my own personal martyrdom.

The prescription was to move slowly toward a confrontation with my trusted friend, Don Baeszler. Above all else, I had to verify that Yukl had in fact given Baeszler the statement as described to me, and that he'd done so spontaneously.

Don was at my desk at nine A.M. Monday, ready to talk. He was excited.

I began by questioning him, in extreme detail, about the time period between when I left the precinct to when Baeszler left the precinct with Yukl. I also had to know exactly what transpired between them after they left the precinct and before Yukl made his statement.

"What time did you take him downtown from the precinct?"

"We left about nine-thirty in the morning," Don answered.

"Did you talk to Yukl before the two of you left the precinct?"

"Yeah." Baeszler nodded.

"What did you talk about?"

Baeszler was growing irritated. "I asked him if he wanted a cup of coffee."

"That's it?" I asked.

"Yeah," he said curtly. "That's it."

"Don," I said, my voice rising, "were you in the room with him for about three hours after I left the precinct?"

"I was in and out . . . yeah," Baeszler confirmed. "Yeah, I was mostly with him during that period."

"All right," I said. "Let's just cut the bullshit. I want to know in detail what you said to him and what he said to you." And then I threw him a cross-examination curve: "How tall are you?"

Baeszler didn't flinch. "Oh, about six foot five."

"Don't you know?" I grilled him. "Are you six feet four and a half or six feet five and a half?"

"No," Baeszler shot right back. "I'm six-five."

"What do you weigh?"

"Two thirty-five." Baeszler smiled. He liked the game.

"Bullshit," I yelled. "You're at least two fifty-five." I wasn't smiling.

Baeszler got a little angry. He was very conscious of his weight. "Okay," he conceded. "So, I'm two fifty-five."

"Okay," I continued. "Now how tall is the defendant?"

"About five foot six."

"And what does he weigh?"

Baeszler stopped me. "What the hell is this shit?"

"Shut up," I said, stopping him. "What the hell does Yukl weigh?"

"About one thirty, one forty . . ."

"Now, were you sitting down or standing with Yukl after I left the precinct?"

"I . . . I . . . I don't know," Baeszler said, fumbling for the answer.

"Why can't you remember what happened two days ago?"

"All right," he said, clearly rattled. "Give me a chance to think. . . ."

"Was the defendant seated at all times?"

"Yes," Baeszler said confidently. "When I was talking to him, he was seated."

"How about you? Were you seated?"

"Most of the time I was seated while we were having coffee and smoking cigarettes."

"All right," I said slowly. "Now tell me what you said to the defendant and what he said to you from the beginning, and don't embarrass yourself by saying that for a total of three hours all this asshole talked about was a cup of coffee."

Baeszler still didn't understand why I was going through all this. But then, in admirable detail, he laid out the conversation, in which Yukl had told him how badly he wanted psychiatric help and that he blamed society for not taking care of him—that he was a person who was crying out for help and not receiving the proper assistance.

After another series of staccato questions, I walked Baeszler through the chronology of events, forcing him to rethink everything that happened at the precinct, on the ride down to the Tombs, and up to the moment when Yukl made the unsolicited statement. Don Baeszler was slowly starting to get my message. I had taken him by surprise, talking to him as I would to an adversary witness, forcing him to recall events in detail and in rapid succession.

He had answered all of my questions. I now felt unburdened by his responses. My misgivings were laid to rest. Don Baeszler was telling the truth.

There was no longer a question of truth or falsity, but now one of legal admissibility. The ultimate question now was whether a judge would construe Keenan's free pass to include the unsolicited spontaneous statement later made by Yukl. Unfortunately, no answers were forthcoming.

It was time to proceed with the investigation. I sent detectives over to Yukl's office to retrieve the table. Although Yukl spoke of the table to Keenan and it was thus inadmissible as evidence, my hope was that we could follow the rule of inevitable discovery which is accepted in New York—the key here being that the police, in the normal course of their criminal investigation, would have found the table anyway.

The next morning, Keenan came into my office. We were preparing to put the case before the grand jury, a required procedure. In order for a felony case to be tried in New York, a grand jury must first hand down an indictment stating that there is legally sufficient evidence for a trial.

"I understand you're going to the grand jury soon," Keenan said. "What are you going to put in?"

"We're going with the statement Yukl made to Baeszler, the table with the mark on it, and the photographs of Schlegel with the marks on her back."

"Wait a minute," Keenan said, surprised. "What about the confession Yukl made to me?"

I advised Keenan that we would not be using the Yukl confession. As I did in every case of this kind, I picked up the phone and dialed the home of the victim's closest relatives. Officially, I represented the People of the State of New York. But I also saw myself as the Schlegels' lawyer.

I explained to both Alfred and Irene Schlegel what they could expect to happen in the next few weeks and months, and that I would keep them informed as to the progress of the case. "Please come in to see me anytime that is convenient," I told them, "but I want you to understand that this case may not even come to trial for a year, at least."

The Schlegels had difficulty containing their initial anger at this delay, and rightfully so. However, I told them that there were approximately six hundred homicides every year in Manhattan, and that our backlog of cases was substantial. "We've got a whole series of hearings coming up in this case," I said, "and I'll let you know the dates if you want to come down."

"Mr. Tanenbaum," said Alfred in a quiet but determined voice. "We very much want to be there."

The Yukl confession to Keenan was not presented to the grand jury when I appeared before them two weeks later. On the basis of the Nancy Weems statements, the Yukl statement to Baeszler, the photo of

Schlegel with the round mark on her back, and the matching table, the grand jury indicted Yukl for murder.

Shortly thereafter, Yukl was arraigned on the indictment, and since Yukl claimed he could not afford his own attorney, the court appointed a lawyer for him.

Yukl's new attorney was Alex Sotis, a former assistant district attorney who was now a solo practitioner, wise in the ways of criminal trials and appeals. Sotis was a contemporary of John Keenan's. They had worked together several years earlier, and now Sotis was handed the case of a freed convicted murderer who had killed again.

In the days following the arraignment, the newspapers focused their attention on why Yukl had been released. None of the three parole board members who approved Yukl's release would talk to the press. But Dr. Emmanuel Feuer, the state psychiatrist who was the last doctor to examine Yukl prior to his release, gave an interview to the *New York Times*.

"He had a good relationship with his wife," he told reporter Selwyn Raab, "and when he left prison he was definitely not mentally ill. . . . We release so many people when they make their required minimum that I didn't have any concern about him," Feuer explained. "We were sure he was rehabilitated, and he was one of the best, brightest, most articulate prisoners I have ever seen. I can't blame the system, there was no way of doing it differently."

Warden Harold Butler also felt compelled to speak out, since some of the blame was aimed at his institution. "I saw him almost every day for two years and I trusted him so much that I probably would have left him alone with my wife or daughter. . . ."

Attorney Sotis also talked to the *Times*. "All this cross fire among different agencies to affix blame for his parole and early release is going to make it difficult to get a fair trial," he suggested. "His guilt has not been established."

After talking to his new client, and despite Yukl's inclination to plead guilty, Sotis saw a great defense opportunity. He jumped into the case, filing motions to set aside the indictment due to legally insufficient evidence before the grand jury. He filed the routine motions of discovery, so as to learn the names and addresses of the People's witnesses, and he filed motions to suppress the table as evidence and to disqualify the statement Yukl had made to Baeszler.

During this time, Yukl was moved across the East River to Riker's Island. He wrote only a few letters—to Irwin Klein, claiming his innocence and asking Klein to send him all the newspaper clippings; to Melanie Chartoff, claiming innocence but admitting his first murder; and to his father.

He told one visitor, "We're going to attempt a not-guilty-by-reason-of-insanity defense, because I don't think I should be punished for something I don't even remember doing."

For the next eighteen months, the legal machinery moved at glacierlike pace as Alex Sotis continued making motions for delays and searching for the right doctor to find Yukl insane—in other words not responsible for Schlegel's murder.

In the meantime, Yukl was part of the regular population on a surveillance ward at Riker's. He existed on a regimen of antidepressants—Elavils—and a tranquilizer called Dalmane, an offshoot of valium. They were all prescribed by prison authorities. He was regularly examined by a battery of Bellevue and prison psychologists and psychiatrists. He attempted suicide three times.

Then at Sotis' request, two Manhattan psychiatrists, Dr. John Baer Train and Dr. John Scanlon, were

appointed by the court to assist Yukl in his defense. It
was expected that following their individual examinations of the defendant, both psychiatrists would, as
expert witnesses for the defense, reach the conclusion
that Charles Yukl was not responsible for his acts.
Instead, and to everyone's surprise, each doctor found
that Yukl was indeed responsible.

The findings confused Yukl. An expert in the art of
talking to psychiatrists, he couldn't believe the shrinks
had not found him insane.

He started to analyze what he had told them. When
his discussion postmortem revealed nothing, he then
concentrated on what he had *not* told them—some of
the key buzzwords that lead to a finding of insanity.
The "Devil Made Me Do It" approach was a good
place to start. But first Yukl needed another doctor.
Sotis found one a few weeks later. His name was Dr.
Victor Teichner, and Sotis had him examine Yukl.

Yukl told Teichner a variation of the same old story—
that he had been hearing voices all his life, that he had
dreams and masturbation fantasies of strangling women.
He also told Teichner that those voices had spoken to
him on the night of Karin Schlegel's murder. "The
voices told me I was bad, that I would be swallowed
up," he told the doctor.

Based on the voices and Yukl's additional revelation of having hallucinations, Teichner concluded that
Yukl was not responsible for his actions. "Defendant
is suffering from a mental illness," Teichner reported,
"that became greatly exacerbated prior to the crime,
causing a disintegration of his personality, loss of contact with reality, and lack of substantial capacity to
know and appreciate the nature and consequence of
the crime and that it was wrong."

At first, Judge Joseph Martinis refused to have the
state pay for this third psychiatrist. "You have had

enough psychiatrists," he told Sotis. "I keep giving them to you. I gave you Train. I gave you Scanlon."

Martinis was one of the most senior and experienced trial judges in New York. He had seen and heard just about everything. He was not a fan of imperfect science, and courtroom psychiatrists always seemed to anger him. On this particular occasion, his sensibilities were offended by the fact that two different court-appointed defense psychiatrists had found the defendant responsible for his actions when the defense, faced with the findings, was bold enough to ask for another bite out of the apple.

He was particularly irritated because it was his view of the law that I would not be allowed to tell the jury about the findings of Train and Scanlan, since Sotis would argue that they were agents of Yukl's defense team, and it would be a violation of Yukl's Sixth Amendment right to effective, competent counsel.

However, I argued that once the defendant placed his state of mind at issue by invoking the insanity defense, the reports of all the doctors were fair game, and the interests of fairness required that the jury be apprised of all the opinions, both favorable and unfavorable. I also told Martinis that if Yukl could afford to buy his own psychiatrist, he would have found Teichner or his equivalent right away.

"Well," Martinis said reluctantly, "if the People have no objection, Dr. Teichner is so appointed."

As I walked out of the courtroom, I bumped into Carol Fahn, founder of "SHOCK," or Survivors Help Organization of Criminal Killings, a support group. "Considering that in 1974, in Manhattan alone, there were over six hundred reported homicides, and that for each homicide victim there are many more survivors," Fahn wrote in a detailed prospectus for the group, "it is an unfortunate fact that at present there is not even *one* program which functions to assist the survivors of homicide victims."

No one had been there in August of 1973 to help Fahn through her grueling personal ordeal when her cousin was brutally murdered during a mugging by an addict who had been a patient at the rehabilitation center where Carol worked. She wanted to make sure others would not have to suffer alone. Finding close relatives of murder victims and joining together with them to form a support group was Carol's way of dealing with her own loss. She had received some preliminary funding for the group, and she found herself attending criminal trials. "I want to reach out and support the other victims," she told me, "the people who loved the people who were viciously killed."

It was Carol's personal obsession. And the Charles Yukl trial would be an opportunity for her to implement her program.

"It's important," Fahn said, shaking my hand, "really important that I be there, to let the parents know that they are not alone."

I told her I agreed with her. "I'll need all the help I can get," I said, trying to be encouraging.

"Well," she said, walking off down the hall, "see you in court!"

CHAPTER TWENTY-ONE

I was able and more than willing to prove Yukl's guilt. Yukl and his defense attorney, Alex Sotis, were equally prepared to prove his insanity. They embarked on a predictable course. Yukl continued to claim that all he wanted was psychiatric treatment. But Sotis needed more than that before a judge and jury. In court he would demand a pretrial hearing and argue that the statements made by Yukl to both Keenan and Baeszler were inadmissible.

If he failed to win a favorable ruling, he would go to trial and attempt to orchestrate a not-guilty-by-reason-of-insanity defense. Sotis could not depend on the testimony of two of his own defense psychiatrists, each of whom had found Yukl responsible for his actions. He had to go with the third, Dr. Teichner, to whom Yukl had told of hearing the voices. It would be a tricky task, but Sotis was a good soldier of courtroom maneuvering. He might not be able to convince a judge of Yukl's insanity in a closed hearing. A jury, however, would be an entirely different matter.

Still, Sotis tried every option. On a number of occasions early in the game, he approached me with an offer for a plea-bargaining deal. "Yukl will plead guilty if you lower the charge to manslaughter one," he once suggested.

"Alex, if he pleads to anything," I told him several times, "it will be to murder. I won't accept a lesser plea."

My mandate was clear: Yukl could not be allowed to manipulate the system again.

But our chances of success were not overwhelming. There were too many obstacles to obtaining a clean conviction. And there was always the probability of a defense appeal.

On the surface, the law is precise. It assumes a person is innocent until proven guilty. It also assumes that a defendant is sane until proven crazy. In a criminal trial, the burden of proving guilt lies with the prosecution. But the burden of rebutting the presumption of sanity lies with the defense.

Insanity is not a psychiatric term. It is a legal definition used to label those who are, without reasonable doubt, mentally incapacitated and unable to be held responsible for their actions. Still, in almost every case involving the insanity plea, it is psychiatry itself that is ultimately on trial.

One of the most corrosive aspects of the criminal justice system is its toleration of the insanity defense. When premeditated killers resort to the insanity defense to avoid responsibility and escape punishment, it shocks the conscience. Legitimate in some few cases, the insanity defense has been rendered farcical through its manipulation by so-called experts.

In virtually every insanity case that goes to trial, each side—the prosecution and the defense—hires its own so-called expert psychiatrist. Both psychiatrists then proceed to give ironclad but divergent opinions regarding the defendant's state of mind. Such testimony is at best conjecture—it is mere opinion and it's neither empirical nor scientific truth. It mocks the truly expert opinion that derives from a reasonable degree of scientific certainty. And it betrays the purpose of a criminal trial, which is the search for truth and the meting out of justice. Instead, the insanity defense gives criminally violent and unpredictable individuals in our community an opportunity to avoid being held accountable for their actions.

In effect, these "insane" criminals are exonerated, not because they have provided a legitimate defense, but because their hired-gun psychiatrists are more convincing than the psychiatrists testifying for the opposition.

For the Yukl case, I had at my disposal a very dependable weapon—Dr. Daniel Schwartz—a courtroom veteran, as much a lawyer as a psychiatrist. Schwartz understood the fundamental differences between the legal definition of insanity and the gray area of conjecture and emotional response. Dan Schwartz also knew, in the interview format, how to get a witness to arrive at a clear and most simple conclusion as to whether a defendant was truly insane at the time of the crime or has later conveniently invented some purposely misleading inconsistencies of behavior. Schwartz comes across in the courtroom the way he does in life—polite and self-assured. He is a star witness without being a star.

On January 7, 1976, Schwartz examined Yukl. Sotis was present during the session. Schwartz began asking his questions at 2:45 in the afternoon.

"How are you feeling?" he commenced.

"Very depressed," Yukl said, in a hushed tone.

"Can you tell me something about that?"

"Well, you mean how I f-f-f—how I feel now?"

"Yes."

Yukl shifted around in his chair. "Um, you know, I

feel very, very depressed, very, very, very, very, yes suicidal. I'm st—you know, I'm st—you know I'm still hearing voices, up at Riker's Island saying how I'm no, you know saying that I'm no good, you know, I'm you know, you know, worthless, that I have to, you know, that I have to commit suicide. I still have hallucinations where I might see my wife standing in the room for, for, you know, ten or fifteen minutes and I'll carry on a conversation with her, but she's not there. But they, you know they put me on new, you know, they did put me on a uh, some new medication, so I wouldn't hear the voices anymore, but I haven't, you know, I haven't had it yet, so I don't know what effect it's going to have."

Schwartz was prepared for this recitation. "Now you say you're still hearing voices—"

"Yes, sir."

"And you're still seeing your wife."

"Yes, sir."

"How long has this been going on?"

"It's been going on approximately six months. As far as Riker's Island is concerned. I've heard voices before then but as far as Riker's Island is concerned. I've always been very anxious . . ."

"You're kind of anxious now too."

"Uh"—Yukl tried to recover—"this is my normal—"

"Mmm-hmm."

"My normal, uh, you know, normal state."

"Would you describe yourself as anxious?"

"Normally, generally, I'm very anxious."

"Generally, oh, I see."

"Very, very anxious," Yukl continued.

"No more so now than usual?"

"I'd say now I'm about like I usually am."

"Do you have any feelings about talking to a psychiatrist?"

"Well," Yukl said, looking away from Schwartz, "I don't trust you."

"Why not?" the doctor asked.

"Because you're supposed to find that I was mentally competent at the time of the crime."

"Well," Schwartz calmly answered, "I'm supposed to examine you; what I'll find, I don't know yet."

"I thought your findings were already foregone."

"Where'd you get that idea from?" Schwartz asked, hoping that Yukl would trap himself.

"I just assume that they are," Yukl said.

"Uh-huh. I'm sorry to hear that."

"That's the way I feel. I'm not going to tell you a lie."

"I'm glad you're not," Schwartz said. "Well, believe it or not, I do have an open mind, uh, and I will be interested in anything you can tell me about what contributed to this situation. But you're right, in the sense that I am here to talk to you ultimately about what your state of mind was at the time of this crime. Again, just for the record, do you know what you're charged with?"

"Yes, sir. I'm charged with murder."

"And do you have some idea of the, uh, severity of such a crime in New York State, what the possible punishment is?"

"Well"—Yukl shrugged—"it's academic, really."

"Why?"

"Because I'm not going to do it anyway."

Schwartz was intrigued. "Tell me more."

"Uh, if I go to upstate prison—either I'll commit suicide or someone else will do it for me. Because, uh, I in my opinion, I really, you know, I don't belong in upstate prison, I know where I belong, and if I don't get the therapy that I need, then I'm not going through and live any longer. Because I've already tried four times to commit suicide, and, uh, I'm just not going to do it if I go back upstate. So it's academic. Whatever. You know, you know, unless I get the help that I need, uh, I'm not going along with it. That's a rational decision."

"Well, in what kind of a place would you imagine you could get the help you needed?"

"In a state hospital."

"Yeah." Schwartz nodded.

"Uh . . . I'm not that naive to think that all the help I need is going to be guaranteed by a state hospital, but I also know that when I want something I'm able to go after it. But I have to be in an environment which is supposed to offer it to begin with. So if I get into a state hospital, I'll be able to get the help that I need. I don't care about the time element. I'm not concerned about getting out. Right now I'm concerned about getting in. I don't care if it takes ten years or twenty years, but it, you know, just can't have this going on again. I don't know why it occurred. I still don't know why it occurred, and I'm not going through life knowing what happened. I think that's a very rational decision on my part."

"Again, just for the record, the 'it' that you're talking about is a murder? Uh, do you know when this happened and, uh, where and how and whom?"

The key was to get Yukl to talk about the crime.

"Yes," Yukl volunteered, then caught himself. "Yes, sir—well, I don't know how, but I know when and where."

"You mean the means of the killing," Schwartz helped him. "I don't mean why yet. But the how."

"Well, strangulation, according to what the newspapers said. I didn't—you know, I didn't know what I must have done. I don't remember doing it, but I know what I must have done."

"And where?"

"It was at one—it was at 120 Waverly Place."

"That was what?"

"New York City."

"No," Schwartz stopped him. "What place is this that you're talking about?"

"That's my apartment."

"And do you know who the, uh, victim was?"

"Yes, sir, it was Karin Schlegel."

"And do you know when this happened?"

"Uh, August the nineteenth, I believe."

"Now, to go back to something you just said; you said you've already tried suicide four times."

"Yes, sir."

"Can you tell me anything about that?"

"First I heard the voices saying that I was no good, worthless, that I must be punished. You know, I should commit suicide, I should hurt myself. But along with that I feel that when I came out of prison the first time I made my wife a promise. I made a promise that this couldn't happen again. And that we would start over again. And I tried. I really tried to start over again. I was going to school. I was working. I don't know why this occurred again. But I—but I feel guilty, because I broke my promise to my wife. And I did the same thing again. I don't know why. I was under the impression that I was doing everything possible so that it wouldn't happen again. But I was wrong. And that's very hard to live with. At least it is for me. I felt that I just didn't deserve to live. If I—I felt that if I can't trust my own behavior, then there's no sense in continuing to exist. And I believe that very strongly. Because obviously I can't trust my own behavior."

"So when was the first time you tried to kill yourself?"

"Uh, it was in—let's see now, February of 1974,

wait a minute, let's see now, no February of 1975. We're in seventy-six now, so it was seventy-five."

"Where were you then?"

"I was in Riker's Island, C-71."

"And what did you actually do?"

"I took sixty-eight Elavils. Sixty-eight fifty-milligram Elavils. Because that was the dose that one of the, you know, I had asked the nurses, you know, kind of joking around with the nurses trying to find out what was the, what was the lethal dose, and they were telling me something like thirty, and thirty-five; so I figured sixty-some-odd would be a reasonable amount."

"What actually happened?"

"Uh, they sent me to East Elmhurst Hospital, and about, and I lost about two or—two or, two or so many days, approximately two or three days, and I woke up. I woke up behind it and uh—"

"You don't remember, I mean there's an absence in your mind of about two or three days."

"About two or three days. All I know is I was very angry when I got up. I was very angry. Cause it's not you know"—he stumbled—"it's a hell of a, hell of a thing when you're feeling that you're going out, and then, to find that you wake up again is, very disturbing. That was the first time. Second time I took seventy-two Dalmanes. And even the nurses said that—"

Schwartz interrupted him. "When was that?"

"That was March, March of seventy-five. These all followed in rapid succession."

"Mmmm-hmmm. Go ahead. When was the third?"

"The third one was around May of seventy-five. That was where I took a combination of Elavils and Dalmanes. And of course the final time was about a month later, June ninth, when I tried to hang myself. And all of these—"

"What stopped—I mean what prevented it?"

Yukl smiled slightly. "A suicide aide made a round when he shouldn't have made a round. It was just—it was just a matter of coincidence that he did what he did. He had made the rounds once, and he wasn't due back again for another forty-five minutes. But for some reason he came back and he cut me down."

"Would this voice that you were describing—would this, uh, come to you in any way before you would get close to your wife?"

"Yes, sir. Whenever it—well, it happened whenever I was in contact with a woman, whenever a woman was around. It was kind of like a—it's it's it's very it's very hard to explain, it was uh, like a prelude, you know to my relationships with women. It—it, you know, I know that it caused me a lot of anxiety, to a point where I would literally start to tremble. And I just couldn't, uh, I just—you know, couldn't get an erection with a woman."

"You say, with a woman. Were there other women besides your wife that you tried to have sex with?"

"No," Yukl answered quickly. "No, but every time a woman—like when I was home and Mom was teaching, wherever a woman came around, I would get that experience. And I would—I would just have to leave, I just couldn't, uh. It still happened even after I was married. My wife—intercourse with my wife was just, uh, a matter of hit and run. There's no—well, I was married for a period of approximately fourteen years, and during that—during that whole time I'd say I had a relationship with my wife maybe about ten times. And that was only because she wanted it."

Now they were going over ground that had been covered by every other psychologist and psychiatrist who had examined Yukl.

"Why do you suppose she, uh, tolerated this little sex for so long?" Schwartz asked.

"She kept hoping I'd change. She kept hoping that, uh, whatever it was that was hanging me up would resolve itself."

"You know there came a time when, uh—was it back in sixty-six when you—the first killing occurred?"

"When I first what, sir?"

"When was the first—there was another girl killed."

"Suzanne Reynolds."

"Yeah, when was that?"

"Yes, sir; sixty-six."

"Sixty-six. And you did some time upstate."

"Yes, sir."

"And I understand you were seeing a psychiatrist there for quite a while."

"Yes, sir, I was taking advantage of everything they had."

"Do you remember anything about your treatment then?"

"Sure. We went into the exhibitionism, why I had—why I had this need to expose myself . . . and it was something that apparently I had to prove my adequacy constantly, and it has—you know, it apparently had something to do with the voice saying I would be swallowed up. You know, to constantly reassure myself that I was still intact. Most of my therapy in prison was not really geared to why I was there in the first place. It was geared on keeping me—keeping my head straight while I was in there. Which was unfortunate."

"Did you describe the, uh—these voices to those doctors?" This was the key question.

"Yes, sir. To Dr. Feuer."

In fact, Yukl had told none of the doctors—not even his own defense-hired psychiatrists in the Suzanne Reynolds case—about the voices. Less than two weeks later, on January 19, 1976, Schwartz wrote:

There is no evidence that at the time of the present offense, as a result of mental disease or defect, the defendant lacked substantial capacity to know or appreciate either the nature and consequence of his conduct or that it was wrong.

In regard to the present offense there is no evidence that the defendant's personality problems or symptoms prevented him from appreciating the nature or consequence of his act: He applied the tie to Karin's neck in a way that effectively caused her death. He describes no command hallucinations or paranoid delusions that might have prevented him from appreciating the wrongfulness of his act. That he hid the body under the bed immediately afterwards, removed it the next day, and disposed of the clothing and film also argues for his appreciation of the wrongfulness of what he had done. While he may have felt so threatened by Karin's open discussion of oral sex that he impulsively killed her and so overwhelmed by the intensity of his emotions that he momentarily blanked out, this would not relieve him of criminal responsibility."

It was the report I wanted.

In late March 1976, we began a series of expected pretrial hearings on admissibility of evidence and Yukl's confession, and on Yukl's competency to stand trial. But Yukl now told Sotis he wasn't even looking for a deal anymore—he just wanted to plead guilty and accept a twenty-five-years-to-life-sentence, but Sotis wouldn't let him. Sotis felt that if he could beat down the Baeszler statement, he stood an excellent chance of going for a mistrial or, at the very least, an insanity defense. Sotis thought the odds were on his side.

Irene and Alfred Schlegel were in the courtroom when Yukl took the stand during the pretrial hearings.

They came because they wanted to see their daughter's killer, to share, strangely, in the experience of a trial that would mete out appropriate justice. And they came to try to glimpse the darkness of a killer's mind, to stare him in the face and release some of their grief.

Yukl appeared unusually calm. In fact, the man was nothing less than a walking drugstore, courtesy of prison authorities. He had been given 500 milligrams of Mellaril, 100 milligrams of Elavil, and 800 milligrams of Thorazine, an extremely high dose.

The Schlegels sat quietly on a bench near the front of the room, in full view of the judge and Yukl. Next to them sat Carol Fahn, providing moral support. Irene appeared nervous. Alfred never took his eyes off Yukl. When their eyes met, Alfred maintained his stare, then lifted up his right index finger, put it on his neck and pulled it across. Schlegel kept pronouncing his own sentence, until Sotis saw it. I saw it too.

Martinis stopped the proceedings and cleared the court, except for the attorneys and the Schlegels. He had them approach the bench. "You are Mr. and Mrs. Schlegel, I presume," he asked, "the parents of Karin Schlegel?"

"Yes," said Irene.

"I certainly appreciate the agonizing experience that you are both going through listening to this testimony," he told them. "You have my wholehearted sympathy in that respect. But, nevertheless, we are required to give the defendant a fair trial. . . . So, for the future you are welcome to stay as long as you want, but please try to withhold your emotions."

The Schlegels nodded quietly, returned to their seats, and the proceedings resumed.

As a witness, Yukl represented himself well. He laid out a scenario in which he had been misled by Keenan and had spoken to Baeszler under the assumption of Keenan's free pass. He was a crafty, clever witness. Sotis had him on the stand for a purpose, and Yukl was delivering.

Martinis had still not ruled on the admissibility of the Train and Scanlan reports, or on Yukl's statement to Baeszler.

By April, we were nearing the end of the hearings. Each day Carol Fahn took what was now considered her assigned space next to the Schlegels.

Under cross-examination, I wanted to get Yukl to go into detail about the manner in which he had killed Suzanne Reynolds. I wasn't interested in the Reynolds case, of course, but I wanted to test Yukl's recollection of the killing, and to unnerve him, to lead him away from the well-rehearsed testimony he had been giving.

First I got Yukl to admit that he had, in fact, made the statement to Baeszler. Then I had him tell the court in detail what he had told Baeszler. Sotis objected at every opportunity, but was mostly denied. I looked over at Martinis. He was growing bored with the game.

I had another plan. While questioning Yukl on the stand, I sent Baeszler out to bring in two of the Bellevue doctors who had examined Yukl. He had never told them about hearing voices. "Isn't it true," I asked him, "that you're a habitual liar and you say anything convenient to help yourself?"

"N-n-n-no," he said. "That's not true."

I wanted Yukl to see them walk into the room, and to assume that they were going to testify that he was a liar.

It worked. The timing was perfect. Just then, as Yukl saw Baeszler enter the courtroom with the two shrinks, he rose in the witness chair. His eyes were fixed on the two men. "You tricked me!" he yelled at me. Yukl then went off on a tangent, a series of incoherent ravings, saying that it was society's fault that he killed— that he asked for help and that society didn't give it to him. Yukl started screaming. Martinis, noting that the witness was "agitated," ordered a short recess.

When we returned to court, Martinis came down with his opinion. "After considering all the attendant circumstances of the arrest and the subsequent events as elicited from the witnesses at this hearing," Martinis ruled, "upon the credible evidence presented, I conclude that the statements made and the communications had by the defendant with Detective Baeszler are entirely voluntary, unsolicited, and not subject to any constitutional infirmities. Thus," he concluded, "the motion to suppress the statements made by the defendant to Detective Baeszler . . . is denied."

The trial of Charles Yukl would begin the next day. Carol Fahn hugged Irene Schlegel. "We will be here tomorrow," Irene Schlegel told me.

"Mrs. Schlegel," I said, "jury selection will take at least two weeks, and there's really no need for you to be here."

"That's right," said Fahn. "But I will be here, and I will call you every day to let you know what happened."

"Thank you for everything, Carol," Irene told her. "I really appreciate you being here."

Carol beamed. She was obsessed with seeing Yukl brought to justice, and she seemed even more determined to complete the mission than did the Schlegels. "That's what I *wanted* to do," Fahn said. "We have to be strong about this."

The next morning, April 20, we assembled for the first day of the trial, and the Schlegels stayed home. Carol Fahn was there, anxiously waiting for the proceedings to begin.

But as soon as Martinis walked into the room, Sotis got into an argument with him over the definition of insanity. "I am not talking about insanity in this case," he told the judge. "This is a case of mental illness or mental defect."

Martinis wasn't feeling well, he had a sore throat and had difficulty speaking. He argued briefly with Sotis, then seemed to accede to Sotis' request that the plea be entered as "not guilty by reason of a mental disease or defect."

I protested, claiming that "what insanity means is defined in the penal law. Whether or not Yukl has a mental disease or defect in and of itself is irrelevant."

Sotis hung tough. "Insanity defense is a newspaper term," he shot back. "It doesn't belong in a courtroom. Every time," he said, "we start mixing bananas with apples, or maybe it should be the other way, apples with bananas . . ." Then he paused slightly, for effect: "The defendant is bananas."

"Your Honor," I continued to argue, "the defendant may very well be bananas. However, as Your Honor has indicated quite properly, the plea in this case is not guilty by reason of insanity . . ."

"The issue is one of criminal responsibility," Sotis interrupted.

"Yes," Martinis agreed. "But the criminal responsibility comes with the purview of not guilty by reason of insanity."

"Well," Sotis chuckled, "why can't I use the word wacky? Is that a proper word . . . wacky?"

Martinis was not amused. "You use what words you want. But the plea is not guilty by reason of insanity."

The volley between Sotis and Martinis continued for the next ten minutes. Finally Martinis said, "I will explain to the jury what the definition of legal insanity is."

"I object to that, Judge," Sotis said.

"If you object," Martinis replied, "you made your objection. Bring the jury in."

The prospective jurors walked into the courtroom. After some preliminary introductions by Martinis, Sotis turned and spoke quietly with Yukl. Then he turned and faced Martinis. "May we step up?" Sotis approached the bench. He tried, once again, and out of earshot of the prospective jurors, to negotiate for a lesser plea.

Martinis looked over to me. "Stop wasting my time," I told Sotis. "Let's get on with the jury selection."

Sotis returned to his seat and spoke again to Yukl.

"May I proceed, Your Honor?" he asked.

Martinis anticipated Sotis' next move.

"Yes. Do you have an application?" Martinis asked him.

"It seems," he told the hushed courtroom, "that after much discussion and associations and confirming on my part with the defendant, the magic moment appears to have arrived and the defendant at this time most respectfully makes application to withdraw his previously interposed plea of not guilty and/or not guilty by reason of mental defect and/or mental illness . . . and wishes to plead guilty to the indictment."

All the maneuvering had culminated in an all-too-quick denouement. Yukl was going to make a deal, and nearly twenty months of interrogation, examination, motions, transcripts, and taxpayers' money would amount to a lessened sentence and a terribly expensive "magic moment."

Yes, he had pleaded guilty. In the process, he was gambling on receiving a smaller sentence. He had spared himself the agony of a trial. And he had denied the victim's parents the cathartic experience of a public trial. It was all over in less than thirty minutes.

Martinis set May 26 for sentencing. Court was adjourned. I turned around to talk to Carol Fahn. But she had disappeared.

The next morning, I called the Schlegels. Surely Carol Fahn would have told them what happened, but I wanted them to hear it from me. "Mr. and Mrs. Schlegel," I began. "I want you to know there's not going to be a trial . . . I . . ."

"What?" Mr. Schlegel interrupted. Surprisingly, Fahn had not told them.

"The defendant is pleading guilty to the indictment," I said.

"What?" he asked again. "How can this man Sotis try to get Yukl off?"

"Mr. Schlegel," I said, "Yukl didn't get off. I gotta tell you that it's the right of every defendant to plead guilty to the crime for which they are charged. That's what he's doing. He's pleading guilty to murder. In a sense"—I tried to soothe them—"this may be a blessing for both of you. You won't have to go through the ordeal of a trial."

There was a long pause. "You're right." Irene Schlegel sighed. "It has been very difficult for us."

I told them that I would let them know when the sentencing hearing would be held.

Irene Schlegel hung up the phone and looked at her husband in silence. She had never felt more alone in her life than she did at that moment. She picked up the phone and dialed Carol Fahn. Fahn had been there, in the courtroom, she reasoned and at least could give her another view of what happened.

"Hello," said a subdued male voice on the other end. It was Carol's brother.

"Is Carol there?" Irene asked.

"No."

"Oh," Irene said, disappointed. "What time will she be back?"

"Uh . . ." there was a pause. "She won't be coming back."

Irene didn't understand.

"What do you mean, she isn't coming back?" she asked.

"Well," said the brother, "Carol died last night. She committed suicide."

CHAPTER TWENTY-TWO

The Schlegels felt abused by the legal system that allowed Yukl to live. The trial they had hoped for, the public exposure of Charles Yukl as a murderer, would not occur. There would not be the final emotional release the trial might have provided them.

The guilty plea took the story right off the front pages, except in Cresskill, where the family received a sympathetic audience from the local paper. Sensational trials make the newspapers. Guilty pleas after nearly two years of hearings rarely do.

Now, the Schlegels' only course of action was to appeal to Martinis to give Yukl the maximum sentence.

I am well aware [began a long letter Alfred Schlegel wrote to the judge] that a Judge in your position, hearing a murder trial, must be somewhat perfunctory. The liberal rationalization that has been prevalent over the past decade or longer must have rubbed off somewhat on the Judiciary of this country. The attitude of the Judiciary which has been guided by the liberal press has caused the citizenry of this country to become virtual prisoners in their own households because it has emboldened the weak criminal to commit his crime. What the heck is a few years in jail for murder? Aren't the criminals being taken care of in a better manner than the poor, elderly, hungry or jobless? Three meals a day, a good clean bed, medical attention and most of all the attention of a Psychiatrist, something few other people can afford.

It sickened me, and my first impression was to wonder: Is this what I risked my life for, fighting and earning four medals answering my country's call to arms, only to have my beloved daughter strangled by a paroled killer who was judged worthy of rejoining society after committing the GHOULISH MURDER of Suzanne Reynolds Then I had to witness the nauseating spectacle of seeing the court-appointed defense attorney Mr. Sotis joke and laugh with this human monster.

The gravity of the charge was not in evidence. I got the impression that the hearings were a circus. It was not a circus however for the victims of this killer. Their last moments must have been agonizing, gasping for oxygen to sustain their lives. I don't and cannot imagine what horror they have suffered. And this is taken so lightly in a court of law?

The Miranda decision, as I see it, cost my daughter's life. The Supreme Court of the United States of America is therefore directly responsible for the horrible death of my beloved daughter. In any action where death occurs, be it on the job, in an auto, airplane, or wherever negligence is proven, the persons responsible can be sued. I hope I can get into the courts and sue someone responsible for the death of my daughter! I hope I will get the same tender consideration that her murderer got in a court of law. I shall see.

When you sentence Yukl keep in mind what he said in your courtroom, which is on record. He indicated quite clearly that this crime which he committed could, and probably would, happen again. Do not sentence another innocent victim to death by giving him freedom in fifteen years.

Also remember his third victim who sat in the courtroom as an observer and later committed suicide. Indirectly she is his third victim. You have no idea of the torture we all have endured. Always remember the victims even though they are buried.

While I was walking in the corridors I overheard one criminal say to another: "I guess you will have to pull another job to pay for the fine you will be getting"; the response was a gleeful roar of laughter. The criminal is in contempt, Your Honor, and what contempt!! It's unbelievable.

Psychiatry was usurped by the Law and the Courts. Is this its function? It represents a grave danger to society because Psychiatrists are permitted, indirectly, to render Judgment through their profession. This MUST STOP lest the people of this country will take note, and then where are you?

Judge Martinis, I implore you to weigh your decision carefully, your wisdom can do a real service to this country.

The Schlegel letter was quickly followed by a few dozen letters from relatives and close Schlegel family friends to Martinis, each urging that Yukl be incarcerated for the rest of his life.

On June 3, 1976—a week later than scheduled—we reassembled for the last time in the case of the People v. Charles Yukl. It was a classic New York County Supreme Court courtroom, with high ceilings and dirty ivory-colored walls. Only twenty people—the usual court buffs and one or two reporters—sat in the long rows of wooden benches designed to hold seventy or more.

The Schlegels were not in the courtroom.

"Charles Yukl," the clerk began, "in the presence of your attorney, Mr. Sotis, you are now being arraigned for sentence upon your conviction to the crime of murder, under indictment #4338 of 1974.

"Before the court imposes sentence on you, either your attorney or both of you may address the court in your behalf, after the People have had an opportunity to be heard."

Martinis looked down at Sotis. "Do you wish to say anything?"

Sotis stood up and faced the judge.

"This defendant is forty-one years of age. He's the product of a broken marriage, not that there aren't hundreds of thousands of people in this country who aren't similarly situated and who have had very difficult childhoods. But it seems to be perfectly clear from the content of the probation reports that the court was kind enough to turn over to me, and in view of my examination of the prior mental history of the defendant, that he, since being a youngster before the age of puberty, showed evidences of mental derangement, mental aberration. One evidence of that would have been when he was a youngster prior to being a teenager, for some strange reason being involved in episodes of arson.

"There is a history of beatings inflicted upon him by an overly severe father, who was charged with raising him when the marriage of his parents broke up.

"His mother was involved in the musical world. Also a very severe, strict disciplinarian. She followed her career ambitions and left her youngster in the hands of her husband, who didn't do the kind of job that would have been necessary to straighten him out if he was capable of being straightened out and put on the correct road.

"Your Honor knows that the defendant, in an effort to make something out of himself in life, enlisted in the United States Navy and made strong efforts to learn a trade.

"He is not an unintelligent person. During the years that he spent with his mother he was trained in music. He is a very capable person in that respect, gifted musically. He was discharged from the navy as the result of a variety of infractions, one of which involved petty thievery, the other being absent without leave. He was discharged under, I think, less than honorable conditions, but then made an application for a review of the discharge because he was very much concerned with the lack of a decent performance in the navy, in the navy's eyes, and upon a review of the case, a review of the strong efforts made by the defendant to adjust his life properly, the navy did award him, he informs me, an honorable discharge."

Sotis continued for the next fifteen minutes reciting the sad history of Charles Yukl and his need for psychiatric help.

Finally he said, "The defendant consigns himself to Your Honor and asks to be helped. . . . What should stand out most is that this defendant wanted to plead guilty, repeated by insisting upon pleading guilty, because he recognized that the only way that he can function is to receive some psychiatric care under proper circumstances. . . . The defendant knew that if he was convicted and received a sentence of twenty-five years to life, he would reach out to do what he has tried to do repeatedly, and that is to kill himself.

"He has a spark of desire in him to continue living, which seems to be overbalanced by this desire to snuff out the light. Some people may not care about that and would probably say, 'What loss to society? Who really cares?' There are other values to be served, and

I'm not going to wax philosophical about that, but I don't think that a well-balanced system involved in the administration of law should lose sight of the fact that when we get an individual as sick as this fellow, whether he comes within the limitations of the penal law or not, that something should be done for him.

"The whole concept of a sentence of fifteen years to life has as a threshold implication that he is salvageable, that after the fifteen years there may be a reason for this release, he may under certain circumstances qualify himself as a very suitable risk.

"Let's not just brush this defendant off," Sotis pleaded. "Because the defendant really can't fight back. The defendant, after I leave him, can do very little for himself, practically nothing. His only recourse is the recourse that he stated to me repeatedly that if he is sent to a state institution where he is ignored and he is not given some psychiatric treatment, and he's there under the influence—"

Martinis was growing tired with this monologue. "We've gone through all this, Mr. Sotis."

"Judge," he said, "I'm talking against the backgound of fifteen years."

"You've been talking for almost a half hour, and I've been very patient in listening to you. We've gone through all this and you should know that I cannot guarantee that he'll go to a psychiatric facility and remain there for the rest of his life."

Sotis sat down. It was now Yukl's turn to speak.

"Your Honor, I believe that the most important factor in this case is that I—that I would receive intensified psychiatric help.

"Now, I asked for psychiatric help, Your Honor, back in 1966. I asked for it in 1967. I asked for it in 1968, all the way up through the year 1973, and I got nothing.

"I believe, you know, the way I look at it, Your Honor, is that I did not really receive what I was supposed to receive, and I don't want the same thing to happen this time, because if I am going to be paroled, which may or may not occur, I don't want this to happen again, and I believe that the only way that this will tend to be precluded would be if I did receive intensified psychiatric help. That's all I have to say."

Now, finally, it was Martinis' turn.

"This court has been besieged with letters, mailgrams, petitions, copies of news editorials and telephone callers critical of our criminal justice system, some requesting that I impose a life sentence, without minimum time, and in other cases even the death penalty has been suggested, to ensure that this defendant will never again be permitted to join our society.

"Many of these communications came from neighbors of the deceased, extolling her virtue, sharing in the suffering of her parents, and deploring the acts of this defendant, who for the second time within ten years has taken the life of a young innocent girl in the prime of life who succumbed to his guile in the hope that he would assist her to gain recognition in her chosen field, only to meet death at his hands.

"I am not unmindful of the suffering and agony of the parents of the victim of this crime who, likewise, wrote to this court, and vehemently protest any consideration for the defendant. I understand their bereavement and my sympathy goes out to them, but nothing I can do can bring back their beloved daughter. I must perform my duty under the circumstances with due regard to all the facts and circumstances in this case.

"While pressures play no part in my imposition of sentence, nor ordinarily are explanations the order of the day, I must live with my conscience to administer justice under the oath of my office.

"However, this is a most unusual case: the commission of a murder, a conviction, imprisonment, parole; and while on parole the commission of another murder in almost the same identical way. The public has a right to be aroused and to have an explanation of the proceedings that led to the final disposition of this case."

Martinis knew well about the weaknesses of the case, first and foremost the fact that we could not have introduced the Keenan confession if there had been a trial. And he knew that I would not accept a lesser plea by Yukl.

But he was also very concerned about a reversal of his decision permitting the Baeszler statement into evidence. He was further concerned about the potential reversible error in allowing me to introduce into evidence the details of the Suzanne Reynolds killing.

Martinis reminded the courtroom that he had presided over the pretrial hearings and was aware that "there was no eyewitness to the commission of this crime; that the People's case was, at best, circumstantial, and as such, a difficult one to prove; but, nonetheless, viable. It was only through the perseverance, tenacity, and persistence of the police, the chief district attorney, and his staff," he said, "that the defendant finally gave a complete, detailed and unequivocal confession that brought to light his perpetration of this horrible and heinous crime.

"Thus, while the crime was solved, the guilty party knew, because of constitutional safeguards that protect individuals charged with crime, this confession would not be admissible at trial. Without this confession, and in light of the insanity defense, the People could have been hard put to establish his guilt beyond any reasonable doubt, either as to the commission of the crime or as to the fact that he was sane at the time he committed the crime.

"So that the district attorney was faced with the possibility of a complete acquittal for lack of sufficient evidence, thereby mandating the immediate release of this defendant to society, which indeed would be a disastrous result; or possibly his acquittal by reason of insanity which would release him to the department of mental hygiene, without any specified period of institutionalization and probable eventual release to society.

"The defendant is articulate, knowledgeable, and understood these possible impediments to his conviction. On the other hand, he also knew that the People had some evidence which might cause his conviction. It was on this dilemma that he offered to plead guilty to the indictment and requested consideration upon sentence, and the district attorney wisely recommended the acceptance of the plea.

"Thus, the defendant, by his plea, stands convicted of the crime of murder in exactly the same way as if he had been tried and found guilty of murder by a jury of his peers. Now we come to the part that concerns us all, the sentence and the significance of the consideration extended to the defendant for his offer to plead guilty and stand convicted of murder without a trial."

The maximum sentence mandated by law for the crime of murder is a life term or life imprisonment. It means that under the law the defendant may be kept in prison for the rest of his life and that he will never be freed from supervision under his sentence. But, considering the weaknesses of the case, Martinis decided not to give Yukl the maximum sentence. Thus, even in pleading guilty, Yukl still had a few cards left in his hand. Martinis sentenced Yukl to fifteen years to life.

"In the instant case, it is my firm belief, under all the facts and circumstances in the case, that to the extent that our law permits, justice is satisfied," he said.

Charles Yukl walked out of the courtroom and headed for initial processing at Sing Sing.

Over the next six years, Yukl was an inmate at Greenhaven, Auburn and Clinton prisons. He continued taking classes at Empire State College in abnormal psychology, hoping for an eventual parole.

Enken divorced him, claiming sexual abandonment and refusal of marital relations.

And, once again, Yukl became a model prisoner. He wrote long memos to state psychiatrists, offering to write papers on interpersonal relationships within the prison system. He wrote some orchestrations for a movie of his mother Dorothea's ballets. He was even asked by one of the psychiatrists to write a critique of René Descartes' theory of the existence of God. Yukl read the material and then lapsed into the same argument he had had with some of the actresses before the Schlegel murder.

"I THINK I have found a glaring contradiction concerning the soul," he wrote to Dr. Jurgen Karker, one of his prison psychiatrists. "Descartes mentions that the soul is nonmaterial and indestructible and that it is located at the base of the pineal gland. My argument is this: If the soul lies at the base of the pineal gland it must take up space. If it occupies space it is, therefore, material. If it is material it is also destructible. If Descartes meant what I think he did then I can shoot him out of the saddle. . . ."

During his last prison interview Yukl chain smoked unfiltered cigarettes as he talked. "You know I'm making progress here," he said. "Before, I only understood my problems on an intellectual level. But now I've learned to understand them on an emotional level. I've asked to work only with women therapists, and I'm not even stuttering anymore. I really think when I leave here I will be as safe a risk as humanly possible." Suddenly, he looked away, and a strange gaze overcame him. "But you never know," he said, focusing on nothing in particular, "it could rain tomorrow."

Yukl's parole eligibility date was officially 1989, though he was convinced he would never make it out of prison through the parole system.

What Yukl *didn't* know was that, once again, the wheels of justice had erred on his side. Despite my letter to the parole authority, and Judge Martinis's statement on record that Yukl never be paroled, a bureauratic error at the Department of Parole had resulted in a five-year reduction of Yukl's sentence, making his parole eligibility date June 7, 1984.

On the morning of Saturday, August 21, 1982, Yukl used his bed to barricade himself in his cell. Psychiatrists talked him out of the room, and he was transferred to an observation cell in the prison hospital.

Shortly after one o'clock the next afternoon, almost eight years to the day after the strangulation of Karin Schlegel, Charles Yukl hanged himself using a piece of mattress cover for a rope.

AUTHOR'S NOTE

The authors spent more than four years researching and reporting this story. More than eighty people were interviewed for this book, ranging from police investigators to childhood friends and classmates, U.S. Navy personnel, psychologists, attorneys, to Charles Yukl himself.

Hundreds of hours of tapes were transcribed, and thousands of pages of court documents, parole reports, and psychiatric evaluations were reviewed. Much source material was obtained through the Freedom of Information Act (U.S. Code 522) as well as from confidential sources within the criminal justice system and the New York State Department of Corrections.

Additional source material was obtained from official New York City police transcripts of precinct interrogations and confession statements, as well as voluminous transcripts from court proceedings and hearings.

Ironically, shortly before his suicide, Charles Yukl himself provided much written material. He also wrote letters to his attorney, probation officer, and psychologist giving them permission to discuss his case in detail. As a result, Yukl's files were made available to the authors.

However, it should be noted that Dorothea Freitag,

Charles Yukl Sr. and John Keenan declined to be interviewed, as did Yukl's last defense attorney. Information and statements pertaining to each of these individuals were obtained from the public record.

ABOUT THE AUTHORS

ROBERT K. TANENBAUM, co-author of the critically acclaimed true-crime thriller, *Badge of the Assassin,* worked in the New York County District Attorney's Office under Frank Hogan. Appointed Deputy Chief Counsel in charge of the investigation into the assassination of President John F. Kennedy, he also served as special consultant to the attorney general for the Hillside Strangler case in 1981. He is the author of *No Lesser Plea* and lives in Los Angeles with his wife and three children.

PETER S. GREENBERG, a former correspondent for *Newsweek,* is a nationally syndicated columnist and television producer. He lives both in New York and Los Angeles.

"POWERFUL, EXCITING . . . BRISTLES
WITH AUTHENTICITY!"

—*Kirkus Reviews*

NO LESSER PLEA
Robert K. Tannebaum

Mandeville Louis has already killed two people in
cold blood and walked away on an insanity plea.
Now handsome D.A. Roger Karp is after Louis, and
his insatiable lust for justice won't let him rest until
he gets a guilty plea. For Karp knows that even in
the relative security of a mental hospital, Louis may
not have finished his killing spree. And Karp knows
he must not let go until he's won this deadly battle
of wits with a smiling psychopath who laughs at the
law while he kills and kills again. . . .

"Strong . . . exceptionally good . . . a raunchy
energy that crackles!"

—*Publishers Weekly*